Corn Flakes for Dinner

A HEARTBREAKING COMEDY ABOUT FAMILY LIFE

Aidan Comerford

Gill Books

Gill Books
Hume Avenue
Park West
Dublin 12
www.gillbooks.ie

Gill Books is an imprint of M.H. Gill and Co.

978 07171 7903 9

Design and print origination by O'K Graphic Design, Dublin
Edited by Síne Quinn
Printed by CPI Group (UK) Ltd, Croydon CRO 4YY

This book is typeset in 11/15 pt Minion, with chapter headings in American Typewriter.

The paper used in this book comes from the wood pulp of managed forests. For every tree felled, at least one tree is planted, thereby renewing natural resources.

A CIP catalogue record for this book is available from the British Library.

5 4 3 2 1

Aidan Comerford won So You Think You're Funny? at the Edinburgh Fringe Festival in 2014. He has also performed at the Montreal Just For Laughs Festival and the Vodafone Comedy Festival. He lives in Ashbourne with his wife Martha and daughters Ailbhe and Sophie.

To Martha!

'To be the father of growing daughters is to understand something of what Yeats evokes with his imperishable phrase "terrible beauty." Nothing can make one so happily exhilarated or so frightened: it's a solid lesson in the limitations of self to realize that your heart is running around inside someone else's body.'

CHRISTOPHER HITCHENS, *Hitch-22: A Memoir*

Introduction

By July 2015, our bedroom is so bedoodled that it looks like Banksy has had a stroke in there, except the artist in question is actually our seven-year-old daughter, Sophie.

She prefers to work with non-traditional materials, and she has a penchant for the permanent. Her 2014 'Handprints with Baby Oil on The Wall' is a fine example. Michelangelo has nothing on her extensive 2012 ceiling masterpiece, 'The Resilience of Ribena', and there is great promise in her early red nail varnish floor work, 'This Cream Carpet Was a Massive Mistake, You Eejits.'

Like a true artiste, she doesn't say much; she lets her art speak for itself. 'What do you think she's trying to tell us, Martha?' I asked my wife, one night. 'I think what she's saying is that she really likes to fuck shit up, Aidan,' said Martha, quite astutely.

Both of our daughters are on the autistic spectrum, although Sophie's nine-year-old sister, Ailbhe (pronounced Alva), is a breeze, whereas Sophie is more like a hurricane with opposable thumbs. She has obliterated any notions of interior design we once had. These days our home decor could be best described as 'Ongoing Burglary.'

We had slightly different reactions after the girls were diagnosed in 2010. Martha doubled down on her post-natal depression and upgraded her pre-existing sleep condition to the 'chronic' package (which comes with a free pillow), although she can function perfectly well so long as she gets twenty-three hours of sleep a day, and a nap.

I started a part-time musical comedy career.

I also lost my job working as a structural draughtsperson (I draw the bits of buildings that make them stand up), and I got a new job, doing the same thing, for half the wages. The pressure of paying our massive mortgage gave me beard alopecia and a hiatal hernia. I would relieve stress by writing silly songs, while dealing with the state of our house the same way I dealt with our mortgage arrears: by closing my eyes tightly and hoping that everything would be okay when I opened them again.

'Not the basis of a sound financial plan' – The Bank, often.

In August 2015, I brought my debut musical comedy show to the month-long Edinburgh Fringe Festival, which Martha was obviously delighted about. 'I'm obviously delighted about this,' she said, which gave me a good opportunity to teach Ailbhe about sarcasm, and marital death threats. Granny and Grandad – Martha's mam and dad, Sheila and Brendan – practically moved in while I was away, and when Martha and Ailbhe flew over to visit in the middle of the festival for a few days, they looked after Sophie at home. I couldn't have gone to Edinburgh without their help.

When I arrived back at the end of the month, they told me to shut my eyes before I went into the bedroom. When I opened them, I saw that it had been beautifully redecorated. They had done everything (with a little help from Martha's uncle Dec) when Martha and Ailbhe were over in Edinburgh with me. This was the first and last time my shutting-my-eyes-and-hoping-it-works-itself-out plan had ever worked.

I looked at Granny and Grandad, and I said, as appreciatively as I could, 'Don't think this doesn't mean I'm not putting you in a home when the time comes.'

We maintain our bedroom now by locking the door during the day to keep Sophie out, although I think, somehow, she understands the consequences of restarting her artistic career: if you ever see an ad looking for a good home for a girl with autism from Ashbourne, you'll know what has happened.

March 2005

The spring sunshine streamed through the translucent bedroom curtains in our compact flat, turning the magnolia walls golden, as I lay on the soft, clean bed, alone, naked from the waist down, forlornly attacking Little Aidan. If I had been merely trying to achieve sexual release I would have ceased badgering myself long before, but I was, in fact, doing my bit for science.

It was nearly a year since we'd been married, and as punishment for failing to impregnate Martha, I had to submit myself to the ignominy of a fertility test. I suspected that I might also have needed to get my ears examined, because when the doctor said, 'We need to check your sperm quality,' what I heard was, 'We strongly suspect that you might not be a real man at all.'

Martha had already been given the full 'Harry Potter' – that's a medical check-up where they put a wand up a woman, shout 'Lumos!' and have a good search around her Forbidden Forest. She had received an 'Exceeds Expectations' grade on that exam, so now they wanted to see if there was any magic in my wand, or if I was just a Muggle with a stick.

When I found out that I had to do the test, I had been appalled at the humiliating prospect of being forced to produce my preciousness in a public facility. Luckily, we were renting a flat in Cabinteely, a suburb of South-East Dublin, which happened to be within half an hour's drive of the hospital that tested sperm for sperminess. This was the magical timeframe that would ensure that my boys would still be in a fit state for their exam by the time I got them there.

We lived in that flat because Martha taught Maths in a school that was a five-minute walk away, and it was on a bus route into the city, for my work. She would have probably been starting her first class of the day at that time. Oh, how I wished that I was in work as well.

When it comes to sins of the flesh, I would not be a professional sinner, but I am an enthusiastic and dedicated amateur, so I had thought that this would be easy. All I would have to do was think some sexy thoughts, produce a sexy sample and then get it to the sexy church on time. However, my brain had decided that the morning's masturbation material would be a panicked recitation of the rules:

> ' ... *if you touch any part of the jar with your penis you must report potential contamination to the laboratory upon submission ...*'

'Contamination?' This wasn't the sort of dirty talk I had been hoping for. It was bad enough that I had to go through the shame of handing a jar of my tepid love juice to a stranger, without also having to tell them that I had failed at one of the fundamentals of living. I had thought the instructions would be simple – like 'Jizz. In. Jar.' simple – but instead, I had been presented with a novella of ejaculatory diktats.

For instance, if I failed to collect the first bit of ejaculate, I would have to report that as well. In terms of potency, that bit is the fire hose of fertilisation, whereas, relatively, what follows afterwards has all the penetrative power of a cracked squirt gun. It would seem obvious, then, that one should insert one's penis a little way into the jar to prevent such a tragedy occurring, especially as one's range of fire could be everything from squeezing out the last of a mayonnaise sachet to going off like a formula one champagne celebration. However, inserting my penis in that manner was fraught, because the aperture of the jar was a joke, leaving only millimetres of play. I'm not bragging, by the way. This had nothing to do with my girth, which could only ever be described as adequate. I thought that they might have given me the wrong jar. Maybe this was the one for collecting tears? If this went on much longer, I could certainly collect some of those. All I could think was *Don't touch the sides, Jesus Christ, DON'T TOUCH THE SIDES*, which is the opposite of what I would normally be thinking.

I held my penis as close to the jar as I dared, and yet there was a gap between the tip and the lip that could be described as 'a distance'. I was hoping for a hole in one, but the closer I got to taking the shot, the more the little caddy in my brain shook his head and said, *Boss, to be honest, I think you're probably going to have to lay up here.*

I paused, took a break, and tried to clear my brain of all the silly rules, and … well, if you're a man, I don't really need to tell you what I thought about next. You know exactly where I went in my head – I went to the place we never tell women about, the fantasy that is deep down inside every man. I went to the place that is far, far away …

> *… I am Luke Skywalker, in my X-wing fighter, barrelling down the trench on the surface of the Death Star, and Darth Vader is closing in behind me. I put away my targeting computer when I hear a ghostly voice tell me to, 'Use The Force, Luke. Let go!' Vader locks on. I am done for; The Rebellion is finished. The Empire will rule in perpetuity. And then, suddenly, out of the sun, comes the Millennium Falcon, and as it blasts Darth out of orbit, the John Williams soundtrack swells in my ears, I throw my head back, close my eyes, and I launch my proton torpedoes straight down the exhaust shaft. It's a direct hit. The Death Star explodes.*

'Great shot, kid, that was one in a million,' shouts Han Solo, in celebration. Thanks, Han, I think, and I breathe a sigh of relief and make my way back to the base, for clean up.

Afterwards, I had to make myself look like a man who had not recently been at himself, which as any man who has recently been at himself (and that is probably most men) will tell you is virtually impossible.

At least I had followed the instruction to fill out the jar's identifying label prior to production, even though I had not understood why I needed to do that. Afterwards, however, I knew exactly why. In the stupefying, shuddering afterglow, I could have been liable to write anything.

NAME: I'm Batman.

I had done the hard part, and now all I had to do was drive to the hospital. I was still red-faced and woozy as I got in the car, and I could taste the metallic tang of adrenaline in my mouth. The countdown was on. I stuck the jar into the pocket of my trousers to keep my boys warm, and alive. It felt like I was on a mission, which made me feel cool – a feeling which I don't often feel, and one that is usually fleeting. Then I missed the ignition with the key … three times, which made my recently successful precision bombing run seem even more miraculous than it had been.

According to AA Routefinder, this trip would take me seven minutes and cost less than a euro in petrol. I had half an hour and a full tank: this was in the bag. (Well, technically, it was out of the bag and in the jar, but there was no time for such semantics.) Soon, this horror show of a morning would be over, and I could get back to work, like a normal person, and never speak of this again.

Three minutes later I had come to a sickening stop at the back of a snaking queue of cars. I had been foiled by the world's evilest organisation: Dún Laoghaire-Rathdown County Council. They had deployed their most diabolical weapon: an Irish Stop-Go system.

With every change of the lights, the queue slithered slowly forward, as I willed it on with every molecule of my body. Some people might have turned to prayer at this point. After all, God can part the Red Sea. God can heal the sick. God can turn water into wine. However, even God would shrug, stultified by a Dún Laoghaire-Rathdown civil servant's idea of acceptable traffic flow. All I could do was wait, and wait, and curse, and wait some more, until finally, I made it through, my seat soaking from the litres of sweat I had just expelled.

I had ten minutes to spare as I drove around the back of the hospital to park. As I approached the barrier, there was a little black Micra ahead of me and I could see empty car parking spaces beyond. I was going to make it.

Then the driver of the Micra stopped too far back from the barrier for the barrier technology to sense the car and open. I didn't panic. They would surely realise their simple error and pull up to the barrier at any moment. Then, the lovely, old-aged, blue-rinsed, wax-jacketed Irish country woman got out of the Micra and tried to make the barrier work ... by looking at it.

'CMMMMmmmmmmnnnnnnnnnn,' I grunted, rocking back and forward. It was possible that I may have been teetering on the edge of my sanity. I took the jar out of my pocket, and it was distressingly less than tepid. I could only imagine the mini-genocide that was occurring in there. I was just about to get out and manhandle the Micra to the kerb when a security guard came over and released the barrier for the lady. Even today, I still have very strong feelings for that man.

I parked the car and ran to reception, where I was greeted by a festival of hospital signage. As I scanned frantically, words melted into each other, and I realised that the term 'blind panic' is a cliché for a reason. I looked at the reception desk and I saw a nurse –

no, not a nurse, an angel – looking back at me. At that point, I was so frantic from my journey that I must have looked like a big, red, sweaty Jelly Baby. Then she said a wonderful word: 'Sample?' She had obviously watched this scene play out a couple of times every day, for years, and I was merely the protagonist of this particular matinee. She gave me some directions, and I thanked her by making the sound of dying badger: 'NNnnngggaaahhhh.'

I sprinted through the labyrinthine hospital, and somehow, I arrived at the right place with five minutes to go. That was when I found out that this was seemingly not exclusively a fertility testing centre. It was possibly a place where they tested all manner of human excretions. I suspected this was true, because Ireland's oldest couple were the only ones ahead of me. If they had fertility problems, I was sure I could identify the issue without the use of samples or wands.

The old man seemed to be the outpatient, and he was flirting with the receptionist in that way that is only socially acceptable because old men are old. (In fairness to this gentleman, it takes balls to flirt with a woman you've just handed a stool sample to.) 'Would ya go way out of that,' said the nurse, giggling, as the man's wife rolled her eyes, clearly well-used to his shenanigans. All the while, I stood there, bug-eyed with the fear of missing my rapidly closing half-hour window of opportunity. My heart quailed at the thought of having to go through all of this again.

I checked my watch. Four minutes left. The man started to tell a tale, as I continued to stand there, agitated, and seemingly unnoticed by the nurse … three minutes … then two minutes … *Jesus Tap-Dancing Christ*, I thought. Then, mid-anecdote, I put all the shame in my poor Catholic soul aside (and that's quite a lot of shame), stepped forward, and …

Bang!

I slapped my sample down on the table.

The man stopped mid-sentence and looked at it.

His wife loo
The nurse looke
I looked at it.
We all knew what it was.
There was a moment of sile
and then the nurse said, 'Oh, right, a
I thought about all that I had been th
'Not a bother,' I said.
'Okay, we'll have the results back to your do
said the nurse.
As I left, I heard the man pick up his story where he le

ked at it.
d at it.

ce for the death of my shame,
id you have any trouble?'
ough that morning.

ctor in a week,'

t off

7

r first
hrough

town of
Ireland,
e of those
ty Carlow
of Ireland.

often forget a.. This is unfair. Go to Carlow. ... losed-down sugar factory to visit. When I was growing up, cy...g my bike to school, I would often be assailed by the romantic, choking smell of sugar production. If someone steamed a sugar beet beneath my nasal passages today, I would be instantly transported to my childhood, and A&E, probably.

Martha grew up in Swords, County Dublin, and she says that it was wonderful, but how could it be when Swords smells of nothing? If you steamed a sugar beet in her vicinity, she wouldn't get nostalgic, she would probably just tell you to stop. Where's the romance in that?

The houses Martha and I grew up in are structurally very similar: three-bedroom semi-ds in suburban estates. I pointed this out to Derm (for Dermot), Martha's younger brother, one day, when he was referring to me as a bogtrotter. He still regards our marriage as an inter-species affair. When we asked him to be the usher at our wedding, he asked, 'But who's going to supply the net?' I was a bit puzzled: 'The net?' 'Yes,' he said, 'The net that I'll have to put up down the aisle to stop your side throwing their own faeces at our side.'

For Dad's birthday, we all went out for a beautiful meal in Kilkea Castle, the hotel that my mam and dad – Mary and Frank – had their wedding reception in, the hotel that Martha and I had our wedding reception in, and the hotel that my sister, Anita, and her husband, Shane, had their wedding reception in. My brother, Kieran, wouldn't have the option of getting married there, even if he'd wanted to, because, years later, the business would go under in the recession. (Or it may have been my parents' fault for not producing enough offspring.)

That night, Martha and I stayed in my parents' house. As we were going to bed, Martha realised that it was, in fact, the optimal night in the month for baby-making, but we were too bloated from food, and frankly too sick of sex (no, I didn't think that was possible either) after a year of fruitless fucking, so we skipped it.

The next morning, when Martha woke up, she was immediately panicked that we would let yet another barren month slip by. She wanted us to at least attempt to have some joyless, perfunctory procreation. However, there was a problem. The house I grew up is basically a three-bedroom anti-masturbation device. It was built in the seventies, when builders would regularly use large sheets of chipboard, instead of proper floorboards, upstairs. So, as a teenager, I never knew when any of my movements would be attended by a chipboard squeak. Consequently, it was virtually impossible for me to build up a head of steam without the house announcing my every stroke. I might start, but the floor would soon scream 'HE'S TOUCHING HIMSELF!' (or so I imagined) so loudly that I was sure everyone in the surrounding counties could hear. And even if the house had merely murmured as I mercilessly mauled myself, it was simply too polite a place to commit the sins of Onan. This is because my Mam is as house-proud as she is appalled by the salacious tone of this paragraph. She regularly declares me to be 'beyond saving', and she's probably not wrong about that.

So, that morning, with my mam and dad milling around downstairs, we just couldn't have sex without the floorboards roaring about it, and I love my parents too much to do that to them. I promised Martha that we would do it twice when we got home that evening. Three times, even! I had thought that that was an acceptable proposition.

Not long after, however, we were seated around the breakfast table, and Mam was laying out the decorative place mats, when Martha asked her, 'Would you mind going out shopping after breakfast this morning? Aidan and I want to do a bit of baby-making.' In the deathly silence that hung there after she said it, I thought that I could hear the Holy Spirit crying, and the Waterford Crystal rattling in the cabinets.

'Well, emmm, yes, of course,' said Mam. This would be the first grandchild for our family (and for Martha's), and as the months moved by with no impregnation, she often told me how she was praying for us. I didn't have the heart to tell her that if she was looking for the preeminent power in the universe, she shouldn't be praying, she should be applying to Dún Laoghaire-Rathdown County Council for permission.

My mam and dad hadn't had any issues when they went about making a family. My sister, Anita, was conceived on the heels of their honeymoon, and was born in July 1975. I arrived fourteen months later, and my brother, Kieran, arrived sixteen months after that. Mam and Dad stopped procreating then, because I think they had made their point. I had thought it would be the same for Martha and me.

Mam and Dad left about ten minutes later, without any of us looking each other directly in the eye. Soon after they were gone,

Martha and I went upstairs. To this day, citizens of the Welsh coast probably still wonder what that awful squeaking noise they heard drifting across the Irish Sea was.

When Mam and Dad came back from shopping, we had arranged ourselves as casually as we could in the sitting room, trying to look like two people who hadn't just done the bad thing, but as any two people who have just done the bad thing would tell you, that's impossible. What could they say? 'Did you have a lovely ride, son?' No, there is only one question that can relieve that sort of tawdry tension:

'Tea?' asked Mam.

'YES!' Martha and I shouted, in unison.

Mam went to make tea, and I pointed to my mam's Dresden doll collection and asked Dad how they made the ceramic lace dresses, even though I knew how they did it, and he knew that I knew, and yet he started into a long explanation, because, Dear God above, please let us speak of something else.

The next week, back in Cabinteely, our phone rang on a Friday evening, just after I came home from work. It was the doctor with my results. Martha was sitting on the couch, looking at me, as I listened.

When I had initially gone to see this doctor, she had asked me to disrobe so she could check my scrotum for lumps. 'Two,' I said, hoping a bit of humour might alleviate the shame of the exploratory fondling I was about to endure. She was very professional, which was lovely, but she also never blinked the whole time while she was examining me, which was slightly odd. Maybe I'm weird, but when someone is rummaging around my ballsack, I find it a little disconcerting if they don't rehydrate their eyeballs from time to time. She had asked me if I had ever had any groin injuries …

… when we were teenagers, Anita and I would regularly engage in jig-acting. (Jig-acting is the messing that Irish kids do that

inevitably leads to an injury.) Jig-acting was our main source of entertainment because no one had invented the internet.

I was having fun with the height and strength advantage that puberty had recently bestowed upon me. I had her in a headlock, and I was rubbing her noggin with my knuckle – a favourite torture technique. Anita was somewhat irked by this, and she cried out in pain, so I released her. I apologised, as anyone who has done too much noggin-knuckling should do. She said it was okay, and we went to hug it out. The next thing I knew, my balls exploded, as if two nuclear devices had been simultaneously set off in their cores. The pain quickly radiated up to my stomach. She had sucker-kneed me. I collapsed in agony.

My Mam came in from the sitting room, asking, 'What's going on?' and she looked at me – her poor, prone, groaning son, cupping his bits – and immediately understood exactly what had happened. She admonished my sister appropriately. Then she said to me, 'Give me a look and I'll see if it's swollen.' She copped her double entendre immediately, and she and my sister spent the next ten minutes doubled up, crying with laughter, while I lay on the floor, doubled up, trying not to laugh, because it hurt too much …

'Not that I can think of,' I said to the doctor.

'Are you sure?' she asked. I must have sounded unsure for some reason …

… I was up at the Chess Club, because I was cool like that. Most of the other kids, including Kieran, only came to the Chess Club to jig-act around the leaky old prefab that passed for a parish centre, but I went because I loved chess. I would play my games, mostly with the adults, and when no one was available, I would quietly study various chess openings. As I said, I was an extremely cool young man.

But one day, I decided to join the jig-acting for a change. I had been hoping to have fun with the height and strength advantage that puberty had recently bestowed upon me. Unfortunately, I was not the only lad that puberty had recently bestowed height and strength upon, and I quickly found myself held by two hairy gorilla types, who had an arm each. I called out to Kieran for help.

I don't know why – and he doesn't know why either – but he ran up ... no ... he took a run up, and bog-toed my balls. They immediately went into high orbit near my ribs, and didn't re-enter the atmosphere until hours later ...

' ... No, definitely not,' I said to the doctor.

The doctor-fondling revealed no lumps, except the two that ought to be there. I thought that my sperm test would reveal that my special brew was as strong as any man's. Growing up as a Catholic, I suspected that if I had even thought about a woman without a condom on she would have been impregnated. But if that were true, how come Martha was not pregnant already?

When she was doing her Higher Diploma in Education, not too long after we first moved in together, she bought a very large academic book called *Infants, Children and Adolescents*, which I suspected was all about infants, children and adolescents. One day, when she was out, I picked it up and flicked through it. When I turned it back to the first page, just before I put it down, I saw that she had written an inscription: 'To myself, for the ones I teach and the ones I'll raise, hopefully.'

The doctor said, 'I'm sorry, Aidan, but you have a very low sperm count.' Martha couldn't hear the doctor, but she could tell from my face as I looked at her that it was bad news, and she looked back at me, stricken. The doctor explained that I would need to get retested, to confirm the result, in a couple of days, in a specialist clinic in the city centre.

How could I apologise to Martha for a failure of my basic biology? I had let our team down, and it wasn't my fault ... and yet, technically, I suppose, it was. Hallmark don't make a card that says, 'I'm sorry, darling, that my balls don't work,' and I don't think it would be a big seller. It would, ironically, take a lot of balls to buy it.

All we could do for the rest of the evening was sit on opposite ends of the couch, and do what a couple who are faced with a seemingly insurmountable problem usually do: we drank a bottle of wine. Each.

For the first time in my life I was faced with the prospect of never having children of my own. The talk and the tears flowed until there was nothing more to talk or cry about, so we said nothing more about it, and we stopped crying.

Instead, to cheer ourselves up, we watched episodes of our favourite television show, *The West Wing*. On TV, the show was up to season six, but we were watching favourite episodes from box sets of seasons one through four. After the end of season four, Aaron Sorkin, the creator, and the man responsible for the whip-smart wit and dialogue that we loved, had left the show, and since then the characters seemed to us to be going through scenes like automata, robbed of the life he breathed into them. As they acted out these strange scripts, you could almost see in the actors' eyes that they felt like their characters were not living the life that was meant for them. (Although maybe that was just us imagining it.) That night, I knew exactly how they felt. I always thought that I would be a father, with my own kids. Always. I didn't like the way this episode of my life was turning out: *Somebody bring back the original writer, please*, I thought.

Later, in bed, free from the pressure of procreation, Martha and I made love and, unable to sleep afterwards, we talked some more. 'The doctor said that exploring other options at this point would be prudent,' I said, trying to be sensible.

'Well, there is this teacher in work that I like,' suggested Martha.

'I think she means something more tried and tested, like IVF or adoption,' I laughed.

'But he *is* tried and tested, his wife just had a baby.'

The other stages being too difficult, Martha had skipped on to the last stage of the infertility grieving process – making jokes at the graveside of your husband's dead balls.

May 2005

I suffered the ignominy of the second test in a clinic in the city centre, which was every bit as awful and awkward as I thought it would be. My favourite bit about it was how the walls of the sample production room were so thin that I could hear the lab technician breathing outside the door, so I had to produce the sample knowing that he could probably hear me too.

A couple of days later, when our doctor called with the results, I was sure that it would just be a courteous conformation of the first test. But the doctor was buoyant. She said that my second set of boys, from the test in the clinic, were Olympic swimmers. Let's not get carried away – Irish Olympic swimmers – but still, strong competitors. They'd probably make it out of the heats. She may not have put it that way, but that was gist. The first test had apparently been erroneous, and you could tell that the doctor didn't quite believe it herself. I think I could actually hear her blinking.

A week later, we were getting ready to go to a sale of work in Martha's school. Martha had been doing woodwork classes – she's good at arts and crafts – and one or two of her pieces were up for auction. Martha was in the bathroom, half-way through her customary two hours of getting ready. When she came out, she still wasn't finished preparing herself for public consumption. I was just about to ask her, nicely, 'What the hell have you been at?' when she took her hand from behind her back and held up a positive pregnancy test. 'Oh my God! Are you sure?' Then she took her other hand from behind her back, to show me another positive test. She said, 'It's early days yet, so be calm.' I calmly pulled the jersey I was wearing over my head and I ran around the flat celebrating. This was last-kick-of-the-game-match-winning-goal stuff. When I thought about it, it made sense: I was never a great footballer, and I had always needed a lot of shots to score a goal. Soon, Martha's net would be bulging.

When we worked it out, we were pretty sure that the golden goal was scored the time that we were down in Carlow, desecrating the Holy Spirit, and rattling the Waterford Crystal.

A couple of weeks later, on a beautiful, blue-sky day, we drove down to Carlow with the windows open, singing our hearts out to the radio, and when we got there I can still remember the look of joy that spread across my Mam's face when I said, 'I've got something to tell you.'

August 2005

'Today we'll be talking about how to look after your hole, and it's not the hole that you're thinking of.'

I loved our antenatal class immediately. It was run by a midwife who seemed to be made entirely of gumption. She was so suited to midwifery, I imagined that if she had been the first of twins to be born, she would have immediately turned around to deliver her sibling.

'Yes, that's right, we're going to be talking about your assholes, and by assholes I don't mean your partners.' Our circle of couples laughed, again. In stand-up comedy terms – which are inexplicably violent – this woman was killing it. There was one couple nearby who didn't laugh, because I think they were expecting soothing tones and essential oils and breathing exercises, not bum jokes. I didn't know it then, but I would find out many, many times later, that as a comedian, even when things are going really well, you are doomed to see only these stony outcrops in a sea of laughing faces.

Martha was determined to have as natural a birth as possible, so she studied the breathing techniques diligently. She did not want to have an epidural. I was in awe of her resolve. As a man, it is hard to find equivalency, but let's say I was tasked with pushing a kiwi fruit down my nasal passage, and someone offered me pain relief, I can't imagine any scenario where I would say, 'No thanks, I'd like to push this kiwi fruit out of my nostril in as natural a way as possible.'

Now, there are, and have been, many fine writers of horror stories – Stephen King, Mary Shelley, Anne Rice and countless other luminaries – but all their works cower under the awesome shadow of Heidi Murkoff and Sharon Mazel's terrifying tome, *What to Expect When You're Expecting*. There isn't a more horrific book you can read, especially if you're in the third trimester of pregnancy, or you're even the slightest bit fond of someone who is.

One night, at around three in the morning, Martha woke me up, and said she couldn't sleep. 'You can't sleep?' I said, puzzled. Martha was usually an epic sleeper. 'What have you done with my wife. How do I know you're not a changeling?' Then Martha licked her finger and stuck it in my ear. I jumped back. 'Ah! Good point, well made.'

She said that she had just been reading a bit in *What to Expect When You're Expecting* about the possibility of having an incompetent cervix. I'd never heard of that, so she explained it as simplistically as she could: 'The womb is like an upside-down bin bag, and the cervix is the drawstring that keeps everything in. If it's incompetent, it would mean that the drawstring wasn't strong enough, you know, Aidan, like those shite own-brand bags you brought home from the shops one day … '

'Are you seriously going to have a go at me about that now?'

She ignored this and continued, ' … as the amount of baby in the bag grows, the seal will eventually fail, the liquid will come out, and the baby will likely die.'

'That's awful. Is that common?' I asked.

'It happens to around one-in-a-million pregnant women,' she said. Despite the ridiculously slim chance, she still needed reassurance that her womb wasn't about to pop like a cheap paddling pool.

'Martha, your cervix is so competent that it could run an international company, while bringing up a family of twelve, on its own. Other cervixes don't know how your cervix crams it all in. And as for liquid retention, if the Hoover Dam ever started to crack, they'd build a new barrier based on the design of your cervix. What I am saying is that you've got an engineering miracle going on between your legs. I'm only surprised that they haven't come to take a cast of it.'

'You say the nicest things,' she laughed.

'Yes, I do. Now, go the fuck to sleep.'

If you absolutely must read *What To Expect When You're Expecting*, have a good work of relatively easy-going fiction nearby, for light relief, like the *Book of Revelation*. I can't be too mad at Murkoff and Mazel, because – much like the Bible – there are one or two redemptive bits in the book, like the inclusion of the passage on perineal massage, which encourages women to let their partners have a good rub of the bit between the two downstairs holes to increase its stretchiness in the weeks leading up to labour. I was doubtful of the effectiveness of this practice, yet I was willing to run some experiments. I'm quite selfless like that.

Because we had found it difficult to conceive, the thought that something would go wrong was ever-present in our minds. However, Martha's pregnancy appeared to be textbook. We sat in most nights, reading scary stories as her belly grew and grew, not believing our luck.

September 2005

The baby was due a couple of weeks after Christmas, but by September we had already got all the essential little things we thought we needed: a buggy, a car seat, a changing table, a Ramones baby T-shirt … and a mortgage.

Our flat in Cabinteely was so small, it was like living inside a puzzle: you had to close some doors to open other ones. We often had to work out how we could move around in some rooms at the same time. We lived our lives in that flat like a couple of Tetris pieces.

The baby, and all its accoutrements, just wouldn't fit. So, once I'd finished victory-lapping after impregnating Martha, we had started hunting for a reasonably priced house, but every time we took a shot at one, we missed.

We went to meet a mortgage adviser, who had the shabby, red-nosed demeanour of a whiskey-soaked private eye. He advised us that with our wages combined we could get a loan approaching half a million euro (if you're reading this book in the distant future, yes, it's true, you could once buy a decent house for the price of a Mars Bar). This was ridiculous. I had a decent job, but I wasn't by any means a high-roller, and Martha was a teacher on a temporary contract, who would soon pop a sprog.

'You've got to be kidding me?'

The mortgage adviser realised that I thought this was a ridiculous amount of money. He said, 'Oh, sorry, I'm sure I can get you more if you want?'

We knew we couldn't afford to pay back that sort of money, long-term, but it was tempting to take it. At first, we looked for a house in Martha's home town, Swords. We soon realised that house-viewing was a contact sport. The job of a Celtic Tiger estate agent seemed to be very like that of a World Wrestling Federation cage match referee. They would open the door and let a hoard of crazed couples in, and the last couple standing would get the keys. We were continually outfought by people with far more financial clout than us.

We realised that if we were to stick to a more modest price tag, we couldn't afford to live in Swords, so we widened our search. Eventually we ended up in Ashbourne, which is a town in County Meath, that is ten miles (16 kilometres) from the North-West edge of County Dublin. Our house was newly built, in what would be a pleasant housing estate when it was finished, with a mid-sized front and back garden, and a kidney-shaped green out front. Most important, the house was ready to move into almost right away, because the previous sale had fallen through, so we'd be in and settled before the baby came along. Perfect.

Okay, not quite perfect; we were a bit further away from the city than we had hoped. Martha's commute until the baby was born would be a two-hours-each-way-arse-muscle-tester, but we had a house – a nice house, with plenty of space – which we would never have to leave if we didn't want to.

A few weeks later, we had signed every form ever printed, and we had the mortgage millstone firmly affixed to our necks. We were delighted.

One night, not too long after we'd moved in, Martha was sitting on an old wicker couch, in the middle of the concrete floor, rubbing her big, pregnant belly, in the bare sitting room, when she looked over at the kitchen table and saw a little mouse on the table top, up on its hind legs, looking back at her.

'I remember when this was all fields,' said the mouse.

I think the pregnancy hormones, and the daily commute, might have been getting to her. The mouse hadn't got the memo that this land was now our land. He didn't seem to understand contracts of sale. He was determined to stay, like a furry little squatter. Martha grew attached to the mouse, of course, because she was feeling maternal, and didn't seem convinced by my insistence that it wasn't sanitary to have a rodent roaming where a pregnant woman was eating. For weeks, that mouse and I had a Roadrunner and Wile E. Coyote relationship. There were so many times I almost had him.

One day, Martha realised she hadn't seen the mouse in a while and she asked me if I thought it was still around. So I told her that the mouse had probably gone back to the farm to be with all his mouse friends.

'You didn't!'

'No, of course not, but if you're going down to Ashbourne, it's probably for the best if you pick up a new sweeping brush.'

December 2005

A month before Martha's due date, on a Friday afternoon, Martha got the bus from the school back into the city, so that she could meet me after work, and we could drive back to Ashbourne together. I got a phone-call in work. I expected it to be Martha, asking if I could get off early. It was Martha, alright, but she was sobbing. In between her sobs, she told me that she had fallen over on the street, and that she was in the maternity hospital waiting to get a scan: 'Aidan, I can't feel the baby moving.'

'Don't worry, I'll be there soon,' I said, already putting on my coat.

She had fallen on a street that happened to be around the corner from the maternity hospital. She had sat on the pavement for a few minutes, without anyone offering her a hand, until two properly raised Eastern European lads had crossed the street to help her up. She assured them she would be okay to walk around to the hospital by herself. When she got there, still sobbing, the outpatients' clinic was just closing. She had intended to speak at the reception desk, but instead she put up her bleeding hands and made a sound like 'Mwwwaahhhhhuhuhuh.' Luckily, this nurse was fluent in the language of Recently-Felled-Pregnant-Woman.

'Did you fall?' she asked Martha, sympathetically. Martha nodded, mournfully, and made a sound like a lost lamb looking for its mother – 'Maaahhhh' – to indicate to the nurse that she had been correct in her assessment of the situation.

'Okay, let's get someone to have a look at you and make sure everything is alright. Try not to worry.'

When I arrived at the hospital and found Martha, she hadn't had the scan yet, which was a good sign. If they were really worried about the baby she would have been brought in immediately, I surmised. But as I sat there comforting her, I had another thought: maybe they were waiting until I got there so they could break the awful news to us together?

'It's going to be okay,' I said, more speaking to myself than to Martha. 'Any movement?' She shook her head. 'How did you fall over?' I asked, but I already knew the answer to that question …

When we first moved in together, we lived in a rented house in the Dublin suburb of Lucan, which is crammed full of starter homes and starter couples. We spent a couple of years there before Martha changed schools, and we moved to the titchy flat in Cabinteely. For most of that time we shared the house with a lean French guy called François, who rented one of the rooms off us. He was a perfect housemate, but he did do one thing that was incredibly odd. Get this: he used to take a bar of chocolate out of the cupboard, eat two squares of it, and then wrap it up and put the rest of it back in the cupboard. 'That's serial killer behaviour,' I said to Martha.

'No, Aidan, I think he's just … healthy?'

Some nights we would all watch Sex and the City *together. He would pretend to be puzzled at some of the frank English phrases used by Carrie and her cohorts. 'What is "skid mark"?' he would ask, and Martha would do her diplomatic damnedest to explain it, while François tried not to smile at her very earnest attempts. One night, though, he over-reached when he asked, 'What is "blow job"?' Everyone knows that the French economy is based on the exchange of cheese, wine and blow jobs. He was rumbled.*

One sunny summer Saturday afternoon, François and I were out in the back garden tossing a tennis ball between each other (this was how we did social media in the days before smartphones, kids). Martha walked out, and as she did, I shouted 'Heads up' and lobbed the ball oh-so-softly towards her. Martha did put her head up, and then made panicked motions with her hands, as if she was drowning on dry land, and the ball passed through her flailing arms and bonked her on the nose. I thought she was joking, but apparently this was her best attempt to catch the ball ...

Martha is what the New Yorkers in *Sex and the City* would call a klutz. There isn't a low-down thing she hasn't stubbed her toe on. There isn't a mid-height edge that hasn't connected with her elbow. For Martha, every corner in the word, in every corner of the world, awaits, ready to attack. There would come a time in our lives when, one day, in an attempt to put on her pyjamas, she would sprain two toes and give herself a near concussion.

So when Martha said, 'I think the footpath jumped up at me,' I didn't question it. I just said, 'Well, it shall be punished. After they make sure everything is fine with the baby, which it will be, I'll ask some of the site guys in work to jackhammer that footpath. And, if it gets re-poured, I'll go out in the night and write rude things in the concrete.'

Then they called us in for the scan.

When Martha had her first scan, after three months, and I looked at the screen, I had an awestruck, inarticulate moment where I thought, *Oh. Wow. Thing. Moving. In. There.* It was suddenly so real. It was actually happening. She was having a baby. As the baby grew, I thought, *What an odd sensation that must be, to feel something squirming inside you.* It's a feeling that is entirely cut off to men, unless the man engages in sordid sexual behaviour involving small furry creatures that you definitely shouldn't google if you've never heard of it.

'What is "gerbilling"?' asked François.

This scan was entirely different, though. This could be our comeuppance for confidently buying baby stuff, and a house, and looking at baby names – we still hadn't chosen one. Now the baby might be ... well, there were two possible universes, one in which our baby was fine, and one in which it wasn't, we just didn't know which one we were living in. It was like that thought experiment with the cat in the box that I couldn't think of the name of right then.

When the technician put the cold gel on, Martha instinctively flinched, but she kept her eyes firmly on the screen. I kept my eyes on the screen too. The scan screen came to life, and so did our baby, so much bigger than the last time. So very, very real now.

'Everything looks fine here,' said the technician, quickly, as she checked around. 'Yes, good healthy heartbeat.'

Suddenly, there was a fetid fug in the room. I had farted in relief. Martha's tear-stained face went from joy to disgust. I could tell that the scanning technician had smelt it too, and was breathing through her mouth as well.

'Was that you?' Martha whispered to me.

'No, I think it was the baby,' I whispered back.

If felt as if everything was going to be okay from here. All I needed to do was work out how many square metres of bubble wrap it would take to cover the entire house, everything in the world that Martha would come close to, and Martha, until the due date.

As I drove us home on that sharp December day, Martha said, 'We should really settle on a name.' I remembered something: 'What do you think of Schrödinger?'

January 2006

It was eleven o'clock at night, and we were just about to go to bed. 'Aidan, I think it's started.' said Martha.

'Okay, are you sure? It could be Braxton-Hicks, couldn't it?' I suggested, very knowledgably. I wanted Martha to know that I was *au fait* with the work of the Hickster, a nineteenth-century preppy prankster who fooled pregnant women into thinking they were in labour, and thus gave his name to phantom labour pains. The Braxmeister and I were tight, because I had skim-read something about him in the pregnancy books. By the time this pregnancy was over, I would be a shoo-in for the Best Husband Ever award.

But Martha seemed sure. 'No, I think this is the real start of it.'

'Okay, I think you should get up and walk around a bit?' I suggested.

'Aidan, you don't need to tell me, I've read the books too. I know that walking around in early labour is a good idea,' she said, pointedly.

'Well yes,' I said, 'but also, I was thinking that the couch is new and the wooden floor is wipe clean.'

She was unimpressed by my quip. 'How about you time the contractions?'

'Yes, I'll do that,' I agreed, feeling like the Best Husband Ever award might be slipping away already.

Counting contractions did not seem to be an exact science. By my timings, our baby would either be born in a few hours, in two days, in three minutes, in the ancient past when the Vikings had invaded Ireland, within seconds, or around about the same time as the Sun died and swallowed the Earth.

'I think we should go,' I said. This was not just because Martha was in labour. I was worried about Martha's dreadful inability to be on time for anything. While Martha thinks that time is merely a suggestion, I think – without being too melodramatic about it – that being late should be classified as a hate crime. So in our marriage it is my job to say, 'I think we should go,' at regular intervals, even if we aren't going anywhere, just in case.

Martha wasn't as anxious as I was. 'You don't want us to be one of those couples who show up way too early, do you?'

'No,' I said, 'but I also don't want to be one of those couples who have their baby on the side of the road. I think we should try to stay out of the papers with this one.'

'I think we should watch an episode of *The West Wing*,' suggested Martha. If Martha wasn't worried, and she was the one having the baby, I decided that I shouldn't be worried either.

'That's *always* a good idea,' I agreed.

'Which one do you want to watch?' she asked.

'Oh, Martha, don't be silly, there's only one episode we can watch at a time like this.' I held up the DVD box.

If you aren't a fan of *The West Wing*, 'Game On' is an episode about an American presidential debate, where a left-of-centre, intellectual, empathetic Democratic incumbent kicks the ass of a right-wing, uninquisitive, empathically inept Republican presidential candidate. You know, liberal porn.

A few *West Wing* episodes later, the contractions were coming at regular intervals, and we thought it would be best to go to the hospital, which was in Dublin city centre.

It took about thirty minutes to get there in the still of night. It was just after two o'clock on a Thursday morning, and we were sure that Martha must be on the cusp of delivery, but when the nurse checked, she found that she was only one centimetre dilated.

One night, in bed, Martha had said to me, while she was reading her pregnancy horror stories, that complete dilation was ten centimetres. 'Ten centimetres?' I said. I needed an appropriate frame of reference to convey my astonishment at that measurement. 'Sure, that's the same width as a house brick.'

Martha looked at me for a few moments, before she said, 'Aidan, I think it might be time for a career change; you've obviously been drawing buildings for too long.'

You could only call one centimetre a brick's-worth of dilation if you were building a *Lego* house. The nurse asked us where we were living.

'Ashbourne,' we said.

'You might be more comfortable if you went home and came back later in the morning,' she suggested. Shit! We *were* one of those couples who had panicked and turned up early.

'I think we should stay,' I said – in a break from my traditional role in our marriage. The reason for my obstinacy was very simple: the Irish government. You see, they had encouraged a property bubble to grow. This in turn made houses prohibitively expensive in the Dublin suburbs, which vastly increased the size of the commuter belt. Young couples were securing monstrous mortgages so they could buy minuscule houses in midlands towns, which property supplements all declared to be within half an hour of the city centre, and yet did not come with their own helipad to make that possible. To pay for these mortgages, most couples needed two salaries, and as most couples didn't work together, they would need two cars, so they could both get to work separately, massively increasing the number of cars on the road. Of course, this would be okay, because surely the Irish government would be competent enough to rectify their initial mistake by providing the Irish public with a world-class public transport system that they could use instead, right? And that might just be the best joke in this book.

I got the bus every morning, because Ashbourne had a decent service, but as the bus trundled down the city centre bus lanes, it would pass car after car stuck in shuffling queues, containing frazzled, singular souls, probably skinning property supplement writers alive in their minds. There were times when I needed the car for work, and I would have to drive into this rush-hour shit-show myself. If Martha and I had to come back in to the city during that morning madness, with the birth of our first child imminent, I would be very, very put out. I might go postal, in that I would probably write a sternly worded letter to the *Irish Times*.

It was time to stand up to The Man. 'Can we stay?' I asked.

'Yes, of course,' said the nurse, 'but it might be a few hours before we can get you a bed.'

'That's fine,' I said. That was her told.

We got a room quite quickly, as it happened, but Martha's cervical dilation was slower than the movement of the continents. As the Best Husband Ever-elect, I was prepared for this eventuality. I opened my bag, and took out a wallet full of live comedy CDs. A friend had given us these, with the thought that maybe Martha could just laugh the baby right out. You know, like 'Ha Ha Ha … Pop.' (I hardly need to mention it, but this friend was single and childless at the time.)

> *'Dad, what was my birth like?'*
>
> *'It was beautiful. There was a cool, winter sun caressing the leaves of the trees outside the window, the birds were performing their mid-morning arias, and Chris Rock was doing a tight five.'*

The hospital had no official car park for patients, so we had to leave the car in a place where it would be gobbled up by the notoriously voracious Dublin clampers after eight o'clock in the morning. (I think they had special parking tickets for that area: 'You've just had a parking fine. It weighs seventy-five euro and no cents. Congratulations!') As it approached eight o'clock that morning, after consulting with the midwife and Martha ('Two centimetres,' and 'It's fine, go'), I thought that it was a good time to run out and move the car to a car park where I wouldn't have to come back to it every few hours to feed change into a meter.

When I left, the delivery room had been like a Wes Anderson movie. When I came back from moving the car, half an hour later, Wes Craven was in the director's chair. Before, we had been dealing with serious issues, but there had been an air of whimsy about the proceedings. Now, while the script was unchanged, there was palpable tension in the air. While I was gone, another midwife had come in, decided that Martha's glacial dilation needed to be pushed along, and manually broke her waters. Prior to this, it seems, her contractions had been like ripples on a pond, whereas now they were crashing in like waves on a stormy day.

Chris Rock had been hooked off stage, so I figured that it was my time to shine. That Best Husband Ever award wasn't going to win itself. I would provide the light entertainment for the rest of the proceedings.

'Hi,' I said, 'so, how have you been keeping?'

'I've been better,' answered Martha. 'Someone broke my waters. What's it like down there?'

I looked. 'It looks like a burst orange.'

'Please don't try to make me laugh,' Martha replied.

'Okay then, I'll tell you some more of my jokes,' I quipped, with a showbiz wiggle as I said it. Martha's facial muscles did not flinch. She looked at me so sternly that it made me think I would never, ever be able to make her laugh again. This was like doing stand-up on a cruise ship, during a typhoon.

I didn't know it then, but this would be very like my first actual comedy club set. The room was small, there was an audience of four or five people, the pay was non-existent, there was an undeniable strong smell, very few laughs, some heckling, and I was ultimately doomed to get upstaged by the headline act at the end.

By nine o'clock, the contractions were coming quickly, and between her heavy breaths she wheezed, 'Aidan, I don't think I can do this any more.'

There was a nurse down at the business end: 'You're nine centimetres dilated. It won't be much longer now until we can start pushing, Mrs Fitzpatrick.' (Martha did not take my name when we got married. Sometimes people call her Mrs Comerford. More often, though, I am called Mr Fitzpatrick.)

She told me afterwards that knowing that she only had a centimetre to go had renewed her. About half an hour later, Martha's cervix had reached full brick. We were on our way, or more precisely, our baby was. Martha started pushing at regular intervals. Then it was ten o'clock. More pushing. Eleven o'clock. Even more pushing. Midday: at around that time, I had a peek at the business end, and I saw the top of the little head inside – they had attached a heart monitor to it (so we could hear the heartbeat in the room, which was immensely reassuring) – and I could see that the baby had hair.

'Our baby has hair!' I said to Martha, almost crying with the wonder of it, as if hair on a human head was the most awesome thing anyone had ever seen in the Universe. I was already high on love.

What I didn't want to tell her was that the baby's head looked incredibly small. I'd seen other babies before, and in my limited experience at that time, I had noticed that babies tend to be mostly head. I take an extra-large cap myself, so it was unlikely that our baby's dome would be unusually small. No one else in the room seemed bothered, but the worry stayed with me, in the back of my mind.

Martha asked me to lean in. I was sure she was going to say something poignant, and I was ready to reply by telling her how well she was doing, how strong she was and that I loved her. 'Don't let me poo myself,' she whispered.

'Eh?'

'I don't want to poo myself, Aidan,' she repeated, a little more loudly and threateningly.

'Okay,' I said. What did she expect me to do? Go get a cork?

They decided that they would have to cut her to try to prevent tearing. Martha was disappointed. She had thought she could get through without the need for stitches. All that perineal massage I had done, selflessly, out of nothing but pure love and dedication, hadn't prevented the need for stitches. (Was it possible that that bit of *What to Expect When You're Expecting* was, ahem, slipped in there by a man?)

One of the staff asked me to look away while they made the incision, but I wasn't going to look away while someone cut my wife. What sort of a wuss they did think I was?

Now, let me assure you that this isn't going to be one of those clichéd labour stories where the partner sees a smidgeon of blood … a lot of blood … woah, actually … quite a lot of blood, and then ousjgakagssss ….

I didn't faint, but I really shouldn't have looked. All I can say, is that just the thought of the things that women go through when they are having babies is enough to blanch my manly heart. Martha had a *good* labour, compared to some of the awful stories I've heard from my female friends. It appears that Wes Craven gets around.

Not long after this, Martha cried, 'Did I just poo myself?'

I checked. She had pooed herself. 'Nope, definitely not,' I said, as the nurses quickly cleaned it up.

'I did,' she whined. 'You lied to me,' she added, in the same tone as a wife who has just walked in on her adulterous husband.

It was one o'clock. *How much more can she take?* I thought.

I think, between contractions, Martha might have fallen asleep for a moment or two around then. She was so exhausted. Waking, she said, 'I *really* don't think I can do this any more.'

'You're nearly there,' I said, and then I somewhat dented the confidence of my assertion by asking the midwife, 'Is she nearly there?'

The midwife looked at me and said, 'Not too far away now, Mr Fitzpatrick.'

Then, the next time Martha pushed, the baby's head started to crown, and as it emerged, I thought, *Oh right, I could only see a little bit of the top of the head before.* The head was big. The head was bigger. *Oh wow, there is so much head*, I thought, as it kept coming. The ratio of head I could see before to head I was seeing now was icebergian. If there is a God who designed this system of making humans, then he's pretty freaky. Even the kinkiest humans know to start with the thin end first.

And, finally, at half-past one, with Martha sucking on painkilling gas, she sprung our sprog.

It was a girl.

She was a girl.

I held my breath until I heard her first cry.

And then she cried.

Ailbhe cried.

I cried.

Martha was too tired to cry.

I couldn't believe after all that trauma that Ailbhe had made it through intact, although she did have some battle scars. Babies that aren't caesarean deliveries are usually a bit bruised in the face, but Ailbhe came out looking like she had lost a nine-month-long boxing match. Yet I would have fought anyone who dared to say that she wasn't the most beautiful baby ever born.

After a few quick checks, they put her on Martha's chest.

Martha said: 'Hello, Ailbhe.'

When she was handed over to me, and I held my baby girl for the first time, my heart expanded like a universe, and in my head, I immediately heard the same three little words that I think all new fathers hear: 'Don't. Drop. It.'

Martha looked at me. I looked at Martha. That was the first time that I noticed that she had burst blood vessels all over her forehead and around her eyes, and I thought, *Well, if she can get through that – if we can get through that – we can get through anything.* I knew that we were going to be good parents, because we were *so* prepared. We were *so* ready.

Then, the midwife came over, and we looked at her, expectantly, like the best students in the class, awaiting instructions, ready to excel at the next thing.

'Okay, can I have a nappy and a Babygro?' she asked us.

I looked at Martha. Martha looked at me. We had forgotten to bring them.

That evening, I was in Martha's parents' house in Swords, the newly-minted Granny and Grandad. The adrenaline of the birth had worn off by the time I walked in the door, and I had suddenly been able to smell myself. I had a much-needed long, hot shower and a much-appreciated meat-and-two-veg dinner. Later, I was up in the box bedroom, getting ready to go to sleep.

Ailbhe was born before we all committed our digital souls to Facebook, and everyone could just 'like' the fact that someone had a baby, so my phone had been buzzing all day with congratulatory texts.

I got a text that said, HOW MUCH DID SHE WEIGH?

I texted back, I'M NOT SURE, BUT I KNOW SHE WAS A LOT LIGHTER AFTER THEY TOOK THE BABY OUT OF HER.

I thought about Martha and Ailbhe in the hospital – my little family. I texted Martha, YOU WERE AWESOME TODAY. I LOVE YOU. She didn't text back. She was probably asleep. I turned off my phone, and I got into the bed. I felt a curious feeling, a sudden rush of endorphins. I was completely happy. In fact, that moment right there, I think, was the happiest moment of my life.

Then I drifted off to sleep.

February 2006

A couple of days later, on a morning so crisp it looked like every person on the street was puffing like a steam engine, it was time to bring Ailbhe home. I had brought a big, fleecy baby suit to put her in.

When I got to the hospital, and we put her in it, it was evident that my baby-measuring skills needed work. It was massive, and it made her look even smaller than she was. We put her into the detachable baby car seat that would slot into the holder in the car, which was parked a couple of streets away. The nurses also wrapped a few blankets around her, and we finished off the ensemble with a matching baby hat. The baby-covering to baby ratio was so high that her little sleeping face looked like a baked bean in a king-sized duvet.

If you've never experienced bringing your first child home from the hospital and you want to know how weird it feels, bounce on a pogo stick for about ten minutes, and then get off and walk around. That eerie, disconcerting feeling in your leg muscles – like you're still bouncing as you walk – is a good guide. Walking out of the hospital doors that day was like stepping out onto a new planet.

When we arrived at the car, five minutes later, Ailbhe was still asleep, or dead. I wasn't sure which one it was, and I didn't think we should be satisfied with not knowing. We had already been the parents who showed up too early, which isn't that bad really, but we didn't want to add to it by being the parents who went straight back to the hospital to say, 'We're sorry, but we appear to have broken our baby,' and yet my inability to detect the inward and outward movement of her little chest under the multiple layers was just a tad troubling.

Martha sat in the back seat beside Ailbhe, and I stood on the footpath, looking in the open door of the car. I didn't want to remove the layers, because, on a cold morning like this, she would surely, instantly freeze to death. Martha said we should just wake her up. What a monster! There was no need to go through that drama. Besides, I had a better plan: 'Give me your make-up mirror.' I would hold the mirror up to Ailbhe's mouth to detect the condensation of her little breaths. Simple.

Martha is an excellent amateur make-up artist, and she's done make-up for many of her friends' weddings. She can do make-up that makes a person glow, while also looking like they're not wearing any make-up at all. Martha always has a make-up mirror. I was looking at Ailbhe, holding out my hand to the side towards Martha, waiting for her to produce the mirror, like a surgeon seeking a vital implement, and yet, given that this was obviously an emergency, it was, oddly, not immediately forthcoming.

Then I looked at Martha to see what the problem was, and that was when I noticed that she had done an excellent job putting on her make-up that morning. It really looked like she wasn't wearing any, at all. Although, she seemed to have mistakenly put the smoky eyeshadow underneath her eyes. She wasn't looking in her bag. She was staring at me intently. 'I don't have a mirror,' she said, as if this was something I should have known.

I realised that it was me who was the panicked parent. In fact, Martha was relatively calm. She was right. It was probably unlikely that we had accidentally smothered Ailbhe, so, reluctantly, I got into the driver's seat and drove home, ninety-nine per cent sure that Ailbhe was still breathing.

After a few minutes, Martha said from the back seat, 'She's opened her eyes.'

'Opened her eyes in a dead, staring sort of way, or in an I'm still alive sort of way?' I asked.

When we got her home, I couldn't stop looking at her. She had a shock of dark-brown hair, a little footballer's haircut, with blonde highlights on the sides. I didn't think that was possible. Near the end of Martha's pregnancy, I had thought that her womb had become quite protuberant. But now, I was surprised that it hadn't been even bigger, given that there must have been a hair-stylist in there with Ailbhe as well. Being outside the womb, with no hair-stylist, she would eventually lose these highlights, naturally.

You know, I think I even loved looking at Ailbhe when I was changing her nap—

'HOLY SHIT, what are you feeding her?' I cried, stepping back from the changing table in horror. Ailbhe had just done her first two-fer. A two-fer is what we called it when it seemed like she had done two poos for the price of one. Ailbhe did a lot of two-fers, and she liked to vary the colours. She had an autumnal arse – lots of yellows, browns and greens. And yet, I quickly got used to it, because nothing was worse than the sight of the first poos she did in the hospital. The Meconium. A monster from the deep. A slick, black mess than looks like it was done by an orc with a deadly tummy bug.

Bathing Ailbhe was my job for the foreseeable future, for two reasons: One, it would be some nice Daddy–Daughter time. Two, and more importantly, Martha had failed the tennis-ball test. Also, quite a few beloved mugs had died by her hand. She was a serial killer of crockery. If she couldn't complete the tennis ball and mug-holding levels of life, she couldn't progress to the Boss Level: wet baby holding.

But I was also worried about dropping Ailbhe, even when she was dry, so deliberately making her slippier seemed to fly in the face of good health and safety practice. To add to my worry, Martha had a bought a baby bath that went on a metal stand, which to my mind was really just a fancy, wobbly sink. The whole enterprise seemed shockingly cavalier.

Before I was a dad, I knew that I had one superpower. Martha calls them my 'Asbestos Fingers'. You know when you cook garlic bread in the oven and when they come out you need to tear them into slices, but you can't even approach them, because they are hotter than the moment of creation? Luckily, the skin on the tips of my fingers is as calloused as my insides – my dead fingers (and insides) coming from years of playing guitar and singing my songs at uninterested crowds – so I could carry out this task without my digits immediately melting to stumps, as would happen to any normal person. As I was getting her ready for her first bath, I discovered that, as a dad, I had a new superpower.

You may have realised by now that my soul is on the sensitive end of the spectrum, but that's nothing compared to my elbows. My elbows are so sensitive I think they might have their own separate feelings. When it came to testing the water to see if it was the right temperature, my two heroes emerged: Elbow One and Elbow Two. These bad boys were better than any thermometer on the market for temperature testing. I dipped them in. Not too hot, not too cold. 'Goldilocks!' they said. (That's their superhero catchphrase.)

When I picked Ailbhe up out of her Moses basket she wriggled a bit, just to test me. Babies at that age usually don't smile, but I swear I could see pleasure on her little face as I lowered her oh-so-gently into the perfectly temperature-controlled water. (Thanks, Elbows.) She was loving this. I looked along her tiny little body, and I saw the water turn golden. Damn, that wasn't pleasure, that was her pee face. So, I had to take her out and start again. She had a lot to learn about bath time etiquette: 'No, Ailbhe, we don't wee in the bath, we wee in the shower.'

I learned a very valuable parenting lesson that day: cherish the beautiful moments with your children as they happen, because they can be very quick to piss all over them.

So I didn't drop her, of course. Well, I did, a little, but that was on purpose. See, as I laid her back into the Moses basket, at the last second, while still holding her, I dropped my hands down quickly, to give her that feeling you get when you drive with speed over a humpback bridge, so I could see her startle reflex. I loved that little reflex. She would throw her arms and legs out and go a little stiff, and then relax and draw her little clenched fists back into her body. However, in my defence, I only did it once … five times in a row. It was a lot of fun (for me) to watch her do it.

Apparently, this reflex is an inbuilt evolutionary mechanism that all babies have, for protection and defence, a leftover from ancient times, in case your tribe are being attacked, or if you're falling from a tree, or if your dad is just being a colossal prick.

March 2006

That first week with Ailbhe was bliss, but then I had to go back to work. That is when some of the advice that is given to new parents becomes a little less practical. For instance, I couldn't imagine my boss being very understanding if he found me slumped over the desk during the afternoon, and I excused myself by saying, 'Sorry, I'm just sleeping when the baby sleeps.'

From what I knew from friends of mine who had become parents, Ailbhe was much like every other baby: you love them with every cell of your being, and they, in turn, try to break you down at a cellular level.

You read about the tiredness, of course, but reading about tiredness is like reading about breaking a bone. I could vividly describe what it is like to have night after night of early morning wake-up calls, in those months before she settled into a more humane sleep pattern, but it would not accurately convey how utterly zombifying the experience actually is.

And there were two of us. What must it be like for single parents? They deserve a medal. Actually, no, they deserve more than a medal. They deserve zero per cent judgement and one hundred per cent support, and, most important, eight hours of sleep a night.

Thankfully, Ailbhe did not take after me. When I first brought her down to see my parents, my Mam said, 'Did I ever tell you that after we brought you home from the hospital you cried for eighteen months solid?'

'Let me think,' I said. 'Oh yes, I remember you telling me … every time we've talked for the last thirty years.'

However, she continued to tell the story. 'And that was after I'd carried you through the summer of 1976, the hottest Irish summer ever. I was fit to drop. You almost drove me into the mental home. We brought you to the doctor so many times, but we couldn't figure out what was wrong with you.'

'Have you figured it out yet?' I asked.

I had wondered why my mam continually brought up that story, but now I finally got it. Eighteen months of solid wailing? I was surprised she didn't have the story tattooed on my face so I would never forget it. I don't remember being like that as a baby, of course, but I think a few months after I had become a dad I called her to apologise. If I didn't, sorry, Mam. Thanks for not putting me in the bin.

Martha was determined to keep breastfeeding, even though she got bad mastitis. I inspected her breasts (professionally) and they were in bad shape. If her boobs were boxers and I was their manager, I would have thrown in the towel.

The first time I heard the word 'mastitis' was when I was a kid, watching the GAA All-Ireland finals. There would be adverts in the half-time break that appealed directly to Irish farming folk. These wouldn't have been as fancy as American Superbowl ads. Most of them consisted of GAA players endorsing a product by holding it or hitting it.

Among these ads were products to alleviate mastitis in ruminants. These would generally show a mad-eyed, terrified cow with a farmer forcing a medicine gun into the side of its mouth. I still have nightmares where I see those terrified cow faces.

And yet, I didn't really know what mastitis actually was until Martha got it. As a possessor of non-functioning breasts, I'd skimmed the breastfeeding bits in the pregnancy books, sure that it could all be summarised as 'put boob in baby.' So when I was watching Martha trying to get a proper latch, with her infected, tender, red boobs, I only had one 'helpful' suggestion: 'I think it's time to take you to the country and get you dosed.' Martha, for her part, would hook her finger into her mouth, and mime the fearful expression of the cow being subjected to the farmer's medicine hook, which would make me laugh, and give me flashbacks.

But she was reluctant to get antibiotics, because she thought it would harm Ailbhe. A friend who had been through the rigmarole of mastitis had told her that Ailbhe would be fine, and that all that would happen would be that her poos would be a bit runnier. We had seen so many shades and textures of poo in the first few weeks that that wasn't a deal-breaker. So Martha got some medicine and I administered it in a slightly more loving fashion than your average Irish farmer.

Even when she had mastitis, it didn't stop me being jealous of Martha's functioning funbags, because I wanted to help with the feeds. But as the old saying goes, you can't get milk from a man's tits.

One day after work, I made an executive decision: I marched into the nearest Mothercare. 'Give me the finest breast pump that you possess.' They showed me the finest one, which was clearly designed to be reassuringly expensive. So I said, 'Okay then, give me the second-finest breast pump that you possess.'

After a little bit of perusal, I went for the mid-range one, which was somewhere between the one that was essentially a gold-plated milking machine, and the one that came with a foot pump.

Over the next few weeks, Martha produced enough milk to supply a Co-Op, and in the freezer, in between the fish fingers and chips, the stash of bottles of frozen breast milk grew. We stored

them up, like Andy Dufresne from *The Shawshank Redemption*
deposited dirt from his escape tunnel in the prison exercise yard,
because, for us, the frozen milk meant freedom.

It meant that I could feed Ailbhe, and Martha could get
a break. But it also meant that Sheila and Brendan could feed
Ailbhe, so we could get a break away together. We were able to
go on my annual college-gang reunion, which was on that St
Patrick's weekend. (There's only one rule on these weekends: no
kids.) We both felt bad about leaving Ailbhe for the first time, so
I made a few compilation CDs of eighties, fluffy-haired anthems
for the car. There is nothing better than eighties songs for singing
away the pain. It is impossible to be sad when you're listening to
REO Speedwagon, and we sang every note of every song all the
way there.

July 2001

Martha and I had been going out for a few weeks, and we were off to a wedding together. This was the first time we would see each other properly dressed up. I had just arrived at Martha's house to pick her up. It was a half-an-hour drive from the house to the venue. My friends were getting married in an hour, exactly. So, if we left within fifteen minutes, we'd be a quarter of an hour early, or as I call it, on time.

When I rang the doorbell I heard Martha shout, 'It's open,' from upstairs, so I walked in and called up, 'It's me.'

'Make yourself some tea, I'll be there in a few minutes.'

Tea? Did I have time for tea? A very quick one, maybe. I clicked on the kettle and came back out to the hall. 'How are you doing?' I called out, trying not to sound too anxious about the time.

'Fine, I'm just doing my make-up … be there in a sec.' I did not know then that Martha's sec and my sec are vastly different units of measurement. We do not have a same secs relationship. (And no, I'm not even a little bit ashamed of that pun.)

In the only long-term relationship I had before Martha, the woman I was with didn't wear make-up, so I didn't know how long the process took, but I'd seen women on commuter buses put it on while the bus bumped over the streets of Dublin, and they did it quickly enough, so on *terra firma* it couldn't take that long, could it? That was when I found out that when it comes to make-up, Martha is an artiste. A piss-artiste, to be precise. She does a beautiful job, but she does that beautiful job by never, ever, EVER being rushed.

Half an hour later we still hadn't left. I had worn myself out pacing, so I had taken a seat out to the hall, placed it by the end of the stairs, and sat down. This was a registry office wedding, which, from start to finish, takes about as long as a Shania Twain song. At this point we wouldn't just be late, we were going to miss the whole thing. I could hear my heart ticking.

A few minutes later, she finally appeared at the top of the stairs. She was worth waiting for. For a moment, the ticking of my heart stopped and it began beating again, loudly.

'Oh wow,' I said. So many superlatives exploded in my mind as she walked down the stairs. She took the steps regally. *Beautiful, Stunning, Resplendent*, I thought, and then *Falling … Oh God, really falling …* When she got to the middle of the stairs, she lost her footing and tumbled straight to the bottom, ending up arse-over-tit, with her dress up around her oxters, and yet, somehow, still holding onto the balustrade. Her make-up did look very good, though.

It was mostly her pride that was hurt. And her elbows. And her knees. Her new tights were ripped and bloody, but otherwise, she was miraculously un-scuffed. I tried to help her up, but it was difficult, because I was laughing too much.

As I drove to the wedding, with a heavy foot, Martha pulled off the tights, rolled them into a ball and stuffed them into the side pocket of my car door.

By the time we got there, she was laughing about her fall too. After I parked, we ran, and we managed to slip in just as the bride was about to enter. Shania Twain was singing, *'Looks like we made it …'*

A week later, Martha brought me to meet her family for the first time. Martha is the eldest, and then there is her sister, Sinéad, and then there is Derm. I wouldn't get to meet Derm for another week or two, when he came to one of my gigs with Martha.

Sinéad was there, though. She answered the door to us. Martha had told me that Sinéad had recently had surgery to get a cyst removed at what Sinéad called the bottom of her back. 'Hi, how's the top of your crack?' was the first thing I said to her. She made an annoyed and amused face. This was going to be fine.

I really wanted Martha's mam and dad to like me. My plan was the same plan I always had back then, when I wanted new people to like me; I would rapidly recite every word I knew in various hilarious combinations. I would be Mr Quippy. I would break world records hiking to the peak of Mount Loquacious, and come back down a hero, loved by all.

After an hour, I thought it was going quite well. Years later, Sheila would say to Martha, 'I never really saw you as a long-term item after I first met him. He was too … emmmmm … '

'Much?' said Martha.

So, when Sheila suggested that some supplies were needed for dinner, Martha very quickly offered my services, 'Aidan will go,' so that everyone could get a break from my one-man show. Sinéad said she'd come along with me, though, because she was obviously keen to hear my full arsenal of arse jokes.

Sinéad is all neatness, and I am not. When she got into the car, she didn't think anything of doing a bit of impromptu tidying up from the passenger seat. (I think she carries her own rubbish bag for such occasions.) When she started tidying, I said, 'Oh no, don't do that.' She said, 'It's no problem,' and as she said it, she put her hand on the pair of balled-up tights in the side pocket of the car. As she went to put them in the bin, they unfurled enough for her to see the bloodied knees. She held them up. She looked at me. I glanced at her. I could see that she had jumped to the conclusion that these tights were the awful aftermath of sin and friction, and for the first time that evening, I was speechless.

I shrugged. She put the tights into the bag, mildly appalled. I didn't address it. Instead I went back to the arse jokes. 'So, what's it like to have two bumholes?'

At least I had only been a garrulous gombeen when I met Sinéad and Martha's folks.

The next day, when Martha and I went to meet my parents, it started well enough. We had a pleasant cup of tea in the sitting room. It was such a lovely afternoon, it was generally agreed that it would be quite nice if we retired to the back garden. As usual, the lawn was neatly manicured, the hedges were wonderfully coiffed, and Martha was commenting appropriately on how well-appointed everything looked, when she spotted my dad's bum.

He was wearing dark trousers, and the seat of the trousers had a fine covering of light-blue fluff, the same shade as the new mohair jumper Martha was wearing for the occasion. She must have been shedding, and he must have sat somewhere she had been sitting.

So, Martha reached out, and started to brush his bum. Because no-one else had seen the fluff, it looked like Martha had just decided to pat her prospective father-in-law's posterior, out of the blue, which isn't generally the custom in Carlow.

Mam jumped in to stop it like a boxing referee: 'It's fine, I'll get it!'

'I must have been moulting,' Martha explained.

Driving back to Dublin that evening, we offered each other some helpful advice on first impressions: 'You know, you should try to relax when you're meeting new people,' Martha suggested.

'You're right,' I replied, 'and you should try not to sexually assault my da.'

April 2006

Sinéad came over to help Martha out with Ailbhe one Friday, so Martha could get some rest. After a day of looking after a three-month-old, Sinéad was tired, so she decided to stay over that night rather than drive back to Swords.

For reasons unknown, Ailbhe cried all through that night, which was unusual for her. In the morning, she needed to be changed and fed. Martha was blearily imploring me to get up, to bring Ailbhe downstairs, and do it. My argument was simple: 'But your boobs are right there.' This very salient point was not the argument-ender I had hoped it would be. Apparently, Martha had been up 'half the night'. I'm not the maths wizard in our marriage, but didn't that mean that I was up for the other half of the night? Eventually, I dragged myself out of bed, cursing the day I went and bought the breast pump, and sure that Martha was breaching some European Union working hours directive by asking me to do this. 'Fine!' I said, in that way people say 'fine' when they are definitely not fine.

I was in a huff. I huffed on my dressing gown. I huffed Ailbhe up into my arms. I huffed out of the room. I huffed down the stairs. I know that you should never run down the stairs. I did not know, however, that huffing down the stairs can be equally dangerous. When I got to the third-last step from the bottom, my foot huffed off the edge of the step, and flew out in front of me. Suddenly, I was airborne, and about to come down with a hefty crash landing. My arms were fully encumbered with Ailbhe, so I couldn't throw them out to save myself. Instead, I gripped her into me, and turned myself as much as I could in that split second so that she would not be hurt.

My lower back smacked off the apex of the step, with all my weight, and I was immediately in agony. I roared. Ailbhe started crying, but luckily, she was not hurt. I think she might just have been shocked by my sudden volume.

Martha came running out of our room, closely followed by Sinéad coming from the spare room. There were three things that were immediately apparent to them: Ailbhe was okay. My skin had literally turned green with the pain. My dressing gown had opened up, and Little Aidan had made an appearance. When Martha got to me, she picked up Ailbhe, and covered up Little Aidan in the process. 'Are you okay? I'm sorry,' she said. 'Been. Better. Sorry. Too,' I wheezed.

Later, I was in bed recuperating, when Sinéad came in to give me a restorative cup of tea. 'Are you feeling better?' she asked.

'I am,' I replied, because I was.

Then she whispered, 'Don't worry, I didn't see much.'

That seemed unlikely. 'But my mouse was entirely out of the house?' I said.

She smiled, 'Yes, as I said, I didn't see much.'

August 2001

I had taken the day off work. It was a Friday morning. Even though it was early, it was already warm, and the sky was a Mediterranean blue. I was about to go away on a weekend that would be hot in more ways than one, with Martha, my new lover, the woman I adored: you will rarely find a finer set of circumstances.

The only thing is that I didn't know where we were going. As Martha couldn't drive, she was going to direct me. She told me not to look as she packed the boot of my car.

We were about six weeks into our relationship, and I don't think we had stopped talking since we'd met. When things are going that well, and the chat is mighty, there is still the worry that one of you will suddenly say something disqualifying. Imagine thinking that you've met the love of your life – you've connected deeply on an emotional and physical level – and then one night, while you are looking lovingly into each other's eyes, the supposed love-of-your-life whispers something slightly off-putting like, 'By the way, I'm not a huge fan of the Jews.' Now, unless 'The Jews' also happens to be the nickname of some obscure football team you haven't heard of, the relationship will probably be in a bit of trouble. Or they might say something even more heinous like, 'I don't completely love the movie *The Princess Bride*,' and then the relationship will cease, immediately. There is no coming back from things like that.

But the chat in the car on the way was easy, and not at all bigoted or racist. *Yes,* I thought, *there was still a very small chance that Martha was a serial killer, and that I was her unwitting victim – perhaps she didn't want me to look in the boot because the only things in there were a shovel and a bag of lime?* Ha! I'd tell her about that thought once we got to whatever well-appointed hotel we were probably going to. That'd be a good laugh.

After driving down the motorway that cuts through the boggy middle of Ireland, she told me to turn off at a roundabout in Edgeworthstown, and the route went from dual carriageway, to national route, to country road, until eventually we arrived at a town called Granard. *Quaint,* I thought, thinking this was our destination. 'Where are we staying?'

'We're not quite there yet.' It was about to get even quainter.

We drove on through the town, and the road became a lane, and then a few turns later, it was a bóithrín with a grass median. On we went, and it became a dirt and gravel road, which went uphill, turned a few corners, and terminated at the gate of a field, with no sight, sound or sniff of civilisation nearby.

'Okay,' I said. 'What now?' Martha smiled and said nothing. She got out of the car and opened the gate, and then walked on and opened another gate about thirty feet beyond that. She shouted back to me to drive through the gates and stop. This all seemed slightly … murder-y.

She got back in the car, and I eyed her suspiciously. She seemed very pleased with herself. As I rounded the last corner, I saw a cute stone cottage. I pulled up right alongside it. In the front, it had two red windows and a red door. Over to the side of the house, there was also a small timber cabin, with a set of swings beside that. 'We're here.'

'Where is here?' I asked, hoping not to hear her say: 'My lair.'

'This is my Uncle Brian's cottage, and just down that hill, beyond the trees is Lough Gowna. We just call it Gowna.' Her

Uncle Brian had bought the house decades previously, when it had been nothing more than a derelict cow shed. Since then he had been steadily restoring it, making it more and more liveable over the years. 'My family came here for summers when I was a kid, and it's ours for the weekend,' said Martha, still smiling.

'It's lovely,' I said, as I opened the boot to discover a packed bag, some food supplies, and no murder-y accoutrements at all. She had brought me to this one-time cow shed house because she loved me, and wanted to share this beloved place with me. I was honoured. It was wonderful. I loved it like I loved Martha: immediately.

When she brought me inside and gave me the tour, I saw a high-ceilinged main room, with white-painted stone walls, and a wide-mouthed fireplace already stacked with timber and ready to be lit. There were lots of vintage ornaments and knick-knacks on a vintage dresser, various shelves and hanging around the walls. To one side of the fireplace, there was a door into a kitchenette, and through the door on the other side, there was a bedroom. The toilet was in an outhouse at the back, near a grove of trees, to the side of the boggy back garden. The shower … was a zinc basin in the middle of the floor. 'Do you fancy a wash?' Martha asked.

'But I'm not dirty?' I said, with a smile.

'Oh, you will be …'

Later that evening, freshly washed, we walked a little way back up the entrance lane, hand in hand. 'I've something to show you.' Just to the right was a gate into a field, which seemed like the entrance-way to heaven. Beyond that gate, the view was of an expansive, green field which rolled down to Lough Gowna, glimmering in the evening sun. Some swans were swimming. On the other side of the lake, the hills undulated away from the shore. 'We'll walk down tomorrow,' said Martha. I leaned on the gate and surveyed the view.

'Thank you for bringing me here,' I said, and I kissed her.

On Saturday evening, I was lying on the couch, drifting into a delicious sleep. I looked over at Martha, in the chair by the roaring fire, wearing only a tie-dyed blanket as a dress, with her legs curled under, devouring a good book, and I thought, 'I am going to marry this woman.' Even if she didn't love *The Princess Bride*, and hadn't been able to do an excellent Inigo Montoya impression …

> '*Hallo! My name is Inigo Montoya. You killed my father. Prepare to die.*'
>
> '*Martha, please, I've said this before, not while we're having sex, okay?*'

… we could work through it.

I imagined Martha and me bringing our kids to Gowna for a summer holiday and how idyllic that would be. I wasn't totally naïve; I knew there'd be struggles – '*Daddy, help! I don't think I have the right number of syllables in my haiku*' – and tantrums – '*Waah! Mammy, you've given me too many choices in this breakfast buffet*' – but between this wonderful woman and me, we would raise our kids to be happy, funny, confident, well-educated, grounded, beloved people. And then, maybe one day, they would bring their kids to Gowna as well – if that's what they wanted, of course. We would never put pressure on them; as far as I was concerned, our kids, Tony, Oscar, Grammy and Nobel, could be whatever they wanted to be.

On the Saturday night, we stood outside in the boggy back garden looking up at the clear night, bewildered by the number of visible stars. Martha was identifying constellations and talking about the Greek gods. *What have I done to deserve this erudite goddess?* I thought. These are the things that she would teach our kids.

For Martha, Gowna was as rustic as she was prepared to go. Whereas, at the time, I was still volunteering as a scout leader. For me, it was like luxury camping. Not long after that first weekend with Martha in Gowna, I went away for a weekend camping with the scouts. Afterwards, I came straight back to Martha's place. She opened the door and went to hug me, but stopped half-way, and took a quick step back. 'Oh my God!' she said, covering her nose with her hand. I realised that she was probably smelling my heady mixture of sweat, campfire and neglect. It was as if generations of onions had perished in my crevices. 'Did you change your clothes once?' Martha asked, noticing that I was returning in the same outfit I had left in.

'Change my clothes? Sure, I was only away for the weekend?' I replied, puzzled.

In an appalled, pinched-nosed voice, Martha asked: 'At least you changed your underpants, right?'

She knew nothing about camping: 'Martha, there are four ways to wear underpants on camp: frontways, backways, inside-out frontways and inside-out backways. There's another couple of days in these bad boys yet!' I replied, snapping at my waistband …

… and these are things that I would teach our kids.

July 2003

We were driving home from Swords, discussing where we would get married. As per most of the population, we were both raised Catholic, but we had drifted away from it. When I say drifted, I don't mean that we were à la carte Catholics; our beliefs were more … off-menu. Some people would call us 'lapsed' Catholics. We would have described ourselves as … 'not'. Not Catholics.

Still, at the time, the options being more limited than now, we could either get married in a church or in a registry office. We decided that for an easy life (because there is nothing like a wedding to strain familial tensions) we would get married in a church. We would, instead, draw our atheistic line in the sand with the kids. They would not be baptised. When they were older they could choose for themselves what to believe or not to believe, and we would try to be understanding and accepting of their choices:

> *'Daddy, I have something to tell you, and you're not going to like it.'*
> *'Darling, you can tell me anything. I will always love you, no matter what.'*
> *'I prefer the Star Wars prequels.'*
> *'You're dead to me.'*

Because we were getting married in a church, it meant that we had to go to a Catholic pre-marriage course. This would be held for three nights over three weeks in the local parish hall. When Martha booked the course she said, 'And, let's say that someone had never been to the parish hall, how would they get there, hypothetically?'

That's how we ended up, on a cold Tuesday night, blinking in the fluorescent light of a room in the parish hall with about twenty other couples. I don't know how the rest of the couples felt about it, but we were sure that after living together for over a year we had discussed everything that needed to be discussed. What could this course teach us?

One of the first exercises was to sit knee-to-knee and talk about what you wanted to bring into your relationship from your family life growing up, and what you didn't. We had already talked about this, but we went through it again because we didn't have anything else better to do: We would eat our meals together, like both our families always did. We wouldn't slap our kids to punish them. We had already opened a joint account where we pooled our money, so we would be either rich or poor together. The hope was that Martha could stay at home while the kids were young and return to work once they went to school. This wasn't because Martha was the possessor of our vagina, it was because, ridiculously, I got paid nearly as much as Martha's school principal; it wasn't biology, it was basic economics. And when we were discussing how long Martha would be out of work we realised that, while we were sure that we both wanted kids, we hadn't ever decided exactly how many kids we wanted to have, which seemed like a slight oversight in preparing to spend the rest of our lives together.

I had the number four in my head. My reasoning was simple. We would pour so much of our love and energy into an only child that they would probably burst. So, to avoid that mess, we could have two children. However, two children would also be a bad idea, because I've read the Bible, and I've learned from it that we could easily end up with a Cain and Abel situation. Three children would be lovely – three being a perfect number – except that would mean that there would be a middle child. Middle children can do terrible, attention-seeking things, like inflicting their 'books' on the general population. There's far too much of that neediness going on already.

Martha asked, 'What do you think about having four?'

'That's what I was thinking,' and after I explained my theories on family sizes and why four was a good number, I added, 'Five or more, that's *Lord of the Flies* time. You couldn't properly parent that. After five, you might as well lob in a conch and kiss Piggy goodbye.'

September 2006

I remember Ailbhe's first roar. It was a Saturday morning, and she was sleeping between us. We both had our heads resting on one elbow, either side of her. We were talking about how lovely she was and how lucky we were to have her. We may have been staring a little too intently, because we set off her proximity sensors. Her eyes suddenly sprang open, she saw our looming faces and went off with a demonic, guttural: 'Guurraahh!'

We both jumped back and let out an: 'Ahhh!' of our own. Then we laughed, and she cried. We decided that in future we might need to give her a few more millimetres of personal space.

Her first word came relatively early. She was about seven or eight months old. It was 'Bear!' We knew that it was an attempt to say 'Bear!' because it was spoken in the exact same cadence and tone as Tutter, the annoying mouse from *Bear in the Big Blue House*. I got into the habit of calling her 'Bear' or 'Ailbhe Bear' and still call her that today. Sometimes I also call her 'Spanner' or 'Crazyface' because, when she is an adult, I want her to have plenty of good material for her psychotherapist.

In that first year, Martha, ever the educator, would mark off the milestones. Early on, Ailbhe could lift her head when she was on her stomach. A few months later, she could roll over – baby's first stunt move. Then she could sit up, unassisted. And then she could crawl. By the time she was eleven months old, we were so happy with her progress. We felt like we were good parents. We started talking about when we would have a second baby.

November 2006

We never discussed whether we could afford a second baby or not. The construction industry was booming, loud and proud. I didn't know then that a few sensible people in the financial sector already knew that the boom was just a blowhard.

At the time, I felt very lucky to be a part of it. I had started out my career by spending two years half-arsing my way through a half-arsed college course in Architectural Graphics. I say it was half-arsed, because we spent most of the time learning on drawing boards when much of the industry had already moved on to Computer Aided Drawing (CAD). (I still have a black dot tattoo from the time I shook one of my technical pens too vigorously and accidentally stabbed myself in the knuckle. I was not good with a pen. I would never have been able to do my job if it weren't for computers.)

In 1995 when I looked for a job after I left college, most of my interviews went something like this:

> 'Can you use CAD?'
> 'I can draw a spanner.'
> 'You are a spanner. Please leave.'

So I was on the dole for about six months, before I got accepted on to a six-month CAD course. When I qualified from that course, I was offered two jobs as a draughtsperson with small architectural practices. After nearly three years of study, including attaining Jedi-level CAD skills, I was to be rewarded with a salary that was a tenner more per week than the dole.

There was also a job with a very small structural engineering consultancy firm in the midlands, which paid twenty quid more than the dole. I wanted that job, not because I knew that much about structural engineering, or was especially interested in it, but because an extra tenner every week would pay for a lot of Dolmio pasta sauce. So I blagged my way through that interview, with all the false bravado of a virgin who says that he has definitely touched a boob, one time, over the top. Surprisingly, they believed me and I was offered the job. I spent the first year desperately trying to learn quickly enough so that I would not be found out.

At my first review, my boss told me he was very happy with my work, so happy that he was going to pay me an extra tenner every week. This was very disappointing, as I had been hoping for a lot more. I was sick of Dolmio. So I started looking for a new job. About six months later I got an interview in Dublin for a job as a draughtsperson with the structural department of a property development company. They offered me a job with a fifty per cent raise. I walked out of that interview feeling like I could buy a Dolmio factory. I moved to Dublin.

By 2006 the company had moved to a bigger office, and I was the head structural draughtsperson. We were struggling to hire sufficiently skilled staff. I knew this was the case because one day I was sitting at a computer with a new draughtsperson, trying to teach him how to draw a section through a building by cutting an apple in half. At one time, we had sought third-level qualifications and years of relevant experience, but as the tower cranes continued to climb across the city sky, and the construction industry went über-viral, our requirements slipped, somewhat. I was pretty sure I could get a job for Ailbhe based on the fact that she had just mastered her pincer grip.

One day, the receptionist called and said an older guy with experience as a draughtsperson had walked in off the street looking for a job. We told her to grab him before he went somewhere else. We were so starved of good candidates that this was like finding a fifty quid note walking across a bog. My boss and I went to meet him immediately.

In the interview room, we met a spry, late-fifty-something Polish guy, in a smart, black suit, and an early-twenty-something, attractive Polish woman. This was an incongruous sight, because we had been used to meeting singular, nervous young lads in ill-fitting shirts and baggy trousers.

Unfortunately, the spry guy would have struggled to order dinner in English. He was far from fluent. His sidekick, however, presented herself as his interpreter: 'I speak for him!' She assured us that he would master English soon: 'He is quick learner.' Unfortunately, she didn't know any technical English, like 'circular hollow section' or 'high-tensile steel' or 'brick'.

After five minutes of misunderstandings, we called in one of our Polish engineers to talk to this odd couple, because we were intrigued. After a short conversation in Polish, our colleague told us that the spry guy had once owned a toilet paper factory in Poland. He had left his wife and his company to follow his new girlfriend (the interpreter), who had come to Ireland to meet Louis Walsh, because she wanted to become a pop star. The spry guy's drawing experience was that he had once used computers to design packaging for his toilet paper products.

We felt it best at this point to excuse ourselves, and go out to the corridor. 'So, what do you think?' I asked, laughing.

My boss laughed too, and then said: 'I think we should hire him.'

I laughed at that, until I realised that he wasn't entirely joking. *I'm going to need a lot more apples*, I thought. We didn't hire him, though. We told him to come back in a few months when his English was better, but we never saw him again.

December 2006

Considering the year of constant riding it took to make Ailbhe, the fact that Martha was in her mid-thirties, and the family of four that we hoped to have, we decided that we really needed to get going on baby number two – so we started trying again at Christmas. That made a lot of sex … I mean sense.

I grew up in the eighties, and these were not the halcyon days of sex education. In fact, my sex education was just one sentence: 'The body is the doorway to hell, and the penis is the handle.'

That's actually a joke I have told on stage many times, but my sex education wasn't, in fact, much more expansive than that. When I was eleven, my parents sat me down and told me that to make babies you had to have sex. 'And how do you have sex?' I asked. My mam replied, 'Well, first you get married … ' 'The Talk' I got after that was functional, pragmatic and very Catholic. I never heard any non-Catholic words like 'libido' or 'clitoris' or 'consent'.

In school, we had an ancient Civics teacher, who was a school fixture, and one of the decent eggs in the teaching clutch. Every year it was his task to give the new brood of first-year boys their sex education, which was to be covered in a single class. I was taught the Irish language for fourteen years, and now, like a lot of Irish people, my knowledge of my native tongue does not extend far beyond asking to go to the toilet: *'An bhfuil cead agam dul go dtí an leithreas?'* By that measure, given the amount of time that was devoted to sex education in school, it's a wonder I can find my own penis.

This Civics teacher walked into the class that day, stood at the top table and said, 'Boys, do you want to know about the facts of life?' The class was aged between eleven and thirteen. I was the youngest. Most of us had just got over the whole Santa Claus isn't real thing. Why couldn't we just talk about Civics? Even learning Irish social history would be preferable to going through this embarrassing experience with one of our teachers. I would much rather have talked about what happened in 1916 than talk about the Rising that was happening in my pants. But, trapped in that musky classroom, all I could do was join in the class's collective mumble: 'Yeees, siiir.'

And then he proceeded: 'The Earth is two hundred and fifty thousand miles from the moon. The Sun is ninety-three million miles from the Earth, the Galaxy is … ' and so on, until he stopped himself, and said, 'Oh, are those not the facts you want?' Then he laughed, very much on his own. I heard afterwards that he did this every year. He was like the stand-up comedian who does the same bad routine, repeatedly, to silence, and then comforts himself after every gig by telling himself (and anyone else who will listen), 'They just weren't my crowd.'

But the real joke was that all he did after that was to describe the biology of sex. Just the nuts and bolts. The ins and outs of it. The structural mechanics. Then he asked us if we had any questions. *Questions?* I didn't know where to start. If I had been at all prescient, I would have asked: 'Sir, if your wife has had a non-existent libido since the conception of your first child, but you want to have another baby, how do you get her excited about having sex again?'

I was excited about having sex with Martha again. I couldn't wait to get back into it, so to speak. I bought Martha some lingerie for Christmas, but in retrospect, that was really just a present for me. She also got me a present that was really a present for her: an industrial-sized tub of non-spermicidal lubricant. It's a perfect present for your lover if you want to tell them that 'you make my soul sing, you make my heart love, you make my brain dream, and yet my nethers remain as parched as a dead lizard.'

Martha wanted a baby, and not just any baby. She wanted an 'Aidan-Baby', as she called it, a little boy who looked like me – the poor chap. She thought that it might take just as long or longer to make an Aidan-Baby than it had taken to make an Ailbhe Bear. Her libido was so low that facing into that much sex felt like beginning *Finnegans Wake* directly after she'd just got through *Ulysses*, whereas I was looking forward to a good bit of heavy booking.

January 2007

In the New Year, our sex life was back on track. Choo! Choo! Full steam ahead!

One night in mid-January, I was in the bed ready to take another ride on the Martha train (the Orient Express of train rides, in my opinion), when she came out of the en suite bathroom, looking shocked. 'Aidan, I'm pregnant!' Our sex life immediately left the rails. There were no survivors.

While I was happy to avoid the frustration of another year of inexplicable infertility, I was unhappy about the impending nine months of sexual frustration. After nearly two years of very little sex, I had hoped that there would be, at least, a few months of a run-up to the impregnation. Big Aidan, upstairs, was delighted … Little Aidan, downstairs, was dejected.

This also meant that our once-faulty equipment had somehow become a well-oiled baby-making machine, so having two more children after this, which we had thought might have been a problem, was now a probability. So there would be a baby, and then lots more baby-making to look forward to, so Little Aidan wasn't too disconsolate.

'I can't believe it happened so quickly,' said Big Aidan and Little Aidan together. While I tried to make sure that Big Aidan's delight was to the fore, Martha still heard Little Aidan's disappointed undertone.

'Oh, Aidan, I know you were looking forward to a bit more sex.'

'No, it's fine,' I said, putting on my bravest face.

Then Martha climbed into bed beside me and said, 'I think we can manage a celebratory ride, what do you think?'

Things were suddenly looking up for Little Aidan. 'I think so.' Choo! Choo!

February 2007

At around thirteen months, Ailbhe passed another developmental milestone: she picked her favourite parent. It was Martha. I took it well: 'Martha. Martha. Martha, Meh, Meh, Meh, I'm so popular,' I whined, like Jan from *The Brady Bunch*.

'She's just a bit mammy-centric,' Martha replied. 'She'll get over it.'

I heard tales of other kids greeting their dads with a hero's welcome or, even more enthusiastically than that, as if he was the star of their favourite YouTube channel. Ailbhe did not so much as raise her head when I came in the door. To Ailbhe, Martha was the fine wine of parenting. When Martha wasn't available, I was acceptable, just like a house red.

At those times, I did all the usual 'Daddy' things with her: the rough and tumble, the tickles and giggles, trying to get her to listen to all the albums I love: 'You need to listen to this one a few times, but after a while, you'll realise that it's genius.' Sitting her beside a chess board and pretending she was beating me – 'Oh, the Sicilian Defence, is it? Interesting choice,' I would say, as she gummed her king to death.

When Martha was there, though, I wasn't even a house red: I was vinegar.

March 2007

Martha is a big fan of the world, and consequently, she has seen a lot of it. The first time we talked about our respective travels, she told me that she had been to Australia for a year; holidayed in Italy and Canada, and got chased by deer when she was in Japan. She stopped the stories of her travels there, not because she was finished, but because she wanted to give me a chance to talk about mine. 'And where have you been?'

'Well, I've spent a few days in Edinburgh, and I went to Brussels, once, for a weekend.'

'And?' she asked.

'And … it was fun,' I said, concluding my story.

We both wanted Ailbhe to be worldly. Ailbhe seemed to be intensely interested in the little plastic animals Martha bought her to play with, so it seemed to us that the excellent BBC documentary *Planet Earth* would be the perfect introduction to the World. *Planet Earth* is voiced by Mister Mellifluous himself, David Attenborough. His smooth, relaxing tones and intelligent commentary are so lovely that they often make grannies feel inappropriate in their big, comfortable pants.

'Can I borrow that DVD when you're finished with it?' – *Martha's mam, often.*

Martha, Ailbhe and I watched the first episode together. There was a lovely scene where a mother polar bear introduces her two baby bears to the world, just like we were introducing our baby bear to the world. *This was a good idea*, I thought.

Ten minutes in, there was a shot from the air of a massive herd of caribou, documenting their ceaseless land migration. Then the shot changed to show the herd being tracked by a ravenous pack of wolves. One wolf successfully split a baby caribou from the pack and chased it. Martha and I exchanged a look that said, 'Maybe this isn't actually that appropriate for our fourteen-month old?'

We had no TV channels in the house, because we didn't watch enough TV to bother getting any TV service, so up to that point Ailbhe had been restricted to children's DVDs. This sort of predator–prey stuff never happened in *Bear in the Big Blue House*. (Although I wouldn't be surprised if there was a lost episode where Treelo, the gentle lemur, finally snaps and tears Tutter a new one.)

My immediate instinct was to find a way to soften the scene for her. 'The wolf just wants to hug the caribou … ' then the wolf caught the caribou and bit it on the back … 'with its mouth and teeth,' I finished.

Martha had no time for my mollycoddling nonsense. She was of a mind that if we were to show the world in all its glory, we couldn't ignore the world in all its gory. There are worse things to expose growing minds to, like, for instance, that awful glory/gory play on words I just did. (That's the sort of thing that makes this book unsuitable for young, fragile minds. Although I think we may have crossed that Rubicon back when I was making love to the Death Star…)

Martha explained what was happening on the screen: 'He's going to catch him.'

Ailbhe repeated this as one word: 'Hesgonnacatchem.'

Martha and I looked at each other. We didn't say anything, but the look of surprise and pride that passed between us said, *Oh, my God, she just said her first sentence!*

And Martha continued, 'he's going to kill him.'

'Hesgonnakillem.'

'He's going to eat him.'

'Hesgonnaeatem,' repeated Ailbhe.

From that point on, 'hesgonnacatchem, hesgonnakillem, hesgonnaeatem,' was Ailbhe's mantra whenever she watched that scene, until the caribou was caught and accepted its part in God's awful plan. Then it became her mantra whenever she watched any scene in *Planet Earth*. It was a bit odd, we thought, but we were mostly delighted and proud that she could make a coherent string of noise.

We would have been a little bit worried about her lack of empathy for the poor baby caribou, had she not liked animals so much. We'd often come in to the sitting room and find the plastic animals paired up neatly across the floor, two by two, but just the mammies and babies. It was like an art installation called 'Fuck you, Daddy.'

'Don't worry, she'll come around,' said Martha one night.

'I'm not worried. This isn't over. It's best of four, remember?'

September 2007

Martha does not have red hair. I do not have red hair. Our parents do not have red hair. None of our siblings has red hair. As far as I know, none of our grandparents had red hair. And yet Sophie was born with a lovely little tuft of red hair on her head. Her hair was red, much like my mate Dee's hair. (Dee for Diarmuid.)

We had gone to Dee and Lisa's house for New Year's Eve, and when we worked out the timing, it was highly likely that Sophie had been conceived then. Up until the point of Sophie's emergence, I had been relatively confident that I was party to that conception. Martha said that she didn't think she had made a baby with Dee, as that seemed like something she would have remembered doing.

I texted a picture message of Sophie to relatives and friends with the typical announcement: SOPHIE, SEVEN POUNDS, TEN OUNCES. I'M DOING FINE, THANKS, but the picture message I texted to Dee was simply captioned, CARE TO EXPLAIN THIS? He texted me back denying carnal knowledge of my wife, but adding that his boys were fine Irish midlands stock, and as such, not only were they good swimmers, they were also good walkers.

Martha and I have a red-haired cousin each, so it's likely that gene is somewhere in the family. I also have a touch of ginger in my upstairs beard, and a lot more in my downstairs beard, although I did not feel it was necessary to share this particular theory with my folks when they came to visit. Mam asked, 'Where did she get the red hair from?'

'I don't know, Mam, but I'll be keeping a closer eye on Dee from now on!'

Relative to Ailbhe's birth, Sophie's birth had been easy. My hand had a bit of cramp from holding Martha's hand, and my feet were slightly sore from standing for the couple of hours it took her to deliver, but otherwise I felt a lot less tired than I had after Ailbhe. I was really getting the hang of this baby-making business.

Martha wasn't doing too badly either. Combined, we were to baby-making what Mr Kipling was to cake-baking: Sophie was an exceedingly good baby. She was utterly scrumptious. Our joy was slightly confined by one slightly troubling issue, though: somewhere in the previous six months, we had become shitty parents.

I was driving Ailbhe into the hospital the next day, hoping that she would see her new baby sister and melt, but I was very pessimistic. During the pregnancy, as Martha's tummy grew, Martha would say, 'baby' and touch her tummy. Ailbhe might say 'baby,' in response, but all invitations to feel the flutter of kicking feet would be curtly rebuffed. She didn't say 'no' – in fact, we had never heard her say 'yes' or 'no' – she would just walk away.

But it wasn't just that. In general, she had gone from being a pleasant baby to a disgruntled toddler. It was difficult to pinpoint when this had started. Her unhappiness just seemed to grow over time, gradually, like bones.

When I stopped at a set of traffic lights, I took the chance to look at her in the rear-view mirror. I know objects appear closer in the rear-view mirror, but I was taken aback by how big she had gotten. When I got home from the hospital the previous day and relieved Sheila and Brendan of their babysitting duties, I looked at Ailbhe and blinked a couple of times. 'Sheila, are you sure she was that size when I left her?' Relative to Sophie, she seemed huge. Then, when I looked at Sophie, it was difficult to believe that Ailbhe had ever been that size.

In the back of the car, Ailbhe held a plastic animal in each hand. She was never without a set now. Since we had left the house, she had been repetitively performing the 'Nemo's swimming out to sea!' scene from *Finding Nemo*. (It's the scene where Nemo touches the 'butt'.) From time to time, Ailbhe alternated with scenes from *Bear in the Big Blue House*, and dialogue from *Planet Earth*. This was what she did almost all the time now.

She had developed dark-purple semi-circles under her eyes. Those seemed to be permanent fixtures too. We thought this was because she had stopped taking her afternoon naps. We had moved Ailbhe into her own room. We did all the things you're supposed to do to try to get a child to settle: making sure the room was pitch black, telling her the monsters would get her if she didn't sleep, giving her a nip of whiskey. Right?

Most nights, Ailbhe slept well, and yet, from the moment she woke up, she was often sullen, and angry. It quickly wore us down, so we were often sullen and angry too. I thought that maybe she was precocious and had graduated early to the terrible twos: that awkward age, where you still have a vague memory of the comfortable womb, and yet you've experienced enough of life to know that everything is not, in fact, awesome. I had seen many toddlers of my acquaintance experiencing a cataclysmic mood change when faced with a new existential crisis, like broccoli – '*It's too terrible, put me back in!*' But the difference with Ailbhe was that she seemed to be so unhappy all of the time – as if the whole world was made of broccoli.

The traffic lights hadn't changed to green. 'Nearly there,' I said, looking over my shoulder, not expecting an acknowledgement, and not getting one. At least, I had avoided a tantrum so far that day. Ailbhe hadn't had a tantrum either.

Kids will have tantrums for lots of different reasons: because they want sweets; or they don't want to stop doing something fun; or they want to be president of the United States.

We thought we knew how to deal with tantrums. When a kid has a tantrum, you don't give them any attention (and you certainly don't vote for them). Much like political candidates, they'll take any attention they can get, even if it's bad press, so long as they are front-page news.

We ignored Ailbhe's tantrums at home, in the supermarket and in the kids' section of the local library. Do you know how hard it is to ignore a child having a tantrum in a library? If you'd like to know what it's like, go out and buy yourself some Blu Tack, duct tape, a smoke alarm and the longest-life batteries you can find. In the library, stick the Blu Tack on the test button; quickly swirl some duct tape around to make sure the button stays depressed, place it on the ground and stand beside it as it loudly wails. Whenever anyone comes over and asks you if there is a problem they can help you with, just smile meekly and say, 'No problem, I just have to wait for this to run out of energy.'

I don't think I've ever sweated as much standing still as when I had to wait out Ailbhe's tantrums in public. What is supposed to happen is that the kid will eventually realise that tantrums don't get them what they want, or any attention at all, so the behaviour stops.

That did not happen with Ailbhe. The more we ignored the tantrums, the more frequent they got. It went from several a week to several a day in no time.

When young men passed me in public places, while Ailbhe was mid-tantrum, I could see that look in their eyes that said, 'I must stock up on contraceptives.' When young women passed me while I waited for Ailbhe to calm down, I could see that look in their eyes that said, 'I must stock up on contraceptives.' No one gets clucky when they see a child having a tantrum.

One day, Martha was leaving a shopping centre, when, for no apparent reason, Ailbhe dropped to the floor and started screaming, right in the entrance lobby. So, Martha stood there and waited for her stop, trying to ignore the people who looked over. At one point, a nice woman gave Martha a sympathetic nod, which said, *'I've been there'* and at the same time, *'That reminds me, I must stock up on contraceptives.'*

The noise of the low-level tantrum I could handle, but as the months went by, Ailbhe found new Mariah Carey-like octaves. It was like climbing a mountain when you didn't know the terrain: just when you thought you were coming to the crest, you would see that there was another crest beyond it. When Ailbhe hit her highest heights, it would make Martha and me flinch.

We might offer Ailbhe some food – 'would you like some apple, or a yogurt?' – and we would get a pained cry, which might quickly develop into a full-on floor display of various angry movements, which we could not decipher. Much like a lot of interpretive dance shows, we were like a trapped audience of two people, looking at this clearly heartfelt performance and thinking, *This is supposed to mean something, right?*

Ignoring this behaviour wasn't working. Consistency is difficult, because, no matter what the books say, there are times when you can't ignore a child having a tantrum, especially if they are somewhere they are liable to hurt themselves, like a playground, or somewhere they are liable to hurt others, like the Oval Office.

Martha said that we should try to find the 'antecedent behaviour'. (She could have just said, 'the cause,' but it was two years since she had been a teacher at that point, so she obviously needed to use highfalutin' education-speak to flex her Higher Diploma in Education muscles.)

So, instead of ignoring Ailbhe's tantrums, we started asking questions like, 'What's wrong?' 'What do you want?' 'Can Daddy help?' 'Oh God, why have you forsaken us?' But all non-specific questions like that were always met with further shrieks. Even the specific ones, 'Are you hungry?' 'Are you tired?' 'Is your nappy wet?' 'Would you like a DVD?' 'Do you want to go in the bin?' would get the same response.

From time to time, as we cycled through Ailbhe's possible needs, we might hit on the right thing by luck. 'Would you like some juice?' and she would cry 'juice!' and after she got juice the tantrum would stop. So why would she just not say juice if that's what she wanted?

Martha was at the checkout with her one day, when a little old lady reached out to pat Ailbhe's head. Ailbhe recoiled and made a sound that can be best described as a bark.

And that wasn't just reserved for strangers. In Carlow one weekend, she was climbing the stairs, which she wasn't allowed to do. My mam reached out to get her, and Ailbhe barked at her too. Mam pulled her hand away, and looked as hurt as if Ailbhe had actually bitten her, which was understandable. You don't expect your first grandchild to act like that around you.

And every time something like that happened, I would tell Ailbhe to say sorry. Then Ailbhe would say 'sorry' in the same tone that I said it to her, never looking at the person she was meant to be apologising to. It had all the sincerity of a celebrity tweeter saying, 'I'm sorry that you felt offended.' People would be kind: they would say things like 'It's fine,' 'Mine did that too,' and 'Don't worry about it,' and 'Don't put her in the bin just yet.' But I was embarrassed by her lack of manners and sincerity.

The non-acknowledgement of my return home from work continued. I would go into the sitting room, lie down beside her and say hello. Ailbhe did not say hello back to me, even though I knew she could say it. I tried to play with the plastic animals with her, but she would just take them off me and go back to babbling out bits of *Finding Nemo* and other movies. I had to wait for her to want to be played with. In contrast, whenever Martha returned from being out of the room for a minute, she would be greeted like a new puppy.

Before Ailbhe was a one-year-old, when Martha's brother Derm was over, he would carry her around singing KT Tunstall songs, which seemed to soothe her, and delighted Derm, but that had stopped too. When he went to pick her up, now, it was like he was trying to pick up an angry wallaby. Ailbhe would force her knees up to his chest and try to spring away, until he had to put her down.

Even bath times, which had once been a source of joy, were now something that I had to take a deep breath before doing. She would often scream out when I touched her head, yet her hair needed to be washed, so I became the world's quickest hair washer. (I wash my own hair very quickly, but that's because I have very little of it.) When she needed her first haircut, there was no way she would sit still enough with that much attention on her head. So we snuck into her bedroom one night, and snipped it quietly, like haircutting ninjas.

We existed on one bar of battery each, trying to work it out in such a way that we didn't both get a battery critical alert at the same time. This was especially tough for Martha, who had been charging for two that year. Even after Sophie was born, Martha seemed to take longer and longer to reach her full charge.

There's a lovely photo of Ailbhe and me in the back garden: she is in my arms and she has a giggle on her face. My mam would often say, 'What's seldom is wonderful,' which is a bit of old Irish Catholic wisdom (with more than a nod to the 'joys' of abstinence). While that doesn't work very well when applied to things like pay cheques and oxygen, those little moments with Ailbhe, when we had fun together, were golden. There were other lovely times too, like peek-a-boos, watching movies together and trips to the zoo. It's just that very often they were ruined by …

BBBBBEEEPPPPPPPP!

Did you forget that I was at the traffic lights? Because I did. The driver behind me leaned on the horn, long and hard, to remind me that green meant go. I looked in my rear-view mirror, and put up my hand, as a gesture to indicate that it was *mea culpa*. He put up his middle finger, as a gesture to indicate that I shouldn't spend my time at traffic lights lost in my thoughts. Then he mouthed a word that succinctly suggested I had an Oedipal relationship with my mother. So I drove on.

After I parked, I briefly contemplated taking the new double buggy contraption out of the boot, but I was still at the stage where putting it together was like wrestling a Transformer. As it was a pleasant autumn day, I decided Ailbhe and I would walk. But when I took her hand, she pulled it away. I tried to hold it again. She pulled it away again. 'Ailbhe, hold Daddy's hand,' I commanded, instantly not up for this shit. She squirmed and pulled it away again. 'The traffic is dangerous, you have to hold my hand,' I shouted. She started to cry. I took her by the wrist instead, and held her arm like a handcuff, all the way to the hospital door.

When we got to the maternity ward, Ailbhe was immediately delighted when she saw Martha sitting up in bed. She bounced up and down beside the bed, desperate to be lifted and cuddled.

'Look, Ailbhe, baby Sophie, your sister,' said Martha in her sing-song mammy voice, pointing at the still surprisingly small Sophie in the cot beside the bed. Sophie seemed to me to be even smaller now that Ailbhe was there for a side-by-side comparison. Ailbhe did not look, though.

'Ailbhe, look,' we both said, pointing. Then Martha leaned over and turned Ailbhe around to look at Sophie. We waited for Ailbhe to be overcome with love. She peered at Sophie for a few seconds, and then turned back to be lifted up on to the bed beside Martha.

Later, when we were leaving, I handcuffed Ailbhe's arm again with my hand, and she cried all the way back to the car.

October 2007

Martha was delighted to get home from the hospital the next day, because she didn't sleep well in the ward. I don't know how new mothers in communal wards get any sleep. 'The baby in the bed next to mine cried like one of the Nazgul from *The Lord of The Rings*,' she said.

Sophie was nothing like that agent of Sauron. She was a sweet-natured baby. 'A doddle,' in parenting terms. At home, she made it simple for us to fall back into the rhythms of looking after a brand-new baby. We had hoped that when Ailbhe realised that this was not a short-term arrangement, she would come to love her sister. I could readily understand some resistance if Sophie happened to be a mewling messenger of Mordor, but with her relaxed nature, her little tuft of red hair, and her exquisite features, she easily clinched that year's title for The World's Most Lovable Baby. And yet, Ailbhe didn't just resist loving her, she mounted a sustained campaign against Sophie, like a guerrilla insurgent trying to drive an invader from her land. We initially put this down to the usual sibling rivalry, but it would prove to be a war of attrition.

Whenever Martha was breastfeeding Sophie, Ailbhe would come over and try to hit Sophie on the head. This was not the sort of interaction that we had been hoping for. Martha had to feed Sophie like a running back, holding her in one hand, while handing off Ailbhe with the other. Unable to breach Martha's defences, Ailbhe had to try a new tactic. One day, when Martha was feeding, she came over with a plastic tiger, and showed it to Sophie like a peace offering. *Awww*, thought Martha. *Finally, she has accepted Sophie. She wants to play.* Then Ailbhe showed the tiger to Sophie's forehead, with a smack. When Sophie cried out in pain, Ailbhe immediately threw the tiger out of her hand, and stood there just looking at Sophie cry.

Ailbhe got the first of her many time-outs for that. She sat on the bottom step of stairs, wailing at the injustice of it all. (It wasn't her – clearly it was the tiger's fault.) When she finally achieved two minutes of continuous sitting on the stairs, I led her back into the sitting room, so she could apply to Sophie for forgiveness.

'Say sorry,' I said.

'Say sorry,' said Ailbhe.

When Martha was looking after the kids by herself in the house, even when Ailbhe was sitting quietly, looking through her picture books – which she did a lot – she couldn't be trusted to be on her own in the room with Sophie. So, when Martha wanted to go to the loo, she had to bring both girls with her. Sometimes she just held it, and waited for me to come back from work. Even though she has a pelvic floor like a steel trap, my key was barely in the door when she would whizz by me in a blur, saying the common prayer of the primary carer: 'Thank Christ you're back.'

She was lying in bed with me one night, so very tired from vigilantly defending Sophie, as if she had been playing rugby against New Zealand on her own all day. Most of the conversation centred on what could be wrong with Ailbhe. We had more theories on what was happening than the fans of that barmy TV programme *Lost*. Just like *Lost*, there seemed to be no satisfying answers, and the more we looked at it the more puzzled we became.

Martha said, 'You know, I love Ailbhe, but … I don't like her.'

When Ailbhe was born, I remember thinking that I couldn't be held responsible for what I would do to anyone who tried to hurt her. I never thought that the person trying to hurt one of my babies might be one of my other babies. So, while that seemed like a dreadful thing for Martha to say of one of her own daughters, I thought *How could anyone ever want to hurt a bundle of delight like Sophie?* and I said, 'Yeah, I know what you mean.'

New Year's Eve 2007

Martha and I usually went to Dee and Lisa's for New Year's Eve. But that year, with Sophie being a few months old, and Ailbhe still carrying out her tactical manoeuvres, we didn't want to inflict our little warzone on them, so we stayed in Ashbourne.

Martha said she was too tired for the trip and, in any case, she didn't feel like being social. She hadn't been out of the house that much since Sophie was born.

Ailbhe went to sleep at a reasonable hour that night, and Sophie was having a snooze, so we started watching a movie. I don't remember the movie. All I remember is that it was so bad that after ten minutes we started chatting.

We started by updating our 'Top Five' list, the five celebrities we would be allowed to sleep with should the opportunity arise. (It is very important for the longevity of any marriage to regularly revisit this list.) While Martha was ruminating over hers, she asked: 'Do Ant and Dec count as one person?' That was a silly question. 'Of course they do!'

As Martha seemed to be in good form that night, I thought it was the right time to tell her that I had been very worried about her for a few weeks. She had seemed very low since Sophie was born. I thought I might know what was wrong. I knew that I would be shitting all over New Year's Eve, but there is never a good time for these things.

There was no way to say it without it sounding like an accusation, but it had to be said.

'How do feel like you are coping, generally?' I asked tentatively, trying to make it sound like a question that I had plucked off the breeze and not a question that had been swirling around inside my head for a while.

'It's tough, but I'm doing okay, I think. Why? Do you think I'm not?' She was immediately suspicious.

'The other day I came in and all three of you were crying at the dinner table … '

'Well, yes, but … ' Martha was trying to interject and shut this down.

' … and there was no dinner,' I continued.

'Do you think I'm not coping because things aren't getting done? Because you're not getting your dinner. Is that it, Aidan?' I wasn't just putting my head into the lion's mouth – I was giving its tonsils the once over.

'No, that's not it. It's just, generally, you seem very … down … I'm worried about you. Do you think that there's a chance that you might have … post-natal depression?' I asked, with a wince.

'What makes you think that?' she warbled, as her eyes began to water and the dam began to break.

'Everything,' I answered. 'You don't seem happy. At all.'

Her annoyance subsided. Then everything that she had been holding so tightly inside her, trying to pretend that she was okay, came flooding out. Keeping up the façade had been exhausting and overwhelming. She collapsed into my arms on the couch, and sobbed every drop of sob in her sob reservoir.

'You need help … we need help,' I suggested. I felt her nodding against my chest.

'I know!'

She told me that on very bad days, there was an incessant, gloomy buzzing of so many voices in her head that she constantly had to work to quell: *You're not good enough, you're lazy, you're a bad mother, why aren't you happy? It's your fault....* Some days, though, it was just too loud. On those days, Martha struggled out of bed. She made phone calls to Swords, casually asking if someone would come over for an hour or two, so she could sleep, trying not to sound too desperate, hoping they would say yes. When Martha said to friends that she felt constantly down, people would say things like, 'Well, you do have a lot on your plate,' which annoyed her because, as she said, 'A lot of people have a lot on their plate, a lot more than me.' Yes, Ailbhe demanded a lot of attention, but Sophie almost made up for that by being so easy to look after. But even that, which should have been some relief, made Martha worry. She thought that because Sophie didn't demand to be heard, she would eventually become used to *not* being heard. She would grow up thinking, *I'm not worth the bother.* Despite knowing that this was an irrational fear to have about a newborn baby, she couldn't stop that voice adding itself to the insistent chorus.

She had another little voice in her head, which said, *You might have post-natal depression.* So when I said those words out loud, I wasn't telling her something she didn't know. All I did for her was bring that voice to the fore.

Technically, I'm not even sure that it could even be called post-natal depression. Martha had told me before that she was an excellent student all through school. When she was in primary school she would sometimes read books under her desk during lessons (which is the single swottiest act of rebellion I've ever heard of). Yet when it came to 5th year, she started drifting. Even though the Leaving Cert was a year away, she barely studied, and she has no idea why she did that. 'I just stopped caring,' she said. She scraped by, and did enough to get herself into college, but there, she said, she often fell asleep in afternoon lectures. She was known for it. She would laugh it off, but it worried her. Even when she got a job working in the labs of Guinness Brewery, years later, she still felt a mysterious fatiguing force. She was going to the gym at the time, at her fittest, but she still fell asleep twice on the job.

Not long after we had moved in together, Martha went into the city to meet me for dinner and drinks with my work crew. She was very much in love. She was enjoying her teaching job. The sun was shining. She was even having a good hair day. There should have been no reason to be down, and yet, when she got off the bus, she couldn't stop crying as she walked down the street to meet me.

When we met up outside my workplace, I said, 'Nice hair,' but then, seeing her tear-stained face, I was concerned. 'Have you been crying?'

'No,' she responded, too quickly, starting to cry again.

'What's wrong?' I asked. She shook her head and shrugged as the tears continued to fall. While she loved her job, she was teaching in a tough school at the time. 'Did one of the kids say something to you?' She continued to shake her head. 'Did you watch that episode of *Buffy the Vampire Slayer* that always gets to you? Haven't we talked about that?' I quipped, trying to make her laugh. She did not laugh, or look up. I searched my brain for something else.

I understood that I was not the best house guest. I had been a pizza-under-the-bed type of twenty-something, so I asked, 'Am I not helping enough around the house?'

That wasn't it, but it was easier for Martha to identify that as a tangible reason for her tears than to say, 'I don't know why I'm crying,' so she said, 'Yes, I need you to do better.' I thought it was a bit of an overreaction to the odd pair of smelly jocks on the floor. Still, I promised to try to do better, because I think we both knew that going down the other avenue would lead to a conversation far too big and terrifying for a nice spring evening, but it was the conversation we should have had.

I remember that when we lived in our compact flat in Cabinteely, when I came home from work, Martha would often be in bed. More than once I referred to her as a recreational sleeper. It was a lie she told herself as well – 'I just enjoy sleeping.' But now, with the added chemicals of labour, the daily grind of looking after a baby and a troublesome toddler, she no longer had the luxury of that time. She had *needed* that sleep before, and without it, she was struggling.

Looking back on Martha's life like that is like the reveal of the twist in *The Sixth Sense*. Spoiler alert: Maybe Martha had been dead (inside) all along.

Either way, whether she had been suffering from depression before or not, she was definitely suffering now. This time we couldn't pretend. We had to do something about it.

January 2008

A s it happened, in the first week of the new year, the nurse was coming to give Martha and Sophie the standard three-month check. Part of that check was a routine post-natal depression test. Martha asked the nurse, 'When the test says, "Do you ever feel like throwing your baby out the window?", would throwing her in the bin count as a *yes*, do you think?'

The nurse squinted a bit. 'Hmmm, if that's how you feel, I think I'd tick *yes* for that one.'

Martha told the nurse about our conversation on New Year's Eve and that, even if the test was negative, she intended to seek help. The nurse looked at the test. Martha had passed the post-natal depression test with flying colours (mostly greys and blacks, though). She said, 'Well, Martha, I'm delighted that you told me that you intend to seek help, because according to these answers, your depression is so profound that I would be compelled to book a doctor's appointment for you, and ensure that you went.'

Martha went to see our doctor. (A lovely man, who was just as nice as our doctor in Cabinteely, but also had the added skill of being able to blink from time to time, which was a vast improvement in bedside manner.) He suggested taking anti-depressants, which Martha would come to call 'Mammy's Little Helpers'.

He also advised her to go to counselling. Martha didn't think she needed to go to counselling. She thought, *I know myself well, and I know my problems. Aidan and I can talk about things, so why would I need to talk to anyone else?* She also thought that the pills might make her fake happy, like the way people laugh at their boss's bad jokes at a stuffy work party: ostensibly amused, yet desperately searching for the handle to the ejector seat on the inside. The doctor suggested she try a drug called Lexapro for a while. 'See how it goes.' She could always come off it in time. Martha acquiesced, and she tried Lexapro, and she has been taking it ever since.

February 2008

Martha decided to bring Ailbhe to the library a few weeks later, 'trying to be a good mother', as she said. It had been a tough morning, with Ailbhe being her usual obstinate self. When Martha was getting Sophie ready to go, putting her into the double buggy (which we could now both put together with a snap of our fingers, like a magic trick), Ailbhe had gone into the sitting room and taken every book off one of the shelves and laid them out in a line across floor. She would do things like that a lot.

By the time they got to the library, Martha was sweating and frazzled, and in that place where you regret every life decision you have ever made that brought you to that point in life. She ran into a woman she knew to see from the breastfeeding group. This woman was a Swedish mother of two and looked like the sort of mother you'd see in a brochure beside a headline that announced, 'Yes, you too can have it all.' She had that Swedish gene that makes the natives glow and makes Irish people who encounter them feel as if they are more closely related to potatoes than Swedes. She made the mistake of asking Martha how she was doing.

Whatever way the question is asked in Ireland – 'How are you getting on?' 'How's it going?' 'How's it hanging?' 'How are the balls of your feet?' – the standard answer is: 'Grand, and yourself?' And the response is: 'Grand, can't complain.' It is something that we stick to religiously, like the responses at Sunday mass. This is the way it has been for ever and ever, Amen. If you want to get adventurous with your response, you might even make a comment about the weather. 'Fierce day out there.' ''Tis!'

But Martha was done with this traditional, polite charade. This was a new year and a new era for her. If she was ever to be well, she thought, she couldn't keep on squashing how she felt. She was not grand.

So she asked, 'Do you ever feel like you've made a terrible mistake?' sure that this Swedish Wonder Woman wouldn't be able to relate. Martha fully expected to get the sympathetic tilt-and-nod of the head, and possibly some patronising advice, maybe even a little embarrassment at her frank question. Instead, the woman's eyes immediately glistened. She leaned in and whispered, 'It is hard, isn't it?'

And when Martha told me about it later, after I came home from work, as I put the books back on the shelf, I asked: 'How many women do you know who are taking medication for depression?'

Martha listed off some women's names, 'And those are the ones that I know of.' It was a lengthy list. Were the housing estates of boom-time Ireland lousy with Lexapro? In the quiet of a weekday morning, was there an underground sea of silent desperation? 'Motherhood is the making of you,' is how you are supposed to feel, but what if it turns out to be the breaking of you? How many women go without help, ashamed to say it? How many mothers stick a pill on their tongues every morning and hope for the best, like Martha? And this was during what people now refer to as 'the good times'. What must it have been like a few years later?

All that I knew for sure was that Martha felt that becoming a mother had gradually made her lose all sense of herself. To me, she was still the intelligent, funny, beautiful woman that

I married. But the depression now seemed to rob her of that perspective, so I would regularly remind her of my perspective, and tell her that I loved her every morning.

I also did what I could, pragmatically. On the weekends, I would take the girls out to give her a break. I was sure that eventually, when Lexapro loosened the grip of her depression, we would all go out together, like other families did. But going out by myself with the girls got to be such a regular occurrence that I would actually become envious of other men walking around with their wives and families.

I missed Martha, but I thought of the situation as a temporary thing. I didn't know, then, that this was just the way it was going to be for us, and it was actually going to get a lot worse.

March 2008

As a baby, Sophie sucked. The moment she got a modicum of control of her arms and hands, everything she grabbed went into her mouth. Countless toys were masticated to death. When her teeth started to emerge, I think the dolls in the sitting room started hiding under the couches. We put away some toys to keep for when she was older and less bite-y. Behind the water tank in our attic, there is still an eerie old toy graveyard.

She seemed to be constantly hungry, but we soon figured out that for her, a finger was as good as a breast (not a philosophy I subscribe to myself). Martha had been adamant that none of our children would have soothers, but Sophie's desire to suck was a lot stronger than Martha's will to deny it. It was Sheila who eventually bought soothers and encouraged us to use them. So, we did. Sophie took to the soother like an office worker takes to the first mouthful of cider on a sunny Friday evening after a hard week at work. She seemed drunk on the joy of it.

After Ailbhe was born, everything she did was precious and new, every moment was cherished, documented and photographed. We were so careful with her. First kids are like new carpets. You will go so far as to put a saucer under your bottle of beer to protect it. This standard of care falls off a little with the second child. To continue the carpet metaphor, with the second child, you still care, but it's more like transporting tomato soup across the carpet in your cupped hands.

With Ailbhe, everything was sterilised. We would even wash our own hands before feeding her – crazy, unsustainable stuff like that. With Sophie, a soother that went on the ground was picked back up, sucked by either one of us, and popped back in her mouth. With Ailbhe, we consulted the books and stuck to the advice. She had a full constitution of care. With Sophie, we barely adhered to the five-second rule.

We still did all the essentials, changing the two-fers, the eye-reddening late-night feeds, using my heroically sensitive elbows to test the bath water. I remember that by the time Sophie was four or five months old, she had a beautiful little giggle and she loved to splash when I washed her, and that despite our slightly more *lassiez-faire* attitude to parenting, she was a very happy baby.

She made us feel like we weren't such shitty parents after all.

April 2008

Kids are to the rustle of a sweet packet at a party as sharks are to a drop of blood in the water. Never open a variety pack of fun-sized chocolate bars at a kids' birthday party if you enjoy having arms. Ailbhe was no different. She would run over and rip you to shreds for a mini Mars Bar as quickly as the next kid. So we weren't worried about her hearing. That wasn't it.

Martha wears glasses. Without them on she cannot read my expression if I'm more than eight feet away, which has led to some misunderstandings when I'm trying to convey sarcasm with my face. So I wouldn't have been surprised if Ailbhe had ocular issues like her mother. However, she could look up in the sky and see a plane flying high up above and say, 'Plane!' Also, on the couple of occasions I brought the girls to the runway viewing road at the back of the airport, when she saw a plane landing, she would exclaim, 'Plane!' Ergo, I had already tested her for long- and short-sightedness. So it wasn't that, either.

There was something up, though. We knew it.

Martha took Ailbhe for a standard development check with the nurse. If a kid were like a new car, this would be like bringing it back to the garage after a couple of years, so someone could kick the tyres and tap the spark plugs. (That's how they check cars, right?)

Ailbhe spent the entirety of that check-up trying to get back up into Martha's arms, while Martha held Sophie, sweated her body weight with stress, and gently tried to guide Ailbhe back to the task with the nurse.

There were some toys there for Ailbhe to play with, to see if she mimicked adult behaviour appropriately: if there was a dolly and a bed, she should put the dolly to bed. If there was a phone, she should pretend to make a call. If there was a white envelope with a window on the front of it, she should pretend to pick it up, throw it in the bin, and curl up in the corner of the room in the foetal position.

But she didn't do any of that in the test, because she didn't do any of that at home. She didn't play like that. For instance, she had just got a set of My Little Ponies, and all she ever did was line them up along the floor in order of size and leave them there. Martha told the nurse about this, by way of explanation for Ailbhe's seeming lack of cooperation.

We'd go to our friends' houses and see their kids, younger than Ailbhe, having, or attempting to have, conversations. Even if it was babble, they were clearly beginning to grasp that to get what they wanted required them to have a bit of back and forward interaction. Ailbhe didn't do that. She didn't say 'Mama' or 'Dada' or 'I' or 'me' or 'Ailbhe' either. Her language seemed to be stuck, and the tantrums were just as bad as they had ever been.

Martha told the nurse about all of it. This was her first chance to bring up her concerns with a health professional, and she was hoping to get some answers. More important, she was hoping to get some help.

When I came home from work that day I asked Martha, 'What did the nurse say?'

Martha said, 'Ailbhe didn't do any of the tests. The nurse said that that was because she thinks she might be a bit spoiled.'

June 2008

They called us all into the middle of the office floor for a meeting. When I had joined the company, there were about 40 people working there. By the time we had that meeting, there were about 130 of us. The number was about to get smaller. A lot smaller. The directors said that there would be some pruning required, which was necessary for the company to survive, but I wasn't fooled. I could see the chainsaws in their eyes.

We would have to accept wage cuts across the board, and redundancies would also be inevitable. We had known that this was coming, of course. The world had got itself into a financial flux, and it was said that Ireland, with its burst property bubble, was one of the countries that was especially fluxed.

I had worked with the company for just over ten years, and I would have been happy to see out my career there. But now, the company was holed below the waterline, and much like Jack and Rose in *Titanic*, all any of us could do now was hang on for as long as we possibly could. We could see the icy water below, and we all knew that this was the beginning of the end.

There had been a low turnover of staff in the company, because we were paid well, and it was a no-aggro environment. Well, it was for me anyway. I loved going to work there. I came in on time (of course), got my work done, and got on with the people I worked with. I had worked with most of them for five years, or more. Some, I had been working with since I started, ten years before, when we were in the crappy old office in Rathmines, looking out at the canal, before we moved into the new, swanky office in the heart of the city.

We often went out for the night after work, and those were often great nights out.

One night, in particular, was the greatest ...

29 June 2001

On Friday evenings, we would usually go across to the Portobello pub to drink death-defying amounts of alcohol. However, one of our most popular colleagues, Kunak, was leaving, so, it being a special occasion, we went across to the Portobello pub to drink death-defying amounts of alcohol.

It had been a hot summer day, hot enough that local kids had been diving into the cool water at the canal lock, while skiving office workers sunned themselves on the lush green banks.

The first pint tasted divine. There were about twenty of us sitting in the snug. The talk and the laughs came easily, as usual. I remember we got into a good game of Six Degrees of Kevin Bacon. (This is a game where you must connect actors to Kevin Bacon in the smallest number of movies; what is referred to as their 'Bacon Number.' Kate Winslet, for instance, has a Bacon number of two, since she was in *The Life of David Gayle* with Laura Linney, who was in *Mystic River* with Kevin Bacon. Laura Linney, therefore, has a Bacon Number of one. Kevin Bacon has a Bacon Number of zero, because he's Kevin Bacon, and you can't get any more Kevin Bacon than that.)

The light smattering of other patrons in the bar grew into a small crowd as other offices closed for the evening, with people gradually coming into the bar in groups.

The door opened. A woman walked in on her own and stood at the door, looking around for someone. My heart sat up in my chest when I saw her. I wanted whoever she was looking for to be me. Then Kunak spotted her and they exchanged a wave. When she walked over, they hugged, and then the woman went to the bar to get a drink. I had heard Kunak say that a friend of hers was coming in, and that she was late. This must be the friend. I started thinking about how I could get this woman to be my friend too.

When she came back from the bar, she sat a few seats down from me, on the same bench, so we couldn't see each other, but I could still hear her.

Weeks later she said: 'I heard you before I saw you. I liked what I heard.'

'You heard me first? So *that's* where I've been going wrong all these years.'

As the night went on, and people between us got up to get pints, or go to the toilet, I noticed that she would move down a bit, until eventually she was sitting beside me. Hello, Martha. Hello, Aidan. Hello, Martha and Aidan. It was like that. Natural. Simple. Wonderful. From the very start.

When we began to talk, we were like two cogs in conversation. Instantly, to me, she was sharp, funny and beautiful. I had a feeling that she liked me. Miraculously, she *liked* me. The first time I made her laugh; the second time I made her laugh; when we laughed together – I wish I could remember those quips. If I could have that night back, in my mind, like a movie scene, I would cherish every syllable that we spoke. I would love to replay that moment, three hours after we met, when we first kissed. Her lips, her perfume. How exciting it all was. How right it felt.

The moment she walked through the door that evening, there was something inexorable about us. I knew it. She knew it. But how could we have known? We were interested in each other. It was lust. It was a shared sense of humour. It was chemistry, applied. And yet, I *did* know. I did. I did not feel it in retrospect, knowing what I know now; I knew it then, at that moment, that this was something special.

We spent the next week together. Seven days later, I told her that I loved her. Stupid. Foolhardy. Ridiculous. And yet, also, the truth. I did love her. And she told me that she loved me back.

July 2008

The first redundancies came soon after the meeting in the middle of the office floor – those who were last in the door, mostly – and the rest of us received ten per cent wage cuts. We grumbled about it, of course, but that was just the start. There would be more wage cuts to come. I rang Martha and told her not to worry: 'It'll be a bit of an adjustment, but we'll be fine.'

We weren't going to be fine, though. After not worrying about money for years, I had done the figures, and saw that things would get tight with the reduced wages, but when I lost my job, as I inevitably would, the house would go with it.

It was a realisation that was as sudden and shocking as a gunshot; the red side of our account sheet started to bleed into the black. I saw no way to stem the wound. I was constantly brimming with regrets. Why had I not planned better for this, insulated myself, insulated us? I felt like a failure.

We weren't spendthrifts. Since our honeymoon, our only foreign holiday had been five days in Paris – Martha surprised me in work, with my bags packed, for my thirtieth birthday.

But we were never exactly frugal, either. When I looked back at our accounts, I could see acres of areas where we could have been a bit more circumspect. We should have built up a bit more of a buffer. There was some arrogance in this coming downfall. I am good at my job. I was a long time working in the company, so I had thought that I would survive any downsizing. I was like the prize cow who thinks it will survive the cull.

As the shadow of our impending financial demise threatened, I tried not to think about the bad decisions we'd made … a lot.

September 2008

Kunak came over to the house for a cup of tea and a chat. Martha told her that she was concerned about Ailbhe's speech.

She had also voiced her concern to other parents, but she was usually answered with an array of anecdotes about kids who didn't talk at all until they were four or five, and had gone on to be President of Everything, or something equally prestigious, but this had not allayed her fears. Ailbhe would be three in January. 'Give her time,' was the typical refrain.

When she said it to Kunak, however, Kunak replied, 'You remember that my mother is a speech therapist, right?' Martha had not remembered.

A few weeks later we were sitting in Eileen's office, Kunak's mother, and Ailbhe was messing with toys at a table in the corner. It was near the end of the hour-long session, and Eileen was explaining to us that Ailbhe didn't understand a lot of what was being said to her. In that moment, we knew how she felt, because we were also not understanding what was being said to us.

Eileen explained that Ailbhe wasn't good at expressing herself, and she was often just repeating words. She showed us that you could ask Ailbhe if she wanted 'sweets or sprouts?' and Ailbhe would say 'sprouts,' not because she wanted sprouts (no one in their right mind would choose Satan's bum nuggets over sweets) but because that was the last word that she had heard, and she was just repeating it.

Ailbhe didn't have purple rings under her eyes because of a lack of sleep. She was permanently exhausted from trying to understand what people were saying and trying to communicate her needs. Ailbhe didn't have tantrums because she was spoiled – she was beyond frustrated at her inability to communicate properly. I completely understood that. It reminded me of how I tried to get by in Paris with my faded Leaving Certificate French – '*Martha, what's the French word for croissant?*' When French people spoke back to me I could often only understand the last word that was said to me too – '*Imbecile.*'

The more that this was explained to us, the more that it made sense. It explained why she couldn't seem to answer a question with 'yes' or 'no.' It explained why, when we asked something like, 'Do you want toast?' she answered with, 'doyouwanttoast?' which we had come to accept as 'yes.' (She said 'no' by crying her eyes out.)

But this didn't explain why most of her speech was repeated from movie scenes and TV babble. We used to say that she spoke ninety-five per cent Pixar. We were then introduced to the word 'echolalia'. This word describes the natural repetition most children do when they are learning to talk, but it can also be a way of dealing with the frustration of not being able to communicate, or the stress of unnerving situations.

We drove home from that meeting happy, armed with some methods to help Ailbhe to start to build sentences, but also, burdened with the shame of not having spotted this ourselves: '*nous sommes les grandes imbeciles!*' To help Ailbhe, we had to break our speech down to its simplest form when we talked to her. No more than two words were allowed. 'Ailbhe want toast' was too much. It had to be, 'Ailbhe want?' or, 'Want toast?' So, for about a year, that's what we did. Sheila and Brendan did it too.

One exercise we did with her involved sitting her on my lap holding her arms, while Martha would sit in front of her and say,

'Mammy want' and touch her chest. Then I would say, 'Ailbhe want' and use Ailbhe's arms to touch her chest, trying to get Ailbhe to mimic me, so that, eventually, she would learn to say 'Ailbhe want … ' by herself.

We got into that mode of speaking so much that even after Ailbhe went to sleep, Martha and I would often keep speaking like that to each other:

'Daddy blowjob?'

'Mammy sleep,'

'Daddy handjob?'

'Mammy dead.'

We thought we had found the root of her unhappiness – a speech delay – and we diligently worked at it. A couple of months later, though, we would come to understand that we were barely scratching the surface.

October 2008

Not long after Sophie turned one, she took to toddling. Like any parents, we were delighted and terrified in equal measure. She had a curious habit of picking a circuit and running around it. A favourite was to go from the sitting room to the kitchen, around the table and back again. Repeatedly. She moved around like a tornado of joy.

She had wonderfully wild red hair and big blue eyes. She didn't smile spontaneously that often, but when she did it was contagious. Everyone thinks their kids are gorgeous, but people used to stop us on the street to say how cherubic Sophie looked.

She rarely stayed still unless she was very tired or in the buggy. If she awoke in the bed with us, she would immediately and voraciously seek out cuddles, especially with Martha. Often, she would press her forehead against Martha's as hard as she could – 'Martha, I think she's trying to get back in.' She did that with me too, sometimes, but what she mostly wanted from me was rough and tumble. Ailbhe liked rough and tumble too, but I had to wait for her to come to me. Sophie could be scooped up, turned upside down, thrown around, at any time of the day and she would be instantly transported to heaven, squealing with paroxysms of glee.

How I wish, now, that I could grow as she grew, so that I would be big and strong enough to do that for her for ever.

Even though she still had a soother, she preferred to examine the world mouth-first. Now that she had greater mobility, it gave her access to so many more things. When I was holding her in my arms on her first birthday, for the 'Happy Birthday to You,' I remember she reached out to try to eat the burning candle on the birthday cake.

She also made some early attempts to start climbing to get at even more things. More delight. More terror. Sophie was born with an independent soul. This sister was doing it for herself. She didn't respond to her name, so our only method of remote control at that stage was a sharp 'Ah! Ah!' in our sternest voices. Once she heard that she wouldn't stop, though, she would simply turn at a ninety-degree angle and keep moving towards the next dangerous thing in her eye-line.

Unlike Ailbhe at that age, Sophie hadn't said a word. *Kids develop differently*, I thought. 'Kids develop differently,' we were told. 'Kids develop differently,' we reassured each other when we talked about it. But there wasn't even a hint of a 'Baa' for the 'Baa Baa Black Sheep'. There was no babbling at all. No pointing. No waving. Lots of giggles, though. She loved to be tickled. She cried, of course, but no more than any other one-year-old would do. And she made some other meaningless, random noises as well as she walked around, but, otherwise, not much of a peep.

That summer, we had been visiting Dee, Lisa and their daughter, Laura. She was born seven months before Ailbhe. They had seen each other often as they grew up. Laura was Ailbhe's second-favourite person after Martha. It was a hot Saturday afternoon. Laura and Ailbhe were running around together at the bottom of the back garden. It was lovely to see Ailbhe happy.

Dee was doing a bit of work to fix one of the swings. Lisa was nearby, looking at the girls playing. Enda, one of the college gang, and one of my best mates, who also lived in Galway, had come over too. We were chatting at the top of the garden. Martha was in the house, in bed, asleep. Sophie was in the buggy beside us, seemingly happy to be sitting there looking around, probably not far away from an afternoon nap.

'She's a fierce placid baby,' said Enda.

'She is,' I replied, 'not a bit of minding on her.'

And we both looked at her and smiled. Enda went back to looking at Laura and Ailbhe running around, but I kept looking at Sophie. She *was* a very placid baby, but was that all it was? She was staring intently at something, but as I followed the gaze of her pretty, blue eyes, I couldn't discern what she was interested in.

My smile faded. She wasn't paying attention to the Laura and Ailbhe show that was going on. In fact, when I looked at her, I thought, *she's not paying attention to anything at all.* Sophie looked like she was lost in thought. Or bored. Or, possibly, in her own little world? I went back to looking at the girls running around and tried to push that thought away.

Give her time, I thought.

May 1995

Near the end of college, one of the lads decided that it was a shame none of our college gang had proper nicknames. He decided to rectify that. Dee got 'Frets' because he was an excellent guitar player (in fact, he can play any instrument he touches, the bastard) but he also worries a lot. Sometimes he does both at the same time. Enda got the nickname of 'JacksHammer' because he would often get up in the middle of night and piss so loudly into the toilet that it sounded like a pneumatic drill. Everyone in his house would be woken up by it.

Both of those nicknames made sense. My nickname was puzzling. They called me 'Furryburger,' which is a euphemism for, well ... I'm sure you can work it out if you don't know. It was never explained to me why I was given this nickname. Maybe the 'furry' referred to the towering brown bouffant headloaf I had at the time, that I called 'a haircut'. Or it could have been an ironic jab at my failure at that point in my life to provide the meat in the euphemistic lady sandwich. Either way, it was a silly, childish, nonsensical nickname, and there was no way that it would ever stick.

November 2008

'**A**h boy, Furry,' said Enda, when he answered my phone call. 'Hi, Enda,' I said, failing to keep a tell-tale, emotional warble out of my voice.

'You okay?' he asked.

I immediately deepened my voice, and concentrated on controlling every syllable: 'Yep, just ringing to see what's going on with you.'

It was a Sunday evening in Brendan and Sheila's house and I had come out to the conservatory. In summer, this south-facing room is like a sauna, but it was late November, so it was cold enough out there to keep a carton of milk fresh for a couple of days. I didn't mind it, though, because the cool air was acting as a salve, relieving the stinging, red-raw skin around my eyes. It had been a difficult couple of days.

Martha would often call me in work, and I could usually tell if she had been crying or not – because she isn't as good at deepening her voice to hide it as I am. I didn't have to be particularly perceptive. At that time, if I asked, 'Have you been crying?' I would have had an excellent chance of being right. A symptom of her depression was that an accumulation of what might seem like small annoyances to someone else would often leave her in misery at the kitchen table, buried by the weight of the question, 'Where do I even begin?'

'Tell me everything is going to be okay,' she said to me on the phone once.

'Everything is going to be okay,' I answered.

'I don't believe you,' she said.

I thought about it for a second. 'What if I tried it in a manlier voice?' And then she made that sound that is simultaneously the end of a sob and the start of a laugh. I love that sound. It's the sound that means that everything is going to be okay, because today, I can still make my wife laugh. It's my second favourite noise that I can make Martha do.

But there were bad days, when she could barely get the words, 'Bad day' out, and I could not hope to playfully cajole her then. On the end of the phone in work, miles away from her, I would feel desperate, stuck between the not unimportant activity of making a salary and keeping my family roofed, and the deep need to be there to help. What would I say to my boss, anyway? 'While I understand that the company is collapsing, and every month people are being let go, would you mind holding my job so that I can stay at home for a while and fix my broken wife?' And even if I could do that, that's when *I* would think, 'Where would I even begin?'

When I picked up the phone that Friday, there was no hello, there was just sobbing, and I thought, 'Shit, this must be a very, very bad day.' 'Is everything okay?' I asked. Stupid question.

The words were a struggle for her, 'Aidan … I … I … think Ailbhe's autistic,' she cried, before her voice was utterly swallowed by tears again.

This was surely just another loss of perspective, I thought.

'Okay,' I said, taking a breath, 'What makes you think that?' It was now my job to make her see sense.

She collected herself a little, and directed me to the website she had been looking at, which listed the signs of autism to look out for. I was sceptical. The internet will tell you all sorts of ridiculous things – the Earth is flat, humans never landed on the Moon, or that there's nothing wrong with eating sweetcorn (or, as I call them, 'pusberries'). But this was a reputable website, and as I read, the case was compelling. It was all there.

Her repetition of movie scenes (echolalia), lining up toys instead of playing with them, how she sometimes barked if she was touched on her head, how we often found her squeezed in between the bed and wall at night, the problems she was having with her speech. And how, even though Martha was crying her eyes out right then, Ailbhe didn't seem concerned about why her mother, her favourite person in the world, was continually leaking from the face.

It was as if a piece of a puzzle I didn't even know I was trying to solve slipped perfectly into place. Now that I could see the whole picture, I really didn't like what I saw. 'I'll come home now, okay?' I said.

'Yes, please, that would be good,' said Martha, collecting herself.

I decided against telling my boss the truth. The statement, 'Sorry, I have to go home because I think my kid is autistic,' might have required a little too much unpacking for a speedy exit. Instead, I opted for 'I have a queasy stomach,' which wasn't a total lie. I added two words to the statement, to make sure that there would be the minimum of questions asked: 'Both ends!'

I had taken the same commuter bus in and out of work since I had moved to Ashbourne, and I had grown accustomed to the familiar faces of other passengers. That Friday afternoon, going home on the afternoon bus, too early, too bright, with a strange crew of people, only added to my discombobulation. I felt as if I had dropped out of my time continuum. I pressed my head against the window as the bus left the city, and weighed the word 'autism' in my mind. It was very heavy.

Before Martha called me, she had been listening to Ailbhe babbling movie scenes. Her worry intensified as she started to think about Raymond from *Rain Man*, repeating: '97X Bam! The future of rock 'n' roll ... ' over and over. At that time, like most people, our knowledge of autism was no more than the standard movie trope; miraculous mathematical abilities married to profoundly disabling social ineptitude. This is what made Martha initially doubt herself. Ailbhe hadn't shown any aptitude for maths. Ailbhe giggled. Ailbhe looked her in the eye.

But she doesn't look anyone else in the eye, even Aidan.

Still, maybe it wasn't autism, maybe it was like the nurse at the check-up had said; maybe we had just spoiled her, given her too much attention? The more Martha read about autism on the website, the more it made sense, and as she read on, the more the myths were dispelled. Soon Martha came to understand that it did explain a lot of Ailbhe's behaviour, even though she desperately didn't want it to.

When I got home, Martha was still sitting at the kitchen table, looking at the computer. In the sitting room, the girls were doing their own thing, separately. It was the same scene as always, but it was as if someone had changed the soundtrack. It was surreal, like Hans Zimmer scoring *Peppa Pig*. Nothing tangible had changed. Ailbhe was watching a DVD and Sophie was gumming a doll to death.

What was different was our feelings, our thoughts and our knowledge. There was autism in the atoms of this scene, and it would be inextricably a part of our lives, for ever. A knot formed in my throat and began to tighten. Even though I was standing perfectly still, just looking at them, I could taste the bitter tang of adrenaline in my mouth. My brain was working as hard as my heart.

Martha got up. We hugged, tightly, and I whispered into her ear the only thing I could think of that would make this situation a bit better: 'Would you like some tea?'

'Yes,' she said, 'you'd better make a pot.'

The talk was mostly about Ailbhe, and how we were going to get her help. We only talked about Sophie as an addendum. We had separately thought, *There's something amiss there, as well*, but we had never really spoken to each other about it properly. 'Give her time', we said. So, when Martha asked, 'What about Sophie? Do you think she might be autistic too?', it didn't come as a surprise to me.

'I don't know,' I replied. Sophie was very young. However, we were never worried about Ailbhe when she was Sophie's age, so we surmised that if we were worried about Sophie already, maybe her issues would be far more profound ... still, *Give her time*, we thought. Give her time.

Sometimes a marriage is just two people taking turns to cry. And that's how it was for us that weekend. The grief came in waves, with every realisation and implication ... would the girls go to a normal school? What about friends? What about college? What about walking them down the aisle? What about their independence? What about our independence? Would Martha and I get to enjoy our retirement, travelling around the world, making the most of our final years, past caring about social conventions, injecting heroin into our eyeballs? (I am joking, of course. There would be no need to travel around the world as well.)

I was also thinking of how I couldn't lose my job on top of all this, and how I would certainly lose my job on top of all this.

The next day we went over to Swords, ostensibly so the girls could be looked after, but also so that we could be looked after. I called my mam as well. She thought we might be jumping to conclusions. 'Yes, Mam, you might be right,' I said, and I hoped she was, but I was pretty sure she wasn't.

And so I had called Enda to tell him about our fears, and for consolation too. But when I heard his voice, my silly nickname (the only one that had persisted over the decades, by the way, even though Dee has worried his way through many guitars, and

Enda still pisses with gusto, making a sound like a waterfall in a bin), I suddenly didn't want to tell him, because he would be the first person outside the family that I had told. I wasn't ready for it to be that … real, yet.

So we talked about work, and how the arse had fallen out of the economy. Dee and Enda had ended up working in the same architectural practice, Dee as an architect and Enda as a draughtsperson, and it looked likely that the company they were working for would go to the wall. They were just waiting for the end, much like everyone else; much like me. And in that conversation, Enda was using phrases that I thought we would never have to use, like: 'three-day week,' 'redundancy,' 'negative equity'.

Even though those were words to be afraid of, they didn't sound as bad to me then as the word 'autism'.

On Monday morning Martha called the doctor and set about the process of getting help. What was to be done? We hadn't a clue.

When I had stepped out the door to walk down to the bus stop that morning, I stopped, and I sucked as many cubic feet of cold November air into my nostrils as I could. I decided that I was done with crying. When I got to the bus stop, I noticed that the queue was a little smaller at the stop, and that a few of my usual crewmates were missing. The great national cull had begun.

The next weekend I called Enda again, to tell him about 'The Hard Weekend', as we've called that weekend ever since. I told him that I had been quite upset, but that I was done with crying now. I was going to try to be positive about it. He said lovely things about how good a father he thought I was.

'If I had to pick the one person who could handle this, it would be you.' It was as if he had designed the perfect statement to make me cry. The bastard.

January 2009

'**A**nd how are you two doing?' asked the nice lady. The nice lady was a health service professional who had come over to our house to assess Ailbhe to see if she fit the criteria for special needs services. She had started off by discussing our worries about Ailbhe's development. Then she had hit us with this sidewinder of a question. It was a question we would often be asked by people in special needs services over the years.

So, how *were* we doing?

By then, in a short couple of months, we had become less of a couple and more like a tag team. Every evening, when I came in, Martha would go straight to bed. On the weekends, she started sleeping into the afternoon. During the week, she struggled to cope, with depression, with abject, ever-present tiredness, with the feeling that things would never change, that they would only get worse. She felt bad, and then she felt bad about feeling bad. She read about parents who couldn't hug their children with autism and thought, *I should appreciate that my girls are affectionate with me.* She thought about people who had tragically lost their children. *I should be happy that my girls are healthy.* She thought about people who couldn't have children, and how we, for what now seemed like a very brief time, thought that that would be us. *We are lucky to have our girls,* and yet, at the time, there was little solace in that thought.

I was stressed, about the girls, about money, about Martha. I had given up trying to couch it, and instead I was trying to impress upon her how precarious our financial situation was, as the money started to dribble away, but it was as if this was one worry too much for her. So I stopped trying. I felt very much alone in dealing with that.

Then I developed a dull pain in my side that would come and go, which at its worst, made it uncomfortable to sit down in work, but I never told Martha about that at the time.

'We're doing okay,' I said to the nice lady, and I looked at Martha sitting across the room as I said it, and she looked back at me, each of us with a pinch beneath our expressions, both of us knowing that I had just told a big lie.

I had bittersweet feelings about this meeting; I wanted Ailbhe to show this lady the behaviour we were worried about, so that she could get the help that we thought she needed, and yet, I didn't want her to do any of those things, because I didn't want her to need help.

As we discussed our concerns about Ailbhe, Sophie was toddling about doing her Sophie things. Near the end of the discussion, Martha pointed at her and said to the nice lady, 'We might be seeing you in a few months about this little girl as well.'

The nice lady didn't hesitate; 'I think we'll put her down now. What's her name?' she asked. *Oh right,* I thought, the nice lady must have been side-eyeing Sophie during the meeting, looking at the tell-tale things that she was and wasn't doing, thinking, *I hope they mention the cute little redhead, or I'll have to.*

Martha was struck by the same thought. 'S-s-sophie ... her name's Sophie,' she stuttered.

At that meeting we were offered two options: early intervention or an assessment. Early intervention meant that the girls would get therapy in a few months' time, but that we would have to wait for a year or so for a diagnosis. An assessment would mean that the diagnostic process would be first, but they would have to wait until after that was finished to begin therapy. (We chose early intervention, because the help seemed more important than the diagnosis at that moment.)

'Couldn't we have both?' I asked in the manner of Oliver Twist asking for some more; a poor, naïve boy who didn't understand how all of this worked yet.

February 2009

Martha went to the doctor and told him about how bad she was feeling, and how, on top of that, she was feeling guilty for feeling bad.

He told her a story about going to conference for teenagers with special needs. Initially, he had been delighted to see that so many grandparents had come along, until he got talking to people and realised that these people were actually the parents.

'Look after yourself,' he said, 'and part of that is allowing yourself to be upset about this. You have to let yourself grieve for the life you thought you had.'

March 2009

It was a Saturday afternoon, and I had been cleaning the house since I got up at seven. I was scrubbing an upstairs toilet, the last of the three terrible toilets, thankfully. Martha was downstairs, looking after Ailbhe and Sophie.

If you saw me then, you might have thought that I was crying, because liquid was leaking from my eyes. I wasn't crying, though, I was just using the really good bleach; you know the one that's so good that it kills the last 0.1% of bacteria, while the fumes strip off your corneas?

As I was scrubbing and not crying – definitely not crying – Martha came upstairs. I suspected that she no longer saw the Clark Kent she had married, but that instead, she saw Superman, on his knees, in a heroic toilet-cleaning pose, not crying. I expected that she would thank me profusely for this, because, before I had cleaned up, the whole place had an air of nuclear aftermath about it.

But she did not do that. Instead, she gently asked me why I was cleaning the toilet with her fancy back brush, when the toilet brush was right beside me: 'What the fuck are you doing?'

I realised what the fuck I was doing immediately, and I reacted by throwing the stupid fucking back brush out the stupid fucking bathroom door, and slamming the stupid fucking toilet seat so hard, that it splintered into stupid fucking smithereens, because it was a fucking stupid, cheap toilet seat and I was Superman.

The Strong One. The Best Husband in The World, Ever. The man who would do everything, who would fix everything, and who definitely wasn't crying. And then, I stomped into the spare room, slammed the door, and slid down to the ground, sitting with my back against the wall. I sobbed, like Clark Kent.

I walked out of the room a few minutes later, and I said, 'So, I think we need to talk.' Martha hugged me.

'Take a couple of days off work at the end of next week; make a long weekend out of it. Get lost for a while,' she said, kindly. Martha had just created our golden rule of parenting children on the autistic spectrum: we can't both be crazy at once.

So we left the chores for the day, and instead, we relaxed with the girls, and Pixar-ed the faces off ourselves. It was wonderful. Since the word autism had come into our lives, I had tried to be the hero, to carry us all along, including myself, but after three months, I was defeated. I really needed the break.

Even Superman needs a duvet day from time to time, right?

I took the next Thursday and Friday off work, and I went for an extra-long weekend to the place in Ireland where everyone who has had a recent mental break goes: Galway.

It was a pleasant spring day when I left Dublin on the train, and I felt a lightness in my chest that I hadn't felt for months. This wasn't just because I was getting away – it was because I had come up with a plan to keep myself sane for the foreseeable future.

I had been a part-time singer-songwriter when Martha and I met. This is why it was good that she heard me instead of saw me first: in my attempts to dress like a serious songwriter, I had ended up looking like I'd just rolled around in the laundry and come out in whatever stuck to me. I was a skinny human bag of unrequited love songs, in sandals. (A few months after we moved in together, my sandals went missing, for ever. Years later, Martha told me that they went to live on the sandal farm with all the other sandals, and that they were very happy.)

The first time I played her one of my songs, she paid me the highest compliment a part-time singer-songwriter can get. She thought the song was written by a full-time singer-songwriter – somebody ... good.

I had started writing songs when I was nineteen years old, for the same reason that every sensitive-souled boy starts writing songs: to make women who I couldn't talk to fall in love with me, which they never did, oddly, no matter how much I sang at them.

When I was unemployed after college, I joined a little acoustic guitar band, and we had a weekly gig in a tiny pub, playing cover songs to college students. Occasionally, though, we'd slip in one of my originals. One night, the barmaid shouted, 'Play "Julia"!' It was the first time anyone had ever requested one of my songs. This song has something in common with the Tracy Chapman song 'Baby Can I Hold You', in that it also rhymes the words 'maybe' and 'baby' in the chorus. This is where the comparison between these two songs abruptly ends. In terms of beauty and popularity, they are both songs in the same way that George Clooney and I are both human males.

Luckily, I didn't take this morsel of validation as encouragement to spend most of my spare time over the next ten years trying to start a serious music career. That would be just too tragic, wouldn't it?

It was nine years.

Martha always thought that I would be successful. So, after we met, as I continued through the usual gauntlet of failed bands and rejection letters, she said that it was just because I was unlucky. She meant it.

Originally, I wanted the same thing every other singer-songwriter wants. A number one hit, leading to world-straddling domination, but eventually my ambitions became a bit smaller.

On the second New Year's Eve Martha and I spent together we went to see one of our favourite bands, The Frames. They were playing in my most beloved venue: the Olympia, a classic old-time theatre in the heart of Dublin. As we were watching, I said, 'All I want is to be able to walk out on that stage once, and play one of my own songs. I could die happy then.'

Eventually, after getting nowhere, and growing bored, I had given up singer-songwriting entirely. It was around the time that Martha was pregnant with Ailbhe, and I hadn't written a song or done a gig since. On the way to Galway I thought, *I will start writing songs again.* I would resurrect my dead singer-songwriter career. Yes, 'career' is a very strong word. 'Hobby' is more apt and accurate. Career implies payment. Payment was never a feature of my 'career'.

But maybe this time it could be more? Before, I had never been deep, or interesting, or profound in any way at all, but now … now, I had proper pain; not the silly teenage-to-twenty-something pain of unreciprocated want. This was proper, grown-up pain; so now I would write proper, grown-up songs that proper grown-ups would listen to while they quaffed their wine and swallowed their feelings, like proper grown-ups are supposed to do.

I was staying with Enda and Sorcha for the first night, and then Dee and Lisa for the two nights after that.

They had all been told that I needed to spend most of my time on my own in Galway, and they understood. I needed the time to create art, and buy an indoor scarf, and a jacket with elbow patches to wear ironically on the beach. Most of all, I needed to be more than a father of two girls with special needs for a few days.

By the Thursday afternoon, I was sitting on a bench in Eyre Square, in the middle of Galway, with a fancy hardback notebook, just purchased from the nearest fancy hardback notebook shop. The glorious smell of it: you could get high sniffing a new notebook. I used to write in ordinary notebooks – even school copybooks – but that would not do anymore. My lyrical beginnings would probably need to be preserved in some sort of future hall of fame, so I thought it for the best to give my nascent musings an appropriately reverential binding. I was steadily scribbling my way to success, slowly becoming the next Leonard Cohen or Tom Waits or Nick Cave. (I wasn't fussy.)

After staying with Enda and Sorcha on Thursday, I went back into the centre of Galway, and sat in a pub on the Friday afternoon, nursing a pint, because that's what poignant people do, I think. By then, I had pages and pages of rhythmic pain in my notebook. As it approached lunchtime, Lisa called me. Lisa is an Englishwoman, who Dee met when he was finishing off his architectural degree in Canterbury. Since she moved to Galway with Dee, she has resisted assimilation, and still says very English things, like 'poorly' and 'bugger' and 'all this land is mine'.

She asked if I want to go for lunch. I thought that I could do with a break from my newfound profundity. Also, it turned out that I really did need to talk, so I talked to Lisa. And I kept talking. I am good at talking. Just ask Lisa: *'He never stops!'*

After lunch, we went back to their new gaff, and Lisa collected Laura from the crèche. Even though she is seven months older than Ailbhe, at that time it seemed like there were, developmentally, years between them. Laura would discuss dinner options with her mother, whereas Ailbhe would cry at her ma and mash food stuff into her face. When I saw Laura, I missed the girls for the first time that weekend. I had been so eager to get away from everything and everyone on Thursday. But barely twenty-four hours later, I would gladly have been on the train back. What a wonderfully awful thing parental love is.

Dee came home from work, we had dinner, he went out to gig with his covers band, came home, had a few drinks and went to bed, and during all that time, I was still talking.

I was drunkenly telling Lisa about my plans to write profound classics, for the purposes of pressure relief and possible world domination. She understood this, because she's a creative person herself – an artist and a photographer. For the first time that day, I took a breath, and Lisa used that sliver of opportunity to say, 'Aidan, I've always loved your melodies, but your lyrics are a bit … shit.' I'm sure she couched it in slightly more diplomatic terms than that, but that's what I heard. Before I had a chance to get out my lyric book and regale her with my newfound, painful (and I mean painful) poetry, she immediately (and I mean immediately) interjected: 'There's never any of your personality in your songs. You're witty, you know … sometimes. Why isn't that in there? It's like you're trying to be someone else.'

Lisa obviously hadn't been listening. Of course I was trying to be someone else! Why would I want to be myself!? Aidan, the boring, normal guy who sometimes refers to himself in the third person. Aidan, so very boring, that he might even do a version of the same 'third-person' joke twice. Aidan, who might even do it thrice, pretentiously using the word 'thrice' instead of saying 'three times', to make himself seem more interesting, when really, he is not. At all. Ever.

However, I thought about that chat with Lisa a lot during my remaining time in Galway, even though she was wrong, and English.

On Sunday, when I got back home to Ashbourne, I was delighted to see Martha and the girls again. It seemed as if they wanted to give me a little bit of extra relaxation that evening: Ailbhe and Sophie fell asleep quickly, and stayed asleep!

So, in the sitting room, I picked up my guitar to write a song, for the first time in years, and I tried to apply memorable melodies to my painful poetry. Martha was sitting at the computer in the kitchen, and the double doors were open, so she heard my multiple frustrated attempts. It was not going well. These lyrics didn't flow. They were hopelessly pretentious. Can you believe that?

Then I got up, took off my indoor scarf, and took out an ordinary refill pad. I would not sully my lovely new notebook with what I was about to do. On the way home on the train, Lisa's suggestion came back to me, and I had an idea for a funny song. I had a go at writing that instead. Within half an hour, it was finished.

In the classic Irish kids' show *Bosco*, they had something called 'the Magic Door'. The presenters would invite us kids to go through the Magic Door, which would then open and bring us to a magical outdoor place (usually Dublin Zoo). As they invited us in, they would say the Magic Door poem. 'Knock, knock, open wide, see what's on the other side. Knock, knock, anymore, come with me through the Magic Door.'

So, it seemed obvious to me that I should take this rhyme and make it into a song about sex, intimating that the Magic Door was … well, you know what. I liked it. More important, Martha liked it. The first time I played it, anyway. As I continued to practise it, Martha, who a few hours earlier had been so glad to see me re-energised after my time away, was now peering at me through narrowed eyes. She said, 'I think from now on we should keep these double doors closed.'

I quickly scribbled down three more ideas for similar types of songs, and that is how I started to become a musical comedian. Although I didn't really know, then, that musical comedy was a thing that sane people could do. I would soon learn that the hierarchy of stage performers goes something like this:

Singers
Actors
Stand-ups
Stage crew who come on to fix mic stands
Stage furniture
Poets
Dust on stage furniture
Musical comedians

While Martha was delighted I had found an outlet, over the next six months, as I wrote more and more and MORE, she began to ask me odd questions like, 'How much would it cost to soundproof the spare room?'

April 2009

Both Ailbhe and Sophie had qualified for early intervention. This meant that we would get the help of Enable Ireland, the organisation that provides services for children with special needs in our area up until the age of six.

Ailbhe's first appointment didn't go smoothly, but that wasn't her fault. Martha called me in work to tell me that as she was driving into the industrial estate where the Enable Ireland office was, a truck had reversed out of one of the other lots, straight into the side of our car. 'Oh My God, are you and Ailbhe okay?' is what I should have said. 'Shite, is it a write-off?' is what I did say, realising that it was the wrong thing to say as it left my mouth. 'We're fine, by the way,' said Martha.

What was happening to me? I have the capacity to be a dick, but not *that* much of a dick. My first thought had been, *We don't have the money to replace the car*, knowing that even if we claimed off the truck driver's insurance, we'd still have to pay over something, because our car had been very old, so it was hardly worth anything, monetarily. We needed a car for Martha to get the girls to their appointments. The pain in my gut intensified.

The previous week the remaining staff in work had been called together so we could be informed of another wage cut: fifteen per cent. The fifty people who were left could fit comfortably in one of the large meeting rooms.

Each round of redundancies were done just before the weekend, so on Friday afternoons we all dreaded our phone ringing, showing the caller ID 'Meeting Room,' because that meant you were being called in to be told that you were out. People would come back from that room, say their goodbyes and drift away. The construction industry had collapsed completely. None of us thought we had much hope of being employed in Ireland for a while. Some people emigrated. Some of the younger ones changed industry.

Martha had to deal with the girls every day, with the weight of depression on top of that. One of the ways I made things a bit more bearable was by working hard and making enough money for us to get by, but we weren't getting by any more. We had started to miss bits of mortgage payments.

I apologised to Martha for being so obtuse about the crash when I got home that day. I explained that we wouldn't be able to buy a new car, because we couldn't get a bank loan, and that I didn't know what to do about that. I also said that initially I had been angry because I had assumed the car crash was her fault. (Just in case you didn't think that I was enough of a dick at this point.) It had taken Martha four attempts to pass her driving test; she had finally done it in 2008, on the same day as Barack Obama was elected. (Martha's achievement was almost as momentous, to me, but it didn't generate half the headlines.)

'I get it, Aidan, you thought it was my fault just because I have spatial needs,' she said, which was a wildly inappropriate, completely unacceptable joke, that also made me laugh for the first time that day.

A few days later, Martha said that her mam and dad were going to add to the insurance pay-out so we could buy a car that wouldn't fall apart the second it left the showroom. 'We can't take that, Martha,' I complained.

'Aidan, we are taking it. Now is not the time for stupid pride.'

May 2009

S ophie toddled out to the back garden and toddled back in a few minutes later, wailing.

This was unusual for her. Sophie was a content little toddler, and she didn't cry much. She certainly didn't have tantrums like Ailbhe. She was not frustrated by her lack of ability to communicate. If I offered her something in my hand, she would take it if she wanted it, and if she didn't, she wouldn't. If she wanted something that wasn't being offered, she would do her best to get it herself.

She had learned how to climb. I was looking after her one day in her bedroom, and I had to go for a wee. I thought she couldn't do much in a minute. I walked back in to find her arse at my head level. She had climbed up a set of shelves beside her wardrobe, which are luckily firmly fixed to the wall. You can see why we started referring to her as 'Danger Baby'.

If Sophie hurt herself, she did her best not to cry, and if she did cry when she was hurt, she didn't cry for long. But she was inconsolable about something that had happened in the back garden. She was in pain, but Martha didn't know where. Sophie couldn't tell her with words, and she didn't point with her hands or her eyes. All Martha could do was cycle through her possible needs as if she was a newborn.

That day, it took Martha a quarter of an hour of Sophie's cataclysmic sorrow to figure out that she had been stung by a wasp – those pointless yellow-and-black bastards of the skies.

When we met with the Enable Ireland team before the first therapy sessions, they asked us what we wanted from therapy for the girls. With Ailbhe, we had a complex list of the areas she needed help with: social interaction, sensitivity to touch, toileting, language development and eye contact. With Ailbhe, we knew what she liked and what she didn't like, and we felt like we had a lot to build on.

With Sophie, we had one request. Martha said, 'I just want her to be able to tell me where it hurts.'

On the evening of Sophie's first therapeutic appointment, when I asked Martha, 'How did it go today?' I was pessimistic about the answer.

Martha, however, shone like a sunbeam. 'Aidan, it was brilliant. The therapist was brilliant. Sophie was brilliant.'

After so many months of Martha's doldrums, I was almost blinded by the enthusiasm of her response. 'What happened?'

Martha had explained that when she went into the room, Sophie was just toddling around as usual, not minding Ciara (the therapist) at all. She was thinking, *This poor woman, trying to get Sophie to interact with her. I don't know how she can possibly stay that enthusiastic for the entire day.*

But then Ciara jumped in front of Sophie, pretending to be a frog. Sophie tried to move away, of course, so Ciara would jump in front of her again, and she kept doing it until Sophie *had* to look at her. When she got Sophie's attention, she immediately turned on a relaxing lamp – you know, one of those ones with bubbling water and lights that change colour. Sophie was drawn to that. She let Sophie look at it for a few seconds, and she tapped her fingers on it as well. Then she turned it off. Sophie looked at the lamp for a few seconds. Ciara asked, 'Again?' a few times, and the second Sophie looked at her, Ciara would turn it on again. And she repeated this sequence, making sure that Sophie looked at her every time.

'I couldn't believe it, Aidan,' said Martha. 'By the end of the session, Sophie was able to ask for something with her eyes.'

These were to be our victories from now on. Compared to other people's kids, they were small victories, but for us, they felt like a stadium-roar. We had expected so little from Sophie, but she had shown us what she was capable of. I should have known better. It wasn't the first time in my life I had underestimated someone with special needs.

I was thirteen and John and I had just discovered a pool table in the centre. 'Do you want a game?' said John. 'Ah no, you're okay,' I said. I was sure it would be an unfair game, even though he was a grown man, because he had stumps where his arms and legs should be. Thalidomide, I think. I was there because my mam and dad had volunteered for the Irish Wheelchair Association, which meant that I had 'volunteered' for the Irish Wheelchair Association.

'I'll go easy on ya,' he said. 'Okay, so,' I said, resolving to miss a few pockets on purpose. I'm not, by any means, a good pool player, but I did feel that I had some obvious advantages over my opponent.

'I'll break,' he said. He held the cue in his mouth, and he aimed using a little white rest that he asked me to place on the table for him. He drew back his head and SMACK! It was a surprisingly powerful break. I came to the table, potted a ball, and then I missed one, on purpose. For the next five minutes, he whirred around in his electric chair, potting ball after ball. As the black ball rolled in, he spat out his cue and said, 'Again?' 'Right so,' I said, resolving to play my best this time. A few minutes later, I was beaten again.

John had the gift of the gab in more ways than one: when I missed my last shot in that game, he said, 'I'm glad you're not wiping my arse, because you'd probably miss the hole.'

We brought the girls to their therapy sessions, and we took home the lessons we learned there. Every time a toy helped the girls to achieve something new, we would buy two of these toys, one for Ashbourne, and one for Granny and Grandad in Swords. Ailbhe had problems with her fine motor skills, so they would encourage us to get Play-Doh and Lego for her. I had no problem with this. On more than one occasion, while distracted with these, I would look up from the kitchen table and think, *where has Ailbhe gone?*

It turned out that a chunky plastic pig with a slot in its back and a belly full of coins would help Ailbhe to develop eye contact. We would hold the coin that she wanted up to our foreheads, which drew her eyes towards ours. Gradually she learned that when she wanted something she would have to look at people. With new people, she still often looks into the space around them, but she has no problem with people she knows. I'm not sure if this is autism, or if she's just inherited my childhood shyness.

Ailbhe had replaced the plastic animals she carried around with Woody and Jessie dolls from *Toy Story*. She didn't make them come to life, like in the movie. She just held them.

'You're going to have to teach her,' they told Martha in one of the sessions.

'You can't teach imagination,' replied Martha.

'Of course you can,' they said. 'You just have to model it for her.'

So at home we would often get on the floor beside her, and perform plays with Woody and Jessie that would put Shakespeare to shame, to our uninterested audience of one (which would prove to be much like putting on an Edinburgh comedy show). We persisted, and eventually she started to copy us, and then to improvise herself.

We tried to do the same thing with Sophie, but she was a far more discerning audience member, and she wouldn't even stay for a minute of the first act. It was clear to us not long after she started going to Enable Ireland that her autism was, indeed, far more profound, as we had suspected; and, added to her determination to do everything for herself, it made therapy with her a lot more challenging.

We tried to induce Sophie to communicate, through pointing, with her hands or her eyes, or through the Holy Grail: speech. What we would do was take things that she liked, and put them into clear plastic containers out of her reach, thereby making it necessary for her to ask for them. This idea spectacularly backfired, and just inspired further feats of daring. We were simply training her to become a one-woman *Mission Impossible* team.

We learned that there is no panacea for autism. It is very difficult to know what will or won't work for any particular child. No one could tell us with any certainty what the girls would or would not be able to do as they grew up. With therapy, there was achievement and frustration and joy and boredom, but most of all there was hope.

Hope that we hadn't had since The Hard Weekend.

Ailbhe and Sophie constantly defied our expectations. Before, we had felt like we were drowning in the shit, but going to Enable Ireland was like a snorkel. Yes, we were still in the shit, but at least we could breathe.

June 2009

The little boy was very angry, so he went into his bedroom, and kicked his bed until it was broken. His parents bought a better, stronger bed. The man who sold them the second bed said that it could not be broken by angry little boys. That week, the angry little boy got very, very angry, and broke that bed as well. So his parents bought a third bed. The third bed was made of metal. The boy could not break this bed, no matter how angry he got. One day, when he wasn't angry, he unscrewed all the bits of the metal bed, and took it apart. He did not do any of this because he was bold, he did this because his autism made him frustrated and inquisitive.

The building had that antiseptic smell that public health buildings often have, an obliterating, bleachy tang that hangs around the nostrils for hours afterwards – they must bulk buy whatever that cleaning fluid is at a national level. From the outside, it was a boxy, dark brick building, a structure that looked like it had never had a heyday, or an architect.

There were twelve other parents doing the course, sitting on a loose circle of standard-issue-metal-leg-plastic-bum school chairs, in a stark meeting room, who looked just as bewildered as us, with every one of them probably thinking the same thing as we were: *How the fuck did we end up here?*

We were there because it was the first night of the parenting course the good folks at Enable Ireland had signed us up for. I know this will make the hearts of soon-to-be-marrieds tremble for their freedom, but it also became our date night. We looked forward to it. It was on every Tuesday, for ten weeks. Brendan and Sheila looked after the girls, and Martha and I would have a good chat and a laugh on the forty-five-minute drive there.

On the first night, the course facilitators had invited an ice-breaker couple; a couple who had been on the last course and were there to tell us about their experience of it. They told us the story of their bed-breaking boy. They said that after he took the metal bed apart, they experienced a bittersweet feeling that parents of children with special needs often feel; a mixture of being proud that he *could* do it, and being apoplectic with rage that he *had* done it. They told us that during those moments, two words that they had learned on the course really helped, and they are two words that I still often say to myself in moments when I need to find a little calmness:

'So what?'

Okay, so he had taken the bed apart – was it really such a big deal? That night they let him sleep on his mattress on the floor and the next day they put the bed back together again. So what?

They also told us about how harrowing a normal trip to the supermarket was with their boy, but that it had also become a little easier over time. Their boy liked public spaces, he just didn't like the other people in them, and he would often have tantrums, but the supermarket staff had become used to their visits, and were very helpful. The mother said that it's not a bad idea to introduce yourself and your child, so at least the staff will know that when your child does have a tantrum, no one is being murdered in aisle number three. As for the other people in the store, their only advice was, 'You just have to ignore the goats who gawp!'

Parents often talk about their children with autism like judges talk about why they can't let recidivists out on bail: 'He's a flight risk.' The dad told us that his boy hated his hand being held, but if he didn't hold it, and he took his eyes off him for a second, he'd be gone. He was what his parents called 'a runner'. To counteract this, the dad had become friendly with the security staff in the local shopping centre, which happened to have a wide and long concourse. On weekend mornings, they would let him and his son in early, before the shops opened and the other people came in, so that the boy could run up and down, banging on the closed shutters. That would last for about an hour, but once that was done, he would be far more manageable for the rest of the day.

After the couple finished telling us their story, the first parent – who was there on her own – told us about her little boy, who had no sense of danger. She found herself locking more and more doors, and putting dangerous implements on high shelves. Then she realised that, in order to protect him, she had made his world so small, and all she could see was how she was making such a little life for her son. She desperately wanted to take him out, to supermarkets, just like the first couple, but she just didn't think she was strong enough to ignore the gawpers. For her, 'So what?' were the hardest two words to say. 'I just want to go around the shops and get my few bits in peace, like everyone else,' and then she cried, and who could blame her? It was such a simple, ordinary, and yet insurmountable request.

Then a dad spoke about his son, and how in a lot of ways he was ostensibly a normal little boy; however, in stressful public situations he would jerk around and move his hands wildly, as a coping mechanism. All this dad wanted was a way to stop that, so that his boy didn't have to live with people looking at him 'like he wasn't normal'.

As we went around the circle, the meeting became like a game of parenting poker, with every hand that was shown one-upping the last. We heard about another little boy who, in a rage, almost pulled the back of a car asunder looking for a beloved toy that had been lost. This was not the first time the toy had gone missing, and every time it happened, the kid would become as focused and violent as Liam Neeson searching for his kidnapped daughter.

We heard about a window being smashed by a toy thrown in anger. We heard about a parent being bitten. We heard about siblings being hurt. We heard about a boy who would bite himself. I knew that the word 'autism' was an umbrella term covering a vast range of disabilities and abilities, like the words 'X-Men' or 'politicians', but I didn't realise that autism was a marquee-sized golf umbrella. These parents were describing so many different behavioural manifestations that it made a nonsense of the stereotypical portrayal in the movies.

I had thought that I would listen to these stories and think, 'That's so like Ailbhe,' or 'Sophie breaks my heart like that too,' but I couldn't identify with a lot of the behaviour they were describing.

Also, except for one other parent, all the other kids were boys, which was anecdotal proof of what I had learned from the reading I had done: the ratio of boys to girls with autism is apparently four to one.

We were the last to go. 'We have two girls with Enable Ireland, one is three, the other eighteen months.' Given the rarity of girls with autism compared to boys with autism, it was an impressive hand. We had won parenting poker with a pair of queens. But hearing about other parents' struggles, it felt like a weak hand to win it on, like we were bluffing. All our beds and windows were intact. Sophie was too small to run away and Ailbhe wasn't a runner.

I had bought a set of catches and safety foamy bits, to childproof some edges and lock the contents of some presses away from Sophie, but the set had languished on the kitchen table, despite my multiple promises to install the various bits in various places. Eventually, like so many packets of filler, pots of paint and tubes of grout, it was lobbed into the shed, where all the rest of my good DIY intentions went to die.

As the weeks of the parenting course went by, we got to know the others, and there would be commiserations and laughter over each other's parenting war stories. Often, the course facilitators would have to shush us, like bold children, so they could move on to the next part of the course.

During one of these discussions, one of the mothers said she had heard someone say, 'Special children only get given to special parents.'

I'm not sure how it works, but when Martha is next to me, I can feel a change in the current when she bristles. I knew she was going to say something, and she did: 'I hate that fucking bullshit!' she exclaimed.

Woah, I thought. That was quite the electrical discharge. But I understood the annoyance. It is one of my pet peeves as well. 'You're so good,' people would say when they heard we had children with special needs, conferring an automatic sainthood on us, as if we were suddenly incapable of being bad at parenting, or planet-sized assholes.

But mostly, it was a very positive experience, and highly recommended. Going home, we would be invigorated by the things we had learned, and how we could use them to help the girls. These were simple things, but so effective. Kneel or bend down to their level and talk to your children face to face. This was also good exercise. Put their name at the start of the request, not the end. 'Ailbhe, make me tea' is better than 'Make me tea, Ailbhe,' because Ailbhe would be alerted by hearing her name and would then hear the most important part of the request: tea. Said the other way, there would be a chance that Ailbhe would only hear her name and not the first (very important) bit, so I would end up with no tea, which is a tragedy. (Obviously, Ailbhe was far too young to get me tea, but it didn't mean that I couldn't practise.)

Instead of giving out by saying, 'Do not', like 'Do not watch that screen all day', say something positive instead, like 'Go out and get a job.' Keep requests simple. Instead of saying, 'Go brush your teeth, get your shoes and put on your coat,' split it into singular requests. 'Go brush your teeth,' and when that is done say, 'Get your shoes,' and so on. There will be less speed, but also less confusion, and there will be more chance that everything gets done. (Martha thought that this method also worked well on me.) Instead of giving out to the children for doing 'bold' things, and speaking to them negatively, catch them doing good things, and praise them for it. Again, a method that works well on me.

On the drive home, we weren't just going to fix our family, we were going to fix the whole damn country. 'They should give this parenting course to kids in secondary school,' Martha suggested, back on her old hobbyhorse of a more holistic education programme.

'Yes, you're right,' I agreed. 'And they should teach kids how to change nappies, and how to fill out tax forms, and how you shouldn't ever drive behind reversing trucks,' I said, keeping my eyes firmly on the road.

'You think being funny will get you out of that one, do you?' she laughed.

'Yes, I do.'

July 2009

I finally told Martha that I had had a persistent pain in my side for some months. She was very understanding about the fact that I didn't want to add to our worries by telling her. 'I'll give you a persistent pain in your side if you don't get down to the doctor tomorrow.'

The doctor sent me for an endoscopy, as I thought he would. That's the camera down the throat, not up the bum, although I wasn't enthusiastic about either option.

I didn't want to take a day off work, because work at that time was like a game of musical chairs. I couldn't be sure that when I came back to work the next day there would be a seat for me. The company was still dwindling down, but I wanted to be in the last dwindle, and I didn't want to give them an excuse to jettison me in the next batch by taking sick days off and demonstrating that I was immediately dispensable, which at that time I certainly was.

In the waiting room that morning I was surrounded by big-eared elderly men. Nobody said anything. What can you say: 'Throat or bum?'

When the staff at the clinic said that I could be back in work that morning if I didn't take the sedative, I said, 'Go on, I'm listening.' I wasn't entirely convinced. Having a tube shoved down my throat while I was fully awake seemed like a slightly idiotic thing to do.

'What's it like?' I asked the nurse.

'It's like a bad trip to the dentist.' (Every trip to dentist for me was a bad trip.)

'I think you'd be well able to go without it,' she said, implying that I'd be less of a man if I did opt for the drugs. I wasn't going to fall for that. I'm totally secure in my manhood.

'Okay, let's go without the sedative, then …'

I lay on my side on the table as the staff fussed about. *I can do this*, I thought. Then they presented me with an horrendously long, thick pipe. *I can't do this*, I thought. It looked like an extreme S&M device. It was certainly not an instrument of love. *That thing is not going inside me,* I thought. I immediately recoiled. Sensing my reticence, the doctor said, 'It's not so bad once it's in.' *You swallow it then,* I thought. Still, after a lot of false starts, I eventually managed it. It is a dreadfully uncomfortable procedure. This book is not meant to be an advisory manual, nevertheless, I can offer you three words that you can live by: Take. The. Sedative.

Ten minutes later, which felt more like an hour to me, after a lot of bilious retching and gagging, the procedure was finally over. The camera came out, and I could properly breathe again. I took a lot of desperate breaths. When I regained a modicum of composure, I looked at the nurse – a shell of the man I had been just minutes before – and I said, 'You really, really need to change your dentist.'

I got a bus from the hospital to work. I have rarely felt as drained in the daylight, so I lay my head against the bus window.

When I got to my desk, I sat down and turned on my computer, but I didn't know how I was going to work. One of my workmates asked me, 'How was it?' with a look of concern that told me that he already knew the answer.

'Not good,' I said.

'Have you looked at yourself in the mirror?' he asked. As anyone who has ever been asked that question will tell you, you can't find a mirror quickly enough once someone says it.

I went into the toilets and I stared at myself. My forehead was covered in broken blood vessels, which was disconcerting enough, but when I looked up, I could see that the lower third of my eyeballs were blanket red, because I had broken blood vessels in them as well, from retching. This wasn't a good look for me. I went home for the rest of the day and slept.

Directly after the endoscopy, when I was still raw of throat and red of eye, the consultant had told me that there was probably nothing to worry about, but that he would confirm that in a couple of weeks after he had got the results back from some biopsies he had taken.

At the follow-up appointment, he told me that I had a hiatal hernia, and showed me some weird pictures of my insides. It wasn't serious enough for surgery. Instead, he prescribed me some acid reduction pills. He told me that I was to look after myself, and that the condition can be exacerbated by stress.

He asked, 'Has your life been particularly stressful of late?'

Well, doctor, I discovered that my daughters are on the autistic spectrum, my wife is suffering from depression, I think I'm going to lose my job and my house, for a while I was worried that I might have stomach cancer, and very recently someone shoved a massive pipe down my throat.

'Yes, a little bit, but nothing I can't handle!'

August 2009

There were many momentous world events in 2009: Barack Obama was inaugurated. Michael Jackson died. Chelsea 'Sully' Sullenberger landed a stricken passenger plane on the Hudson river, using his gigantic pilot's balls as flotation devices. And with almost equal courage and skill, after a three-year hiatus, I started doing gigs again.

I hadn't intended to start again. That summer, since my little mental break in Galway, I had been steadily writing silly songs. There was a lot of chaff in those, but the wheatier songs I recorded in my bedroom. I put them up on Myspace, under the name 'The Guilty Folk'. I thought 'Aidan Comerford' sounded less like someone who would regale you with witty songs, and more like someone from Kilkenny who would 'hurl the head off ya'. This was to be a one-man band, like The Divine Comedy, or Simply Red, or Badly Drawn Boy, or, more accurately, considering the sort of songs I was putting up, one of those blokes with cymbals attached to his knees.

As with most recorded-in-the-bedroom-and-immediately-uploaded songs, mine languished in internet obscurity. A 'viral' day for me was when my listens went into double figures. Then I got my first message from a fan.

It said, 'I love your songs … ' *Excellent, I wonder if they are a record producer or a music video maker?* I thought as I read on ' … I have a fantastic opportunity for you … ' *Brilliant! Go on* ' … you could make thousands of dollars a week if you act immediately … ' *Shit! Spam!*

For months, that's the only sort of response I got.

That was until July, when I got a message that started, 'I love your songs … ' I was about to delete it, like I had with all the rest, when the next line caught my eye. 'There's a gig I think you'd be perfect for.' The message turned out to be from a lovely artist called Dorothy, who was also a one-woman band, writing and performing quirky, witty songs under the name Eleventyfour. She told me about a new cabaret night called 'The Brown Bread Mixtape'. Dorothy said that she could get in touch with the guys who ran it. A gig? My bowels flipped over.

'Martha, someone's offered me a gig, will I do it?' Martha had been listening to me writing and rewriting songs since March.

'Yes, I think it would do you good to get out of the house for a night,' she concurred, a little too enthusiastically.

So, a couple of weeks later, I was hanging out in a hot, sweaty basement, nervously waiting to go on. The other acts were brilliant, as were the presenters, who interspersed this wonderful variety show with very well-written, acerbic comedy sketches. It was a small crowd of about fifteen people, but they were loving it! I was sure that I would come on and be a downer.

When the lads introduced me as The Guilty Folk, I suddenly wanted to run away, but instead my legs carried me to the stage. I looked at the audience, said nothing, and started to play and sing 'The Magic Door'. The first laugh was such a rush that I relaxed and really enjoyed the rest of the set. I didn't even mind it when some of the lyrical jokes I'd written turned out to be duds. It was still fun, and the audience was very forgiving.

After I had performed, a woman came up to me who I recognised. It was Sarah, who I knew from the singer-songwriter circuit years previously. After a conversational round of 'and-how-are-you-getting-on-yourself?' she said that if I ever needed someone to sing with to give her a call.

I probably shouldn't have driven home that night, because I was high on gig fever. As I drove, I was delighting in the lines that had worked and already rewriting the ones that hadn't. I had forgotten how much I once loved gigging. But this time it was even better, for two reasons: with sandal-serious-singer-song-writing, unless the audience aren't listening to you at all, you always get a round of applause at the end of the song. It's hard to know if you've done really well. But with comedy songs, there was an instant 'yes' or 'no' from the audience. They either laughed, or they didn't. It was as simple as that. No sandals required. (Thanks to Martha, the sandal-killer, I no longer owned a pair.) If it went well, there was a huge payoff, and if it didn't, there was no safety net. I would come to realise that bad gigs hurt. But far from being frightened of that, it drove me to try and write better and better songs, to make my set bulletproof.

The second reason was that when I was gigging that night, for the first time since The Hard Weekend, I was just a guy with a guitar trying to make people laugh. This would be something that was mine alone, free from the pressure of family life. It felt precious. It felt … necessary. It felt as if I wouldn't be breaking any toilet seats for a while.

When I got home, Martha was in bed. 'How did it go tonight?' I asked her.

'Soph's just gone to sleep,' she yawned.

'Oh shit, that was a late one.'

'How did it go for you?' she asked. I spent the next fifteen minutes telling her. 'So, it went well then,' she said, cutting me off mid-sentence.

'Yes, I have to do that again.'

The night after that first gig, I sat in the sitting room after Martha had gone to sleep, thinking about Sarah's offer.

I started writing a duet.

September 2009

Ailbhe started her free pre-school year in the crèche around the corner. I remember starting primary school around her age. I was just about to turn four, and my parents thought that because I was a very quiet, anxious child, it would be a good idea to put me in school as early as possible, so that it would force me to be more socially interactive. This is akin to teaching a child to swim by dropping them from a helicopter into the Pacific. I wouldn't speak much until I got to college, but I was never unhappy. I mostly tried to keep my head below the parapet.

Ailbhe was not like that. Almost every day, when Martha went to pick her up, the teacher told her a story about something Ailbhe had done, or had refused to do, that was disruptive.

Soon after she started, we had to meet with the staff to try to work out some methods that would help Ailbhe be less of a handful. We were worried that if this didn't work, they would ask us kindly to find a more suitable crèche.

I heard a story from another parent that when you have children with autism, it is advisable to start them in pre-schools or after-school clubs about fifty kilometres away, so that when you are inevitably told that they don't have the facilities to deal with your child, you can move to the next school or after-school club that is a little closer to home. Hopefully, by the time you have sorted out the behavioural issues, you'll be going somewhere close to your doorstep.

Ailbhe had the same attitude to personal space as whoever decides how many carriages are necessary on an Irish commuter train. Out of curiosity, she would sometimes attempt to poke other children in the eyes. We blew raspberries on her tummy at home. She didn't understand why she couldn't blow raspberries on a classmate's tummy. Some kids understand that sort of thing innately. We had to teach Ailbhe.

Her main issue was that she didn't really understand the 'first/then' principle. For example, 'first', you get up before the sun, drag your weary carcass to work for eight hours. 'Then' you crawl back home in the dark, living your life like a mushroom. You get the reward of hanging out in your pants on the couch, watching your favourite box set, and falling asleep half way through the episode you had been dying to watch all day. This is the fundamental deal that we all make with ourselves, and yet it was difficult to explain it to Ailbhe, almost as if it didn't make sense. She didn't understand why you just couldn't do what you wanted all the time.

> 'Well, Bear, some older people can do that, but that's because they are baby boomers, and a lot of them have retired handsomely on their pensions and the profits from the equity in their primary residence, while Daddy is stuck trying to work his way out of this negative equity cesspit.'

The people at Enable Ireland had suggested using a visual schedule with Ailbhe. If you were going to demonstrate the 'first/then' principle to an adult, using a visual schedule, you would draw a person wasting their life away at a nine-to-five job, and put it beside the front cover of the *Breaking Bad* box set. You would point to the pictures and say, '*First*, you keep it together for eight hours. *Then*, you get to go home and watch another man slowing falling apart, for fun.'

For Ailbhe, it was, *first*, you do what the teacher wants you to do (counting, writing ... things like that), *then* you get to play with plastic animals or run around for a bit, but the principle was essentially the same. The visual schedule worked. Steadily, she started to settle down.

Over the summer, Ailbhe's speech, mood and concentration had begun to improve. She called a truce with Sophie. She had to. She had also developed a strong dislike for our disapproval. We had won that war. This did not mean that they played together. There was no interaction. They kept themselves to their own hemispheres of whatever room they happened to be in. It was merely a cessation of hostilities, and yet a huge improvement in our lives.

Ailbhe's tantrums still happened, but far less frequently. Her echolalia, her repetition of television and movies, was fading, and eventually would cease completely, although she said the word 'sorry' quite a lot, for no apparent reason. Maybe she was making up for all the insincere apologies of the past? Maybe this was just genetic. I said the word 'sorry' a lot when I was growing up, when someone ran into me on the street, on dates, after sex (although often that was with very good reason).

Ailbhe always knew a lot of words, by themselves, but gradually, with help, she was learning to build her own sentences. We were told at one speech therapy session that a sign of good language development is when a kid can join up two unrelated concepts to make a name for something they don't know the word for. For example, we heard a story about a little boy who had hurt himself in the crook of his elbow, who said, 'I hurt my elbow-pit,' because, like a lot of kids, he was able to take the word 'armpit' apart, and apply the 'pit' bit to his elbow. (I have called this part of my body my elbow-pit ever since.) Very early on, Dee and Lisa's daughter Laura called her bellybutton her 'tummy nipple'. (Show-off!)

One day, just after she turned four, Ailbhe was looking for a toy on the mantelpiece, except she didn't know the word 'mantelpiece'. 'Where is it?' asked Martha.

Ailbhe pointed at the mantelpiece and said: 'Fireshelf!'

April 2010

When she was just over four years old, we were interviewed as part of Ailbhe's diagnostic process. They talked to us about our family history and environmental factors. Martha told them about our initial fears of infertility, and how she drank an entire bottle of wine very early in her pregnancy. Wine causes drunkenness, and a strong desire to re-watch *Sex and the City*. I like wine, and my favourite episode of *SATC* is 'One' (where Miranda and Steve kiss at Brady's first birthday party), but there is no evidence that it causes autism. Martha knew that.

She told them that she had fallen over in late pregnancy. She told them that she'd had a headache in the first trimester and taken a Nurofen Plus. She told them about the stomach bug we both got in her second trimester that was so bad that at one point we had to share the one bathroom in Cabinteely, her on the toilet and me in the shower. 'So, you have a good relationship then?' asked the therapist, at once smiling and appalled.

I laughed. 'Well, yes, once you've seen someone's most anguished poo face, there's no going back, is there?'

Then Martha told them about her depression. And then she cried.

One of the therapists offered Martha a tissue, and Martha dabbed at the wet bits of her face, while I told the other therapist that I had been a socially awkward boy in school, but that I overcame that in my late teens. There was a snotty snort of laughter from Martha.

I can see now that we were looking for something to blame, something that we had done, or hadn't done, or something about us, separately or combined, that we should have known would mean that our children were bound to be on the autistic spectrum. There is such a strong desire to identify a cause that it is understandable that some parents can latch on to erroneous theories about where autism comes from. There is something so unsatisfying about, 'We don't know what causes it.' Also, if you can't identify a cause, it's very difficult to come up with a cure.

A few weeks later, we were back in Enable Ireland to discuss the results. 'But will she ever *not* have autism?' I asked. Martha and the two therapists looked at me, puzzled.

Then one of the therapists spoke. 'Aidan, Autism Spectrum Disorder is a lifelong condition,' she said, slowly, like someone who is not sure that all their words are landing, as if she were talking to a kid who had trouble understanding her.

'Yes, I know. But. Em. It's Just. Em. What I'm trying to say is … does she get to take a retest later in life?' If life were a game of football, my manager would have been shouting at his staff on the sidelines, 'Get that eejit off before he hurts himself.'

The therapists looked at each other. 'No, this is her diagnosis, she will always be on the spectrum.'

'Right, got it,' I murmured.

'Are you sure?' said the other.

'Sorry, I just wanted to … check … and stuff,' I said.

'Okay, well if there's anything in the report that you disagree with, please let us know,' she said, looking very pointedly at Martha, as if she were the only adult in our relationship.

I remember that at our antenatal course, the midwife told us that she had delivered a baby boy who looked a bit odd, so she suspected that he might have some issues. She said, 'I was just about to call the doctor over, when I looked at the baby's dad, who was, let's say, a unique-looking man, and I realised that there was nothing at all wrong with the baby, he was just his father's son.'

I suspected that this is how the therapists were regarding me now, and they might be wondering if they had properly factored for 'the dad's oddness' in their results.

We were given copies of Ailbhe's report, which was comprehensive. We were asked to read it to see if it accurately reflected what we knew of Ailbhe. The word 'difficulties' appeared a lot. I found the hardest thing to read were the tables of figures. I had thought that the first time my children would be measured for potential would be the Leaving Certificate, at the end of school. The words 'lower percentile' appeared a lot in the conclusions. But from time to time, my eye also picked out the word 'improvements'. This is what I had awkwardly tried to ask earlier: 'How much will she improve?' is what I had meant.

'How much will she improve?' asked Martha. 'What will she be like as an adult?'

'Every child responds differently to therapy,' answered one of the therapists. Another unknown. So many unknowns.

But at least we had a diagnosis, now, and that meant that we had a chance of Ailbhe getting help when she went to primary school. So we weren't upset by the diagnosis. In fact, we were relieved. Martha had told me stories about kids in secondary school who obviously needed help, but who couldn't get it because they didn't have a report like the one we were holding in our hands.

A few months later, we had another meeting so that we could get Sophie's report. She was on the spectrum, of course. Her results showed up that she was far more profoundly affected than Ailbhe. In many cases she wasn't competent enough to take certain tests. This report was just confirming what we already knew. We weren't upset. In fact, I remember we were happy to get the report, and that we did a lot of laughing in that meeting, which I'm sure made for a pleasant change for the therapists.

I cannot begin to count the amount of times I have photocopied those reports over the years to attach to various applications. You can probably see the dent we put in a rain forest somewhere from space.

August 2010

When Sophie was about to turn three, she said her first word. It was 'bye.'

That wasn't surprising. We had been trying to get her to say 'bye bye' when people were leaving. She associated it with people going away, so eventually, she would come to use it when she *wanted* people to go away, which is something that she wanted a lot. She would eventually combine this with a 'talk to the hand' style wave, which is just a fully extended arm and an outstretched dismissive hand. 'Bye, Daddy' does not mean that she wishes me well in my adventures, it means 'I am done with you, serf, and it would please me greatly if you would kindly fuck off at your earliest convenience.'

Over the next couple of years, she would develop a limited two-word vocabulary. Then her language would stop developing. She acquired just enough to make her needs known. 'Want Ribena!' 'Snuggle Mammy!' 'Supermarket?' Simple and easy to understand. One of her favourite phrases is 'Daddy trampoline,' which means that she would like me to bounce on the trampoline with her until my legs are nothing but bloody stumps.

She eventually acquired about fifty stock phrases. It's obviously not a perfect system, and there are times when she can't say what she wants, or we don't understand, especially when she is trying to request an obscure YouTube video. That will generally lead to wailing, out of frustration. Ironically, she is usually at her most coherent when she is angry. She is a conversational Hulk: 'I hate that!' 'I'm so angry!'

Her receptive language is a lot better. She can understand important requests like, 'Sophie put your seatbelt back on' and 'Sophie, get back in that window now!' and 'Snap on the kettle and make Daddy a cup of tea.' (Tragically, that last one was just a joke.)

But she cannot hold a conversation. It is as if she sees no need for it. (After all, why would one want to consort with the downstairs staff?) But just because she is not talkative it doesn't mean that she is quiet. She became a dedicated babbler.

She runs around her circuits, excitedly, with arms and head doing their own thing, like a sentient drum kit, and she will emit a stream of sounds as she goes. I think most of this is down to echolalia, but it's not as coherent as Ailbhe's was. It is the tones of the scene she is repeating rather than the words of it, and it often sounds like there is someone in her head rapidly changing the channel.

Unlike Ailbhe as a toddler, she can sometimes use this echolalia appropriately. One night, I said, 'It's time for bed.' She instantly replied, 'I am not sleepy and I will not go to bed,' in the exact same English accent as Lola from *Charlie and Lola*, which she was mimicking. I laughed, and put this down to coincidence, but as I tried to put her to bed, she got angry, and let me know in no uncertain terms that she really meant it: 'Go away, Daddy!'

September 2010

A s the years go by it is difficult to remember what you got and gave from one birthday to the next, but I can still remember what I got for my thirty-fourth birthday: Redundancy.

They really shouldn't have. It's the thought that counts, so they really should have just thought about it and left it there. It wasn't a surprise, though; there had been nothing for me to do for a very long time. I was either going to get made redundant, or pass away from boredom. Still, as the managing director mouthed off the usual platitudes, I thought, *surely it should be illegal to do this on my birthday?*

The previous Christmas, the thirty-odd structural staff that we had had at the height of the boom had been whittled down to three. After that, I had survived for nine months, but when the music stopped this time, I was the one left without a chair.

Even though I had been ready for it, as I walked out of the office that morning, it felt surreal. I had worked continuously for nearly fourteen years, and now that was over, probably for a few years. I was scared about what would happen. I was sure we would lose the house.

I had one good thought as I walked down the road to get the bus home for the last time: *now I'm finally a full-time musician, just as I'd always dreamed.* It wasn't as exciting as I'd hoped. Sarah and I were gigging away as The Guilty Folk, but there was the slightly sobering fact that we had yet to be paid for doing a gig. I suspected that my 'performance artist' pay packet would leave a slight shortfall in our monthly mortgage payment.

'I might not get another job in engineering for a few years. I think I might look at doing something in computers,' I suggested to Martha.

She had a different idea. 'I think you should dig the garden.'

This was an unexpected response. 'How much does it pay?'

'Uncle Dec says he'll pay for a patio to be put in if we dig the garden first. Sophie needs somewhere to play!' she said.

Our back garden was eternally boggy, and Sophie, who loved to be outside, would sink up to her ankles in it after a heavy rain.

'Martha, I still need to send emails, apply for jobs, that sort of thing.'

'I thought you said there were no jobs.'

'Well, yes, but I have to try.'

'I know, Aidan, but while you're trying, dig the garden.'

'Look, I'm not digging a garden in a house that the bank will take off us in a couple of years.' I was firm about that.

'The bank won't take the house.' She thought she was being optimistic. I thought she was being naïve.

I was reading stories about our generation lobbing keys into their letterboxes and heading for the airport. Martha had stopped reading the news, so she had no idea about those stories. There was no arguing with her, so I stormed off upstairs to stab out some job-seeking emails. I definitely was not going to do something so pointless and idiotic as digging the garden.

A few days later, I was out digging the garden. I was tired of looking at my inbox and seeing 'no unread emails'. It was only a few days, and I had already begun to feel useless. *What will I be like after a few years of this?* I thought. Reluctantly, I accepted that digging the garden had been a good idea. First, Martha was getting the garden done, which she had wanted for a while, but second, she had given me something useful to do, which stopped me sitting at my computer, getting depressed, endlessly refreshing jobs websites, which is exactly what I would have done.

There is a huge loss of identity attached to the loss of a profession. It affects how you think of yourself: *I am a something*, whereas when you are unemployed you think: *I am a nothing*. It would be all too easy to slip into that rut. If Martha had not had the foresight to give me something to do, I probably would have come to her after a couple of weeks like Colonel Brandon in *Sense and Sensibility*, and asked her to, 'Give me an occupation, or I shall run mad.'

A couple of months later, it was a Wednesday morning, and I was due to start a computer programming course the next Monday. Sinéad's wedding was on that weekend, and I was looking forward to going to that. The new patio area was two-thirds dug. My mobile phone buzzed in my pocket. It was my ex-boss, who had been let go around Christmas of 2008.

He was working a three-day week in a Dublin-based company that was doing structural work in the Middle East, and he had three days of drawing work that needed to be done. He wondered if I would be interested. I was interested in it like a drowning man is interested in a life buoy.

The next day, I was at that office at eight, wondering if I still remembered how to do my job. The project was a modular piece of drawing work (i.e. a lot of copying of previous work could be done). I asked, 'If I can do this in two days, will you give me a permanent job?' One of the managing directors of that company said he would, but he couldn't guarantee that he would be able to keep me on for more than a couple of months. The pay was less than half of what I had been on, but it was a lot better than the pay I was getting for digging the garden, or performing with The Guilty Folk. It meant that there would be a chance, albeit slim, of keeping the house. It wasn't going to be enough on its own, but it was a start.

A year later, I was still working for that company, the garden was still two-thirds dug, and our mortgage was deep under water.

March 2011

I had been watching an entropic Champions League football match, which was spiralling towards a seemingly inevitable stalemate. I was delighted that Soph had gone to sleep early, so that I could fall asleep in front of the match in peace.

Soph had only gone to sleep early because I had cheated. Instead of putting her to sleep in her bed, I had put her to sleep in our bed, which meant that she would go to sleep quicker. This was supposed to be a week where we tried to make sure she stayed in her own bed at night. Earlier, Martha had driven over to Swords, so she could have a break for the evening. I thought, since Martha was having some time off, it was only fair that I should give myself a break too. *One night, what's the harm?* I squashed any thoughts I had of the many other nights I had immediately relented and let Sophie go to sleep in our bed as well.

That night, it had worked beautifully. I read her a story in our bed. Then I went to have a wee in the en suite, and when I came back, her eyes were lidded, her body was still and she was breathing in and out in a rhythmic way. She was asleep, I thought. My heart did a little dance, and I carefully shut the door and went downstairs. Match time!

Half an hour later, as I lay on the couch, watching sideways soccer, I saw something curious in my peripheral vision, out the window, that looked like a little bird. However, in my experience, birds usually fly side to side, and this one had a very definite, unrecoverable up-to-down trajectory. I got up to open the sitting room window, expecting the sad detritus of dead bird on the ground.

Martha's mobile was ringing in Swords.

Just as I opened the window, I saw another object fall from above and hit the ground. It was a coin. I heard Sophie's unmistakeable delighted gurgle, and it sounded very much like she was outside. Except she wasn't! I knew exactly where she was. *Shit!* I thought, and turned and sprinted.

Martha answered her phone. A neighbour, who lives in a house facing ours on the opposite side of our green, had spotted something that she thought worth mentioning to Martha: 'Sophie is kneeling on your windowsill, naked. The window is fully open and she's throwing stuff out.'

'I'm not there, I'll ring Aidan, thank you,' said Martha, and she immediately hung up and rang home.

As I was running up the stairs, I heard the phone ringing. Every time my foot hit the step, a clipped, breathless *shit* went off in my head. *Shit! Shit! Shit!* I was bounding so hard – I think it only took ten *shits* to get from the sitting room window to our bedroom door. When I opened it, Sophie was not in the bed, and the curtains were closed. Ostensibly, it looked like an empty room, but then I heard an unmistakeable, delighted little screech from behind the curtain. I pulled back the curtain to see Sophie kneeling on the jamb of the fully-open window. There was a decorative ceramic jar with coins and assorted crap in it, and she had been lobbing those out the window. If she had overbalanced even slightly, she would have fallen out.

I grabbed her and fell back on the bed, with Soph in one arm, simultaneously grabbing the phone with the other. All I heard when I answered was a rapid shout of: 'AIDANSOPHSATTHEOPENWINDOW!'

'It's okay. I've got her. I'm sorry. I thought she was asleep. She was asleep,' I said, breathlessly.

'I'm coming home,' said Martha.

'No. There's no need, I have her now. Stay there.' But I had fucked up, and my trust-o-meter was a little low right then, so she did come home.

Sophie had had an unhealthy interest in windows since she could toddle up to them. But we put our faith in the fact that a girl who couldn't speak well probably couldn't figure out the mechanism to open them. Clearly, that era was over.

After Martha put down the phone, I shouted, 'Sophie, Bold!'

'Bold!' she shouted back, and giggled.

'Shit,' I said under my breath.

'Shit,' she said under her breath.

The next day, we had to get someone in to fix the windows so they couldn't be opened fully with ease. To open a window fully now, you must reach up to the top of the window and unclasp a little latch. That should hold her until she's about thirteen. After that … I don't know.

When I pass a house on a nice summer day, with all the windows fully open, and the sound of carefree children happily playing within drifting out, I feel a stab of envy.

April 2011

The eighth wonder of the world is the capacity of Ailbhe's bladder. She was a reedy five-year old, but when it came to holding her piss she was like a Wee-Tardis.

We gave her plenty of liquids, and she drank them, and yet she could go up to twenty-four hours without weeing:

'She is literally taking the piss,' said Martha.

'Yes, Martha, but what is she doing with it? That is the question.'

Because of Ailbhe's diagnosis, we were able to avail of a second free pre-school year, which we were glad of, because we didn't think she was ready for primary school after her first year of pre-school. One of the reasons we didn't want her to go yet was because she couldn't *go*, yet. She wasn't toilet-trained.

This had become my bugbear. I didn't want my kid going to their first day of proper school wearing a nappy, and September was looming.

When your child has special needs, and they are over three and not toilet trained, you can apply to the Irish government to provide you with free nappies. After we were approved for that scheme, Martha drove to Navan to collect the boxes of nappies every couple of months. They filled the boot of the car. 'That is literally a shitload of nappies,' I said the first time I saw them.

And when Ailbhe did a wee in one of those nappies, it would be an unbelievably voluminous grey mass. When it was wrapped up for disposal, it felt as a heavy as a gravitational singularity, and it made an impressive 'thunk!' when it was thrown into the bin.

And then there were the shits – the epic man shits. They were like the unending poos that your dad would do on a Sunday afternoon, while perusing the sports section, except somehow, unbelievably, bigger.

The infrequency of her movements and the apparent size of her bladder made toilet-training an almost impossible task. It was like trying to train a camel to drink. But try, I did. I tried with a potty, but Ailbhe looked at it with a face that said, *'You want me to piss in a fancy basin on the floor, are you serious?'* She wouldn't spend a minute on it, let alone a penny. I think Sophie used the potty as a hat for a while before we threw it into the toy graveyard in the attic.

So I got a toddler toilet seat that fitted into the ring of the big toilet seat, made so that toddlers with their small bums wouldn't fall through. That seat was cushioned. Cushioned! Short of angels playing lutes while she whizzed, what more incentive could she want?

Then Martha read that children who are prone to being anxious about using a toilet may find it hard to relax and wee because their feet are dangling. While I do understand the joy of being able to plant one's feet squarely on a surface, for leverage, while one is defecating, I was sceptical. We bought a plastic toilet step. It didn't work. I now suspect this theory was a capitalist ruse by the Big Plastic Toilet Step Industry.

Although, the step did work well for Sophie when she took it out of the bathroom to stand up on it so she could reach a scissors and cut her hair. (Even though the step went the same way as the potty, Sophie would still find a way to climb up and get a scissors to cut chunks out of her hair on the morning of my brother's wedding. In the photos, she has a strategically placed hairband.)

Eventually, I installed a new toilet seat, with an inbuilt toddler toilet seat in the middle that could be flipped out when needed. It reminded me of the scene in the movie *Alien*, when the Alien opens its mouth to threaten Ripley and then a second Alien baby mouth pops out. Oddly, Ailbhe wouldn't put her arse near it, at first.

Eventually, I got her to sit on it, at timed intervals, but she would never wee. 'I can't,' she'd say. I would counter with the very persuasive, 'But you have to.' After ten minutes, our little negotiations would break down, and I would let her off, frustrated. I would do that with her for about a week, before I'd lose patience. It was a pain in the hole for me. It was literally a pain in the hole for her.

One Sunday morning in April, I said, 'Martha, I'm worried about Ailbhe going to school in a nappy.'

Martha didn't seem as bothered. 'You don't have to worry about that … the school won't *let* her go if she's not trained. She'll figure it out, though, don't worry.'

I blew out my cheeks. 'Right then, she's going to figure it out today, I have a plan.'

Martha rolled her eyes. 'Why do I get the feeling Ailbhe will be talking about this plan of yours in therapy when she's an adult?'

Ailbhe had expressed a strong interest in going to see the movie *Gnomeo & Juliet*. The movie was just out, and I had already planned to take her. I went to Ailbhe's room, where she was playing. 'Ailbhe do you want to go to the cinema today?'

'Yes!' she answered, excitedly.

'Okay,' I agreed, 'But no nappy. Wee in the toilet first.'

I sat on the edge of the bath. She sat on the Alien-mouth toilet, not weeing. 'I can't,' she cried, eventually.

'Okay, we will try again in ten minutes.' We weren't going to be beaten. The movie was in an hour, at half-twelve, in the local cinema. We had time.

But she could not wee. I gave her some water, we waited ten minutes, and tried again. We kept this up, until the time for the start of the movie passed. 'It's okay, it's on again at three,' I said, 'we'll make that.'

We did not make that.

There was one last showing at five-thirty. Surely we would make that? And yet, every ten minutes, we tried and we failed.

We had one last go at quarter-past-five. If she didn't wee now, which was likely, this unending day of dryness would be a waste. The whole point was that she would be well-rewarded for weeing in the toilet, she would go out in public with no nappy and see how good that feels, and she would forever associate weeing in the toilet with good times. Yes, maybe that would lead to some questionable practices in later life, but I was prepared to take that risk. And yet, it still wasn't happening. I sat on the edge of the bath, with my chin cupped in my hand, falling asleep, defeated.

And then, out of nowhere, strong and true, I heard 'Pssssssssssssss'. Ailbhe did a piss and a half. It was a wonderful, magical, fantastic, horse piss.

Ailbhe was delighted. 'I'm doing it!' she said.

'You are!' I exclaimed, and hugged her, while she was still weeing. So, yeah, there may be some psychological damage.

As she finished, I looked at my watch. Ten minutes to movie time. I was so desperate to get to the cinema that I was washing her hands before I pulled her pants up. I barrelled out the door, carrying her, lobbing her into the car seat, and making it to the cinema just in time for the opening credits.

The movie was good, but it would have been better if I hadn't spent the entire time bursting to go for a wee.

May 2011

Martha, Sophie and I waited outside the principal's office for the head of the autism unit attached to the school to come and meet us. It was a boys' school, but it was a co-ed autism unit. We had come to see if it would be a good fit for Sophie. If it was, she would be able to do her pre-school years as well as her primary schooling here, and we wouldn't need to move her to a new school for years to come.

The only drawback was that this school was a forty-five-minute drive from our house, and as I now needed the car to get to work, we'd have to apply for the school bus. It would mean a lot of travelling every day for Sophie.

I was inspecting the notice board, looking at the usual announcements of school fundraising efforts and past achievements. Sophie was sitting in a seat beside Martha, swinging her legs. I hoped the wait wouldn't be too long. By the time she was coming up on four years old, she could produce a sizeable tantrum if we tried to hold her still for too long. Even though she wasn't half as able to communicate as Ailbhe had been at her age, she didn't seem to be as frequently frustrated. Also, we were better able to deal with them, but still, I would rather that the school's first impression of her would not be 'Redheaded Air Raid Siren.'

A gaggle of happy-headed little boys passed by. I looked at them, and then I looked over at Martha. Our eyes met, and I knew that we were thinking the same thing …

A few weeks earlier, we had been lying on our bed talking, face to face. The girls were asleep. It had been a good day. 'Aidan, what do you think about having another kid?' This was a ridiculous question. There were so many reasons not to have another kid, not least the fact that when you have two children on the autistic spectrum, the likelihood of having another one increases massively. Martha knew that, but she still wanted an Aidan-baby. A little boy.

'I don't think so,' I said. Martha was trying to rationalise it. 'I could handle another kid like Ailbhe. Maybe even a kid like Sophie. But if the kid is more profoundly affected than Sophie … I mean, the way things are going, our next kid might just be a head.' I laughed and I put the back of my hand against the underside of my chin and moved my fingers, pretending to be an Octobaby – just a head and tentacles – and in a warbling alien voice, I said, 'Mammmyyy, whhhy don't you looove me?' Martha laughed.

In my previous company (which I missed hugely) we had a silly competition where we had to identify baby pictures of our colleagues. Everyone got my picture right, because my face had never changed. That was why Martha could well imagine what our little boy, an 'Aidan-Baby', would look like. He would look like me, when I was a baby, and on my wedding day, and now.

And I wanted a little boy too. I still wanted our family of four. Also, and I'll be totally honest, I could have done with a ride. But it would have needed to be the Space-Shuttle-Take-Off of rides to be worth it, because I thought having another kid would break us. Even a kid who wasn't on the autistic spectrum. If he or she didn't break us emotionally, he or she would surely deal a death blow to our bank account, which was already critically injured, and might not survive in any case.

So, I took my hand down from my chin, and I was firm: 'We can't have any more kids.'

'Yes, I know,' she agreed, 'but it doesn't stop me wanting them.'

'Me neither,' I said. Martha was melancholy. 'I just wanted to know if you were feeling the same way I was feeling.'

'I am, but we cannot have any more kids, Martha.' I used my sternest tone to underline the statement and placed a big, black full stop at the end of it. The foot was down. The decision was made. We wouldn't discuss it again, I thought.

Then the schoolboys passed into the bowels of the school and the corridor was quiet again. 'So, why were you sent to the principal?' I asked Martha.

'Marrying a Carlow man,' she replied.

'Oh, you're going to get a lot of detention later for that.'

'You wish.'

'I do,' I smiled.

Just as I scoffed, a bespectacled, wiry South African woman came around the corner. She was the head of the autism unit – enthusiasm personified – and she was immediately lovely with Sophie.

We walked out through the empty boys' school playground and went to a one-storey, prefabricated structure out the back, which had its own gated playground off to the side.

It being almost the end of the school year, most of the kids from the unit were out on school tours, so the buildings were empty, except for a few staff. We were shown around the classrooms, which were much like every other primary school classroom I've ever seen, with art around the walls and the like. Except there would only be six or seven children in each class. The layout of the room was different too: there was a central table and separate little cubicles all around the walls, each cubicle having some learning toys and visual schedules. 'I suppose this might look at bit odd, at first,' she said.

'Actually, it doesn't,' I said. 'I saw something very similar recently when I visited the Google offices.'

Eventually, we went out to the playground, which Sophie had been very eager to get out to. She ran around trying out the various playground equipment. There was one other kid there with a special needs assistant looking on nearby. His class was out on a day trip at the cinema, but he didn't like the cinema, so they were looking after him at the school. When he saw us, he climbed into one end of a crawling tube and did not come out the other.

'Do any of the kids ever go on to mainstream school?' I asked.

She tapped her glasses and said, 'These are my eighth pair since I started in the school.' She explained that there was a boy who liked to punch when he was frustrated, and that she had been the recipient of a lot of these punches, but that after years of being in the unit, he was going to go to mainstream school, with some assistance, in the new term. While she told the story, I wondered why anyone would choose her profession. How many pairs of glasses would I go through before I gave up? The answer to that was easy. One. Tops.

Just as she finished telling us this, there was a startling sound – a human klaxon. It was coming from, and amplified by, the crawling tube. We all looked over and I scanned around and didn't see Sophie. While we had been talking, she must have got in with the boy.

'Oh, we'd better get her,' said the head of the unit with a little alarm, and I thought, 'if *this* woman is alarmed … ' and I ran over, but as I did, Sophie was emerging from the tube, backwards, unhurt.

I looked in and I saw a very agitated boy sitting in there. His little world inside the tube was just fine for him until Sophie came along and ruined it. Normally, Sophie would laugh at loud roars, but she wasn't laughing at this one. She knew enough to back away from the boy. I wanted to apologise to him, but I had the feeling that it would just set him off again, so I said nothing.

We did discuss having kids again, many times, but when we did I always thought about that boy in the tube. What if he was our son? We would not have been able to deal with that. Sophie would also become more challenging as she grew. We realised that we wouldn't be able to look after another kid like her either. That was it. No matter how we felt, we simply couldn't have any more kids. There would be no Aidan-baby.

When Martha had resigned herself to that, she said, through her tears, 'You know, Aidan, I think I might always resent Sophie for this.'

August 2011

We were going on holidays for a week. This was our first time to bring the girls to Gowna. Just before we went, Martha said to Ailbhe, 'Bring something to eat for the car.' Ailbhe looked puzzled. 'What do cars eat?'

It was a sunny day when we set out. If one of the days of our holiday happened to be rainy, we had money for a trip to the cinema in Longford, which was about half an hour's drive away. But there was not much else to do, so I really hoped the weather was going to be good that week, and that the girls would love Gowna as much as we did.

I knew from past experience of trips to Galway with the girls that Sophie's patience would usually run out after about an hour and a half in the car. Martha had thought of that and had brought an emergency bag of Jelly Snakes. On the way down, I ate the emergency bag of Jelly Snakes, but Martha had thought of that as well, and had a second emergency bag of Jelly Snakes. That day, though, Sophie seemed mesmerised by the scenery that went by, as the road changed from motorway, to country lane, to bóithrín, as it wound its way to Gowna.

The sight of the stone cottage did my heart good. When I let Sophie out, she immediately ran around to the boggy back garden, and started to spin and spin and spin. Spinning means, 'I'm very happy'. Then she ran back around to the front and discovered the swing set. She spent the next hour on that. *This was a great idea.*

Ailbhe was less enthusiastic about the outside part of Gowna than Sophie. As a pale-skinned child, like me, she had to wear a lot of sun cream – trying to put sun cream on our girls is like trying to butter a kangaroo. But Ailbhe was delighted with the inside of the house, because of four things: the TV, the chair that spins and reclines, the open fireplace and her bed for the week, which was a bunk bed on top of the wardrobe in the bedroom. For a kid who slept in a normal bed, a bed that you can kill yourself by falling off is the height of adventure.

I saw that there was a small cabin across from the house that had been newly installed by Martha's Uncle Brian, which had a washer and a dryer and a shower. *Sacrilege!* I thought. I wouldn't have a chance to teach the girls about the ins and outs of underpant preservation in the countryside, my best scouting skill. Also, it meant that the zinc basin for bathing was defunct. I spotted it, now a little rusted, sitting out among the trees. To me, it looked like it belonged in a modern art museum with a label, 'The Death of Romance'.

Later, while Martha got the dinner ready, I brought the girls down the hill to the rocky shore of the lake, which was a picture of serenity in the orange evening sun. I saw some swans, and I wondered if they were the same family of swans that were there when I first came to Gowna all those years ago. I thought, *How long do swans live …*

SPLASH!

I realised that I had taken my eyes off Sophie for a moment and she had somehow managed to pick up a big rock and throw it into the water. Then she turned and tried to pick up a rock bigger than her head.

I picked it up for her. 'More?' I asked. She didn't say anything.

'More?' I repeated. Then she looked at me. 'More?' I said, again. She started to get upset as I waited for her to say, 'More.'

Then I admonished myself internally: *No therapy today, Aidan, this is a holiday*, and I threw the rock as far as I could, like a very weak shot putter with an appropriate grunt. It splashed like a depth charge in the deeper part of the lake. Sophie squealed with delight. 'Woah!' Even Ailbhe was impressed.

Then I said, 'Sophie do it,' and Sophie started picking up smaller rocks and throwing them in. While she did that, I tried to show Ailbhe how to skim a stone. I found a lovely flat one and it skipped eight times. I had just enough time to be pleased with myself, when Sophie ran into the water up to the middle of her calves, before I was able to reach over and grab her.

On the way back up the hill, I had Sophie on my shoulders, her legs dangling, drying and cleaning themselves on the front of my top as we went. I had a hand on one of her legs and I was holding Ailbhe's hand with the other.

As we came back up out of the trees near the lake, I saw that there was a herd of about twenty cows in the field that hadn't been there on the way down. *The farmer must have driven them in a few minutes ago,* I thought. I could hear the faint hum of a tractor. As we walked, Sophie started squealing in delight at the sight, which made the cows notice and walk towards us.

'Daddy, I'm scared,' said Ailbhe.

'Cows are harmless,' I said to Ailbhe, simultaneously Googling my brain: *Are cows harmless?*

Sophie kept squealing and the cows kept coming. 'Let's just go a little quicker,' I suggested to Ailbhe, as one or two of them broke into a trot, which made Sophie squeal even more. They cut off our path to the gate, but it was only then that I saw that the farmer was there with some supplementary cow feed. 'Hello,' I called out.

'Hhmm,' he said with a smile. He had seen my frightened trot with my family, and obviously thought I was some sort of soft city lad who was afraid of cows – which wasn't the truth at all.

'How did it go?' asked Martha when we got back.

'I skimmed a stone eight times, Sophie ran into the lake and we almost got killed by some cows. What's for dinner?'

I already knew the answer to that. I'm not saying that the girls don't have a varied dinner diet. They'll eat spaghetti, tagliatelle, penne …. What was for dinner was the only thing both of them would eat. 'Spag bol,' said Martha, 'but I snuck some grated carrot into it,' she winked.

That night, we all sat on the couch and watched a movie together. I could feel the heat of the day on my forehead. A bit of sunburn, despite the sun cream. I put my hand to my head. I had forgotten than I had more forehead than I used to have – *'Daddy, why do you have a hole in your hair?' Ailbhe would ask me one day.*

After the movie finished, Ailbhe climbed into her bunk bed, and I put Sophie in the bed beside me. A couple of hours later they finally fell asleep. When I went back into the sitting room, Martha had fallen asleep with a book by the fire.

A couple of days later, the girls were a little bit bored, so I decided to put them in the car and drive slowly around the house, with them taking turns to sit on my lap, pretending to steer. On the last circuit of the house, I went a bit wide, and drove right into the boggy back garden, and the car got stuck. With the girls still in the car, I got out and tried to push the car but it was stuck fast. I knew I could walk the fifteen minutes down to the nearest farm and ask the farmer to give the car a tow with his tractor, but then I would be forever confirmed as the soft city eejit that he thought I was. So I wouldn't do that. I would get the car out myself.

I spent half an hour, sweating and grunting uselessly without the car budging at all. Then I was assaulted by a wasp! He waited until I was at my lowest moment before he swooped down to sting me right on the tip of my ear, for no reason at all, except that all wasps are bastards.

As I walked down the road, I met the farmer in his tractor. 'Hi, I'm after getting my car stuck, can you give me a tow?'

'Hhmm,' he muttered, and he drove on around the corner.

When I got back up to the house Martha said, 'Well?'

'I think he said yes.'

A couple of minutes later, he drove in on his tractor. He saw the car. 'Hhmm,' he laughed.

September 2011

There are some days when you look at your kids and you think *wow, they're getting so big*, as if they had stretched by inches overnight. The week that Ailbhe and Sophie went to their respective schools, when they put on school uniforms for the first time, they looked so small all over again.

Ailbhe had already spent two years in pre-school, and she would be six years old in the New Year. So, on her first day in primary school, or 'the big school' as she called it, she was the eldest in the class. She would have a small amount of time every day with a special needs assistant to help her with zips and buttons and focusing on what was happening in class, as well as some hours with a resource teacher.

I remembered how, on The Hard Weekend, we didn't think either of them would ever go to mainstream school, but Ailbhe had improved so much with the help of Enable Ireland, the exercises we did with her and her innate ability to learn quickly. We were so proud of her. The school is a ten-minute walk from our house, and Ailbhe skipped down the street as Martha walked her over. We have a photo of her on her first day, where she is looking back over her shoulder, holding a Lego brick, smiling, delighted with herself.

I took a couple of hours off work a few mornings later, so I could stay behind to see Sophie off on her first day of pre-school; her first day on the bus. 'You're going to school, Sophie,' said Martha. We had explained it to her, but we didn't think she understood. Martha had been worried the night before. 'What if she wants to come home straight away?'

'Well, then, they'll call me in work and I'll go.'

'Yes, but you're over an hour away.'

'Look, I'm sure she'll love it,' I said.

'Are you just saying that to make me feel better?' she asked.

'No, I'm saying that to make me feel better.'

'The Big Blue Bus', as Sophie would eventually come to call the minibus that collects her for school, arrived bang on time, at eight o'clock. There were no other kids on it. We lived the furthest away from the school, so Sophie was the first to be collected. Martha walked down the driveway with her, and handed her over to Francis, the bus assistant, a kindly-looking grey-haired man. When Sophie was on the bus and the door was shut, Martha immediately turned around and walked back up the driveway. She didn't want Sophie to see her sobbing.

I waved from the door, but Sophie didn't wave or look back. The bus pulled away, around the corner, and it was gone.

At the door, I hugged Martha, and she wailed into my chest. I could feel her knees go weak. 'She'll love it,' I said, to her, and myself, as a tear rolled down my cheek.

When Sophie came back that afternoon, she could not tell Martha about her day. She has never been able to tell a story. Instead, Martha and Sophie's teachers would use a communication book, which went in Sophie's bag every day. They would write us a short paragraph about how Sophie got on and Martha would write helpful notes like, 'She might be a little cranky; she only slept for an hour last night.'

But even without her telling us, we knew that she loved going to school. Soon, she would skip down the driveway into Francis's arms every morning.

October 2011

When she was nearly six, Ailbhe asked if she could have a cat. Every day. I always answered her the same way: 'You can't have a cat because Mammy is allergic, and because cats are spawned in the seventh circle of hell. Don't be fooled by the cuteness of kittens, they are Satan's minions.' She looked at me like I was weird.

One Saturday we went on the bus to the city. It was a rare and special day for the two of us without Soph. We went to the cinema (which she loved), and I had to do a little shopping (which she did not love).

Ailbhe held my hand as we walked back to the house after getting off the bus. As we walked up the road, we were having one of those light-hearted conversations that every parent will have with their child at some point … about death.

She asked, 'Are Granny and Grandad going to die?'

I always want to be honest with her, so I said, 'One day they will, yes, but not soon, hopefully.'

After a short pause, where I could almost see the little cogs in her head working it out, she asked, 'Are you going to die?'

'Yes, one day I will die, but way off in the future, probably.'

She computed that as well, and she seemed fine with it. But then she worked something else out which made her eyes water. 'Is Mammy going to die?' she asked, with rising panic and upset.

'Yes, one day, she will die too.' And then she started crying. I stopped to get a tissue out of my bag.

As I did, she looked up at me with big tears in her eyes, and she said, 'And then can I get a cat?'

December 2011

How do you know if someone has run a marathon? Don't worry, they will tell you. That's how the old joke goes. Thankfully, I'm not one of those awful people who have to slip their exact best marathon time into every conversation, no matter how incongruous. Those three-hour-thirty-four-minute-and-sixteen-seconds people are the worst, aren't they?

Another way to know when someone is a runner is to check their nipples. They probably won't have any.

One Sunday afternoon I went for a longer run than I had intended, and it started to rain. Not long after it did, I got sore around two very specific, protuberant points on my chest. The tips of my nipples, to be precise. With the combination of hoodie, white cotton shirt and lack of nipple lubricant, by the time I finished my run, my nipples had been almost entirely rubbed out.

When I got home, Martha asked, 'Where have you been?'

'Sorry,' I said, as I zipped open my hoody to reveal that my white cotton t-shirt now came with two blood-red nipple tassels.

'Jesus Christ, Aidan!' exclaimed Martha.

'No, Martha, I'm pretty sure the stigmata were on the hands and the feet,' I said, cementing my place in hell. From then on, I lubed my nipples with Vaseline before every run.

After the hiatal hernia diagnosis, Martha had been especially worried about my health. She expressed this worry by saying heartfelt things like, 'Don't you dare leave me alone with these kids.' She needled me to go for a general check-up with our doctor.

'Fine, I'll go, but if he checks my prostate then I'm going to check your prostate.'

'You wish,' said Martha.

'Yes, I do.'

'Mmmmm,' said the doctor, when he wrote down my weight. This wasn't the 'mmmmm' you hear when someone eats something delicious, this was the 'mmmmm' of someone who was worried about someone who had eaten too many delicious things. 'You need to start doing something about your BMI,' he said. 'Technically, you're obese.'

Obese? OBESE! *Jesus, Doc, why don't you just stick a finger up my bum and be done with it*, I thought.

So I had started running that September. I did a little running as a teenager, and I had heard the term 'muscle memory' so I assumed that my muscles would simply remember how to run once I started again. After the first kilometre, on my first run, when I felt like I was about to shit out my lungs, it was clear that my muscles weren't remembering my teenage pursuits. Instead, they had post-traumatic stress from the twenty years of pizza, Coke and biscuits I had eaten since then. *Why am I doing this to myself?* I thought.

There were three reasons. One, Sarah and I had made a video of my song 'Lovelocked', which is about a couple who get stuck into each other, and then get stuck *in* each other: mid-coitus. For this, we would get into the same pair of gigantic pants, and sing the song crotch-to-crotch, with me on the ukulele. Because I was in profile, all I could see in that video was how big my belly had become.

Two. Sophie had learned to scoot, and while she could not outrun me, she could certainly out-scoot me. I worried when I took her around the estate that she would roll out onto the road and get hit by a car, so I had to get fit enough to keep up, so that I could grab her if she looked like she wasn't going to stop. And one day, I knew, if I didn't train, she wouldn't need a scooter. She'd be faster than me just using her own two legs.

Three, I ran because there was so little that I could fix about our lives. My health was one of the only things I could actually control.

It wasn't just good for the health below my neck, either. At first, I would run with music in my ears, but eventually I stopped wearing headphones and I ran to the soundtrack of my thoughts. In my mind I wrote lyrics for new songs, I calmed down, I resolved arguments with Martha, I thought about how fast I was going (or not). I might remember a fun day out with the girls, or a good gig, or Martha touching my leaner legs in bed and saying something very nice about them. When I was training for a marathon, on a weekend morning I would often wake before the sun and drive out to Swords. I'd run out to Malahide and down the coast road as dawn broke over the sea. On those mornings, I didn't think about much but the scenery.

January 2012

Getting Sophie to go to sleep at night got tougher and tougher.

We tried everything, consulted therapists, followed advice from books, but getting her to stay in her own bed was like trying to capture a storm in a duvet.

Eventually, I would sit, sentry-like, outside her door, ready to put her back when she would inevitably shoot out the door for the umpteenth time.

When she did go to sleep early, that wasn't always good news. She might wake up after a couple of hours of a power nap and be ready to go again. She was like a little Margaret Thatcher – sleep being for the weak – destroying our sanity, breaking our union … and closing our coal mines.

There have been nights when we have been watching a movie in the sitting room, after Sophie has gloriously gone to sleep early, when it suddenly starts raining through the spotlights. I would run up the stairs to find Sophie standing beside an overflowing sink. 'Oh, wet!' she'd say. Consequently, our sitting room ceiling looks like it has many tales to tell.

And if we are in bed when she awakes, she makes repeated attempts to get into the room. Continually carrying a decent-sized, resistant four-year-old back to her own bed is utterly exhausting. We are often defeated, so we relent and let her sleep between us.

I wake up and hit the snooze on the stupid morning alarm. It is still dark outside. As I turn over, I see Soph in the dark between us, and let out a sigh. I remember her last performance in the early hours of the morning, complete with lots of repetitious babbling. Unfortunately, she has not figured out the meaning of the word 'shush' yet.

As I stand in the bath, under the shower, with my head against the tiles, I try not to think about how much sleep I didn't get last night. I am lucky, in a way, that I don't have much hair left to wash, as our shower has pathetic pressure. Martha, who still has an enviable head of hair, often dreams about the day when we can get what she calls 'a proper shower'. I have not investigated the cost of this so as not to get Martha's hopes up, because unless it comes for free we can't afford it.

I tell myself to *not* think about the mortgage arrears. Then I think about the mortgage arrears. I tell myself to think about something else. I still think about the mortgage arrears. Maybe I could give up gigging and get a job in the evening? But Martha is already finding it hard to deal with the evenings when I go out for a gig. She seems to be tired all the time now – so taking a regular part-time job doesn't seem feasible.

Then an idea for a song for The Guilty Folk pops into my head, like a fart. I must capture it quickly, so that it doesn't escape. A couple of rhyming couplets come to me. This could be a good one.

It's only when the water starts to run a little colder that I think, *fuck, what time is it?* I jump out of the shower and check the phone in my jeans pocket. Shit, I'm going to be late.

I storm around the bedroom looking among the mess for things I need, which are never where I think I left them. I accidentally wake Sophie up. 'Sorry, I love you,' I say to Martha as I kiss her cheek.

'I love you too,' she replies, with her eyes still closed, hoping that it isn't really morning.

I can tell from the tone of the words Sophie is trying to say that she is babbling something from the *Sesame Street* videos we watch together. She likes the ones that have the celebrities in them. The one with Natalie Portman being an elephant, especially, makes her squeal with laughter.

'Shush,' Martha says to Sophie, while Sophie is already into her second rendition of 'The Princess and the Elephant.' There is no shushing Soph.

As I drive to work, I am humming a tune for my new song and trying out some lyrics. I join the motorway, and a little way down I hear the toll bridge tag beep, taking another couple of euro from our account. *Death by a thousand cuts* I think, and the question that is always lurking these days comes to the fore again, and I stop humming.

It's always in my brain, like tinnitus: *What am I going to do about the mortgage arrears?*

February 2012

Martha and I were sitting in the bank, waiting to meet a mortgage adviser. There are only two types of meeting you can have with a mortgage adviser. This was not the good one. This was about our mortgage arrears, which were expanding like a mushroom cloud. As we watched other people carry out day-to-day transactions, I hoped that I was only person who could smell the whiff of my sweat. I was very nervous. Martha leaned over and whispered:

'It smells like stale people in here.'

'Yeah, they should really do something about that.'

She was looking good, in sharp clothes and even sharper make-up. She looked like she was ready for battle. I was wearing my best suit, which was also my only suit. My pants were itchy. I have a nervous habit of bouncing my foot when I'm sitting. I rarely sit entirely still. Martha was looking at my foot; 'I know where Sophie gets it from now!'

A rumpled sack of a man appeared around the corner. 'Martha and Aidan?' he asked, trying to sound friendly and not quite getting it right.

'Yes,' answered Martha. I nodded, feeling sick.

He introduced himself as we went up the stairs. 'I'm Clive'. (His name was not Clive, but moments after he said his name, I forgot it.) Clive had the look of the sort of man whose wife rolls over in bed after a twenty-five-year marriage and says, 'Oh, are you still here?' Architecturally speaking, he had all the personality of a windowless, magnolia four-storey gable wall.

As we walked up to his office, he asked us how our journey was (this was our local bank, and we had a five-minute drive). 'Fine,' I muttered. I imagined that Clive had a whiskey-cheeked, well-connected uncle who got him a job in the bank straight out of school, after which they tried him out in the full *Kama Sutra* of bank positions. He failed miserably at every entry-level job, so they called him a middle manager and stuck him in a broom cupboard-sized office. Every year, for the last thirty years, they would forget to put his name in the office Kris Kindle, but he says nothing and no one notices.

Obviously, I couldn't have known any of this about Clive – after all, I had forgotten the man's name – but these were just my first impressions. I was probably biased though, because I hated Clive. I hated that we were there, in this stupid-sized office, talking about how we hadn't been able to pay our stupidly big mortgage. And I was pretty sure that Clive hated us too. He had probably been ticking off the days until early retirement, eating his cheese sandwiches in his drab office, picking away at the erotic novel he'd been writing for the last ten years. Then the recession came along, and the bank suddenly had thousands of problem mortgages to deal with, so they dusted off their Army of Clives and told them that they were now mortgage advisers.

His office was not built for meetings. We had to rearrange the chairs so that the door could be closed. When we were all seated, Clive asked, 'So, what seems to be the problem?' 'Don't you have our file there?' I asked, already irked.

A couple of weeks previously we had completed a twelve-page form that delved deeply into the nitty gritty of our lives. By the time we had finished filling it out, the bank probably knew which way my penis hung in my pants.

'Oh yes,' said Clive, and he turned to a vintage computer that reminded me of the chunky Amstrad 464 I had as a teenager. I wouldn't have been surprised if there was a tape deck on the side of it. After a minute of attacking the keyboard, Clive turned to us, sounding exasperated. 'I'm sorry, I can't get into the system this morning for some reason.' I looked at him, and thought, *I'm pretty sure mashing the keys like you've been doing just there is not a Windows shortcut.* Clive was a bad actor. Either he knew the system wasn't working, or he couldn't find our file. I didn't want to argue with him about it, so instead I dipped into my bag and I pulled out a photocopy of the form. 'Oh great,' Clive said.

As Clive looked through the form, Martha told our story, about the girls, me losing my job and ending up on half pay, and her depression, and then she cried. I got a lump in my throat listening to her, but I didn't want to cry because crying is not a good strategy when you're trying to come away from the negotiating table with a win. ('"I'm going all in,"' the poker player sobbed,' is not a story that ends well.)

Clive tried to be comforting, but he was too uncomfortable in his own skin to do it properly. I bet he was thinking, *I hate it when they cry.* 'Let's look at this form and see what we can do,' he said, and he took out a very nice pen, and ran down the boxes. As he went down the form, and saw the figures, he made faces like he was reading a recipe for poo pie.

Then he looked up from the form and started reminiscing about how little it cost him to buy his house in the seventies, in relation to how much they cost during the boom, and how at least the recession might help his kids make it onto the property ladder. I knew he was going to say it, and, for once in his life, Clive didn't disappoint: 'We all lost the run of ourselves a bit during the boom, didn't we?'

I've heard the 'we all partied' line so many times. I wanted to say that all I did was marry the woman I loved, have a couple of kids, and buy a house and a car. In my experience, that is not a party. Well, at least, not a very exciting party. That's just living. Am I not, as a reasonably well-educated, hard-working person, entitled to think that the arse won't fall out of my world? I didn't want to argue, though, I just needed it to stop hurting every time I thought about the house, so I said, 'Yes, I suppose,' because I was eager to get to the part of the meeting where he helped us to solve our financial problems.

'How old is your car?' he asked.

'Ten years,' I answered. I knew what he was getting at. We wouldn't be able to afford a new car when it inevitably broke down, unless we didn't pay the mortgage for a few months. Then Clive told us about how it was more economically sensible to buy a new car every year, although he also said that he hadn't been able to do that himself this year because he hadn't got his bonus. He was so obtuse that Martha's tears were stunned into stopping.

When we were driving up to the bank that morning I'd said to Martha, 'These people are not our friends. They won't help us. This is just a box-ticking exercise.' I am prone to making pronouncements about how I think things will go which don't always turn out to be true. ('De Gea won't be a good keeper for United,' 'President Donald Trump? Pah! He won't even get close to the nomination,' 'Skinny jeans!? They'll never catch on.') Martha was justified in telling me not to pre-judge.

'It might go better than we hope,' she said, hopefully. As Clive went back to the figures on the form, muttering, I looked at Martha, and shrugged my shoulders. She nodded her head. That was as close to a 'You were right,' as I was going to get.

About halfway through the form, Clive just skipped to the back page. He was bored. 'These are the really important figures,' he said, pointing out the totals of incoming and outgoing at the end. The disparity was obvious. This was not a crack in our finances; this was a chasm.

'So what do you think we should do?' I asked. Clive sat back, arched his fingers. He was thinking. Maybe I had misjudged him? Maybe he would help us?

Then Clive said: 'Okay, what I think you need to do here is to try to make more money than you're spending.'

March 2012

After Ailbhe turned six years old, she was discharged from Enable Ireland, which meant that, henceforth, her therapy would be provided by the Irish Health Service Executive (the HSE, our version of Britain's NHS, or America's Hunger Games). This was like going from a loving embrace to a punch in the gut. Her name was put on very long waiting lists. The same thing would happen to Sophie a couple of years later.

Sophie was still with Enable Ireland at that time, but, steadily, over the previous year, they had stopped offering appointments as frequently. Some staff had left. They didn't seem to be replaced. The organisation was stretched, and we could only surmise that this was because of the recession, which was biting everyone, everywhere, all over.

We would have loved to be able to pay for private therapy sessions, but it was impossible. The mortgage arrears were accruing every month. Soon, it would be into five figures. Our bank account was burning down. I got a very small pay raise, but as for dealing with our debts, the little bit of extra money had all the impact of spitting at the sun.

So, one night, I said to Martha that she needed to go back to work. As a teacher, she would have made more money than I was making at the time. It would be a steadier job. I would stay at home, and get a part-time job, or do some drawing nixers in the morning when the girls were at school.

'Or I could keep my job, and you could get a part-time job in the mornings?' I suggested to her, very strongly. The only upside to the girls' appointments becoming more infrequent was that Martha's mornings would usually be free. We needed something to bridge the gap in our finances. She seemed strangely reluctant, even though my plans made a lot of sense to my mind. The only issue would be finding a job. Unemployment was rife at the time, but Martha was good at her job, and she had a lot of experience of working part-time jobs on her travels in Australia. She could do this.

I signed up for a teaching jobs website, on her behalf, and the pickings were expectedly paltry, but I did spot one job that would suit her maths and chemistry background. I got the form and asked her to apply for it.

'But I haven't done an interview in years, I won't get it,' Martha moaned.

'I believe in you. You have to start somewhere,' I said, doing my best impression of a living inspirational wall poster.

'I can't, Aidan.' She was starting to get upset.

'Just start by filling out the form,' I told her.

She got as far as filling out her name and address, and then she started to have what I later understood to be a panic attack. She was crying so hard that she couldn't breathe properly.

It was frightening to see her falling apart like that. When she regained her composure, she told me something that I didn't know.

'I sleep through the mornings. All morning. And when I get up I'm still tired. I can't do this.'

'Why didn't you tell me?'

'Because, Aidan, I'm ashamed. I understand that we need to do something to save the house, but I don't know what to do.'

'Neither do I …'

On a scale between coma and cocaine, Martha's level of wakefulness is at 'enduring-a-day-long-Powerpoint presentation-with-no-breaks.' Anyone who's ever had to go to one of those will know that no matter how much you struggle to stay awake, as the presenter reads every bullet point on the hundreds of slides he has prepared for the day, verbatim, in a bored monotone, resistance is futile. You are doomed to sleep.

It was after the get-a-job panic attack that we started to take Martha's problem with sleep more seriously. Correction – that *I* started to take it more seriously. Like everyone else, and to my eternal shame, I had doubted its reality, and more than once attributed her predilection for horizontal unconsciousness to being lazy. She had known that she'd had some sort of problem for a long time, but it had never been this bad. (I just really hope she was fully awake on our wedding day.)

She got placed on a waiting list for a sleep study, and she started pinning her hopes on having sleep apnoea, because that would mean there would be a cure. She would have gladly plugged her face into a machine every night if it meant she could have the same number of productive hours as most people.

By the time the sleep study came along, Martha had convinced herself that that was what it was. When she got the results, and she was told that she didn't have sleep apnoea, she was devastated, and she started to doubt herself: *maybe this is all in my head?*

It would take two years to get a diagnosis.

When she got the second test, she texted me a photo of herself from the hospital, looking disgruntled. She was a mess of pads and wires, all running to some sort of monitoring device in the front. I FEEL LIKE I'M BEING ASSIMILATED BY THE BORG.

I texted back, YOU LOOK LIKE YOU'RE BEING ASSIMILATED BY THE BORG. IS EVERYTHING OKAY?

YES, I'M JUST GOING FOR A SLEEP NOW.

IS IT WRONG THAT I FIND THIS A BIT HOT?

She texted back two words. YES. VERY.

Her sleep was monitored overnight, and she got a good eight hours. The next day they woke her at seven. After that, every two hours, she was brought to a quiet bedroom, where they would reattach her to the collective, and ask her to try to fall asleep again. She was given a quarter of an hour to fall asleep. If she fell asleep, they'd let her sleep for half an hour before waking her. They did that six times. She fell asleep six times.

After her final nap, when the nurse woke her, Martha realised that this diligent woman had being calmly doing her nursing duties all day long, while she was sleeping. She felt ashamed, and she started to cry. 'Is there something wrong?' asked the nurse.

'I'm so ashamed,' gulped Martha, 'What if there's nothing wrong with me?' This was Martha's biggest fear: that the doctors would tell her that it was all in her head.

The nurse said, 'No one can fall asleep six times in the day without there being something wrong. You can't fake that.'

After the test was done, her dad came to pick her up, because I was in work. On the way home in the car, Martha fell asleep again.

A few weeks later, she went back to the consultant for the results, where she was told that she had idiopathic hypersomnia. Like most people, I had never heard of it before. I actually like the sound of the words. Idiopathic hypersomnia. They belong in that group of words which are nice to say, but actually describe something quite unpleasant, like syphilis, or Oscar Pistorius. When you break down the Latin, it means excessive sleepiness with no known cause. The Wikipedia page is not light reading. The words 'lifelong chronic disorder' are there, and those words are neither fun to say nor describe something pleasant.

The 'solution' the consultant gave her was, 'Take these pills, which may or may not work,' in so many words. Martha calls them her Wakey Pills. They do help her to stay awake, but they give her bad headaches and make her irritable and anxious, so she can't take them every day, but if she has a lot to do she will take one. Martha used to joke that if you ever have a taciturn table of retirees all you had to do was ask them what medication they were on, and the conversation would continue from there until the wee hours. With her medication for hypersomnia and depression, my thirty-eight-year-old wife invested in a pill box.

She doesn't make that joke anymore.

She went back to the consultant six months after she got the pills to talk to him about the side effects and ask him if there was anything else that could be done. His response was, 'That's just the way it is for you now,' in so many words.

The irony is that I sometimes go through periods of insomnia, and I am generally able to function perfectly well on not much sleep. 'We were meant for each other,' I quipped one night. Combined, we have a normal sleep cycle, and if I could take a dial and push it to balance our need for sleep, I would. It seems though, that we are doomed to be the Yin and Yang of slumber until we die.

April 2012

I became an expert in bringing the girls to the movies. I don't remember what the first movie I brought them to was, probably because, early on, trips to the cinema were less about me enjoying the movie with them and more an exercise in crowd control. I first started bringing them together around the time Sophie was two years old. She found it hard to sit still and often tried to play whack-a-mole with the heads in front of us, while Ailbhe would loudly attempt to narrate the movie. We were not the people who you would have wanted to sit beside.

Then, I had a Eureka moment: cinemas have corners! I was a 'near-the-back-in-the-middle' guy before I was a dad, but I realised that if I booked the three seats up in one of the very top corners I could corral Sophie at the end, and, if the movie wasn't too popular, there wouldn't be too many people around us to be annoyed by Ailbhe's cinema-seat direction. Those early stressful trips were worth it, though, because they both settled down (although Ailbhe is still prone to the odd loud declaration) and it became one of my favourite things to do with them.

I went with the girls as often as I could afford it. I think I might have seen most of the kids' movies that have come out. Some of these movies are timeless masterpieces, like *Up*, *Tangled*, and *Fantastic Mr. Fox*, and I'm delighted I had kids as an excuse to go to see them on the big screen. However, some of the movies come back to me in my darker moments. I'm looking at you, *Happy Feet Two*.

I loved the cinema before I had kids, and I loved it even more after I had them, because the movies taught Ailbhe how to cry. One of the things that upset Martha the most about Ailbhe when she was young was her seeming lack of empathy. When Martha cried at home – which, as you've gathered by now, happened a lot – Ailbhe continued to be unbothered by it. Eventually, Martha said to her, 'When someone is crying it's good to pat them on the back or give them a hug.' After that, if Ailbhe saw Martha crying, she'd go over and give her a few of the most perfunctory pats possible, and walk away. She was as likely to give similar comfort for a paper cut as a lost finger. She did *want* to be kind. Over the years we were able to teach her to be more empathetic, by simply explaining what to do in certain situations: 'At an Irish funeral you say, "sorry for your loss" and get out as soon as you can.'

In fact, it would be Sophie who would one day go and get Martha a tissue for her tears, unbidden. Martha was sitting watching a kids' movie during the day, and crying at an emotional scene. (Probably *Up*. A stone would weep at the start of that movie.) She looked up, and Sophie was looking at her with a perturbed expression on her face. Martha was waiting for Sophie to smile, or laugh, or react in some other inappropriate way. Then Sophie said, 'I get tissue.' Martha was stunned, as Sophie got a tissue from the box and offered it to her. Ironically, this made Martha cry even more.

When we went to the movies and people heard crying coming from the corners, and they looked around to see who it was, it was usually me. Especially *Toy Story 3*. Inconsolable, I was. It was okay, though: Ailbhe gave me three very even pats on the back to make me feel better.

One of the great things about having kids is showing them all the movies that you loved as a child. However, you should always watch the movie again as an adult before you show it to them. You'd be surprised how many times you will put on an old kids' movie and think, this is actually horrific and racist. I'm looking at you, *Pinocchio*.

I did not watch the movie *Willow* again as an adult before I showed it to Ailbhe. It turned out to be the first movie she ever cried at.

Ailbhe was sitting between Martha and me in our bed, and we were watching the movie on the laptop. It was supposed to be a treat. Very near the start of the movie, there's a scene where a woman with a baby is being chased by some ravenous, evil dog creatures. I'd forgotten about that. She sacrifices herself to save the baby by placing it in a basket on the river. Ailbhe bawled at that like she had never bawled before, so much so that I had to turn the movie off. Martha and I were delighted, though, that she had shown genuine empathy. I think she might have picked up on our delight. We didn't hide it very well. We may have high-fived.

Since then, when she cries at movies, she cries dramatically, as if she wants to make sure that I'll notice. I noticed that she wouldn't cry at every emotional moment – like me – she only cried at bits in movies which involved a child losing a mother. However, kid's movie makers are the masters of matricide, so she got a lot of practice.

I have decided that to save her from death by dehydration she is never allowed to watch the movie *Bambi* unless she's hooked up to an IV line first.

May 2012

Sophie's teacher sent a note home with her, asking if we were thinking of toilet training Sophie soon. We weren't. It had been such a struggle with Ailbhe that I thought Sophie, with a similar cavernous bladder but fewer communication skills, would take years longer. They weren't as pessimistic as us though, and were sure that she would be able. They asked us to start sending her in on the bus without nappies. They put an incontinence sheet under her for the first week.

She got the hang of going to the toilet after a few days. Yet again, we had underestimated her. Sophie understands a lot more of what is being said to her than she can say back, and it is easy to forget that. And that was how, after six years, we finally said goodbye to the nappies. I never, ever want to see one again.

It was just over eight years since we'd been married and in that time our promises had gone from: 'In sickness and in health' to, 'If you become incontinent in old age, you're changing your nappies on your own.'

September 2012

I got an email from a theatre director by the name of Una McKevitt. She had seen The Guilty Folk performing the previous night, and she was wondering if we'd be interested in being a part of her theatre show *Singlehood*.

Una's oeuvre involved interviewing people and creating theatre from their testimonies. For *Singlehood*, she asked perennial singletons, divorcees and some married people to talk about their perceptions of single life. She, and her writer friend Dave Coffey, had edited these responses into a script. The cast would deliver this script and add some of their personal experiences to the show.

'We wouldn't be massively involved,' I said to Martha later. 'We'd really just have to know when to come out and sing from time to time.'

'Theatre, is it?' she said, 'You're not going to go around incorrectly using words like oeuvre, are you?'

'God no, that wouldn't be my oeuvre at all.'

'Are you getting paid?' she asked.

'Yes, we are getting paid … in exposure.'

When I came back from the first rehearsal I said to Martha, 'So, we're a little bit more involved than we first thought.'

'Define a little bit, Aidan.'

'Well, we'd be on the stage the whole time, there might be about seven or eight songs in the show, and we have to teach the cast to sing some of them.'

'And how much rehearsal is that?' she asked.

'Not much. A few weeknights … some weekends … throughout August.'

'That sounds like a lot,' she said.

'Obviously, we won't do any gigs while it's going on.' We weren't exactly flooded with offers for gigs, so this wasn't in fact that much of a sacrifice. 'It's a good show. I really want to be involved.'

I saw Martha growing tired before my eyes at just the thought of that much time on her own looking after the girls, but she never wanted to say no to any gig I wanted to do – and she was proud, and very happy for me also – so she agreed. 'Yes, okay, but I reserve the right to be monumentally pissed off at the time.'

'That's fair enough!'

The show was on in the Dublin Fringe Theatre Festival for a week in September, in a venue that held 150 people, and it was completely sold out. We had gone from being the odd act out at sparsely populated singer-songwriter nights to making full houses laugh. It was fantastic.

When the run ended, we went back to doing the usual gigs. I missed the camaraderie of the cast during rehearsals and the buzz of doing the shows with everyone. 'I miss *Singlehood*,' I told Martha.

'I miss singlehood, too,' said Martha.

'You're not talking about the show, though, are you?'

She shook her head.

October 2012

One Saturday, for a change, Martha decided to take the kids to the library while I got some stuff done in the house. Ailbhe insisted on getting a Katie Price 'Perfect Ponies' book, and Sophie did a poo in the play castle. Martha doesn't take them there anymore.

January 2013

One of my favourite things to do is to chase Sophie around the house with a sword. Don't call social services just yet.

'It wasn't just the sword thing, though, the entire book was a cry for help,' said the concerned citizen.

It's not a real sword. I wouldn't chase Sophie around with a real sword, unless she was very bold.

It is Ailbhe's foam Minecraft Iron Sword, which is broad enough to make a satisfying smack. Sophie runs away from me on the balls of her feet, with her arms in the air, tense, and her hands squeezed into balls of excitement. When the sword connects, her giggles are interrupted by a high-pitched 'heeee!' and she jumps up, but keeps running in the air.

I started this game one Saturday morning. I forget when, exactly. I was threatening Ailbhe with the sword and as Sophie bounded by on one of her usual circuits, I tapped her on the bum with it, and surprisingly, she giggled and said, 'Bum!' and ran away. The chase was on!

We played this game so much that the sword eventually broke – Sophie's arse being made of stronger stuff, apparently – and we had to buy a new one. Ailbhe advised us at the time that it would be better to get a foam replica of a Minecraft Diamond sword, because Diamond Foam is the strongest foam there is, apparently.

As I chase Sophie, I smack the sword off various bits of the house and I sing the *Lord of the Rings* theme tune through a series of da-da-das. You know how it goes:

'Da-da-daaa-da-da-daaa-da-da-daaaaaa-daa-daa-daaaa-daaaa-da-da-da … ' (I accept no liability for this tune being stuck in your head for the rest of the day. Sue the director, Peter Jackson, or Howard Shore, the composer.)

Sophie at once becomes my terrified-yet-strangely-excited little halfling prey, and I am Daddy the Balrog, intent on dealing death by ten thousand arse smacks. (It truly is the worst way to go.)

At first, I did not think she understood the depth of this little scene I had created for her, on the basis that great artistes are never fully appreciated in their own lifetimes – especially by their kids. Then, one Saturday morning, I cornered her in the kitchen, and instead of going for the traditional arse smack, I pretended, in glorious *Matrix*-like slow motion, to swish my sword across her stomach and sever my beautiful little halfling in twain.

Without any prompts from me, Sophie dramatically fell to the floor and lay on the ground. 'Oh no, Sophie dead!' I said, in a sing-song voice.

She said, 'bleurgh, blood, blood, blood, blood,' and she stuck out her tongue and 'died'. It was such an unexpected piece of playing along that I almost broke character. (Of course I didn't, though, as I am a true professional.)

When Sophie wants me to chase her, she comes to me and says, 'Daddy Sword.' One day, a few weeks after Sophie's debut death scene, I was getting a bit tired of chasing, so, I stopped and handed her the sword, and said, 'Sophie Sword?' She took it off me and started chasing, and as she did, *she* sang the *Lord of the Rings* theme tune. I couldn't run for laughing.

The only downside to this game is that it can tend to disturb the Slumbering Grump, in the Land of Nod above our heads.

With the combination of my Oscar-worthy roars and Sophie's various 'squeals' of delight, we can be very loud. This is not our fault; as any thespian worth his tights knows, 'You must project or die, darlings.'

One morning, Sophie chased me around the sitting room, and I ran out and pretended to be cornered in the kitchen. 'No, Sophie, no!' I cried. (It was a truly heart-breaking performance.) She thrust the sword towards the crook of my arm and plunged it in. I duly played my part in this production, by falling to my knees, rolling my eyes, and tipping over onto my back, flat on the ground, with the sword sticking out. I gave a last few deeply-emotional half-roars, and then, to complete this epic death scene, I stuck out my tongue and 'died.' I wouldn't have been surprised if I had heard applause.

Instead, I heard the unmistakeable clunk of the kitchen door opening. 'No Soph!' I shouted, but once she is beyond the Door-Of-No-Fucking-Resistance-Whatsoever and running up the Stairs of Doom, my magical parenting powers are useless. I struggled to a standing position (noting how going from lying on the floor to standing up has become a mini workout for my aging body). I ran into the Great Hall, and I took the the Stairs of Doom two steps at a time as I chased after her, desperate to reach her before she reached the Grump's chamber.

The Stairs of Doom is well worth a visit if you're ever in our house. Stop and enjoy its many fine landmarks. The Forgotten Paint Tester Wall is a treat. You will see there four mysterious daubs of paint. Legend has it that the wall was once to be repainted, but that the task passed out of the minds of men – well, one man, in particular – and now, no one would ever be able to identify the make and colour of these daubs. It will for ever remain one of the world's great mysteries.

The Gnawed Balustrade Balls are well worth a moment's contemplation. How did these balls get gnawed? There is a gnawed ball on each turn of the balustrade on the Stairs of Doom. They were once finely painted with a white, glossy sheen. A craftsperson, as unappreciated as he was inexperienced, toiled over their completion for many an age, until the commissioner of the artwork told him he was finished by saying, 'I suppose that will have to do.' And they did do, until one day the paint was partially stripped with teeth marks. I suspect the halfling, but I have no proof.

Finally, there is the Inexplicable Remnants of the Impenetrable Baby Gate. Once upon time, there was a great gate at the top of the Stairs of Doom that was said to have been erected to keep relentless little baby monsters at bay. The gate was removed long ago, but the fixings for the gate remain. It is a monument to apathy, indolence and procrastination.

Sophie does not stop to admire these landmarks, though, and I will not catch her in time. She bursts through the door into the Grump's Chamber, and launches herself onto the bed and under the duvet in one balletic movement. The Grump's slumber is disturbed. The Grump grumbles menacingly.

There is nothing for it now. I must become a Prince, for a Grump can only be turned into a Princess with a true love's kiss. Some of you may have noticed this by now, but real life is not often like a Disney fairy tale, and the actual administration of a true love's kiss is not at all done the way that it is depicted in the sanitised kids' movies. In real life, a soft peck on the lips is nonsensical. How is something so measly supposed to break a spell?

A real true love's kiss is performed by removing the Duvet of Warmness, pulling down the Knickers Of Maximum Coverage, placing the lips squarely and firmly on the butt cheek of the Grump and blowing a massive, wet raspberry. Be careful, though; this kiss will not work if administered too early in the morning. If this mistake is made, instead of giggling to life, the Grump will surely dismember the poor prince.

This morning, though, I am in luck. 'Ah! Stop it!' giggles the Grump, at once metamorphosing into my love, Martha.

'Neck bubbles!' shouts Sophie, popping her head out of the duvet. She wants Martha to blow raspberries on her neck. Sophie is ticklish there. Martha obliges, and Sophie squirms and squeals in delight. I climb into the bed behind Sophie, so that she is between us. This is her nirvana. She is so happy that she is practically effervescent.

'Sophie squeeze!' she cries, and Martha and I grab arms and squeeze Sophie between us. 'Again!' she says. We squeeze again. 'Again!' she says, over and over, until Martha says, 'Last time.' At that moment, Ailbhe walks in. She has been in her room most of the morning, playing Minecraft on her computer. She jumps into the bed.

Immediately, I become Ailbhe's greatest nemesis: 'Daddy Monster!' I indicate my change of character by roaring the only thing that Daddy Monster can say: 'MONSTOR!' (The sound of this monster goes up to eleven.)

'Oh, I have a bit of headache,' winces Martha.

I roar 'MONSTOR!' again. (This monster goes up to four or five, max.)

I jump out of the bed, pick up a pillow, and begin to pummel Ailbhe. 'No, no, no,' she says, and she attempts to fight back. Eventually, Monstor lets his guard down, Ailbhe swings a devastating pillow blow to Monstor's chops and Monstor goes down, defeated. Ailbhe sits atop her prize.

But wait, maybe life *is* like a Disney movie after all. The Monstor, magically, comes back to life. He has been reincarnated as a Daddy Jedi.

Again, being a Jedi in real life is nothing like it is depicted in the movies. In real life, there are no light sabres. But this does not mean that a Daddy Jedi does not possess a deadly weapon:

'In a Galaxy Far, Far, Away …

FART WARS!'

I feel the force … rumbling inside my bowels. I jump up, and pin Ailbhe to the floor, by putting my arse lightly on her head, and I let go with a deadly assault. I would never do this to Sophie, because Sophie does not understand how to fight back in this game. I knew that Ailbhe would figure it out, though. One day, when I was quietly lying on the couch, watching a movie, not suspecting a thing. Ailbhe came over, turned around and farted in my face. I am sure to get my Father of the Year award any day now.

After playing with Sophie, Martha is breathing heavily. 'Oh no, you're in trouble now, Ailbhe. It's Martha Vader!'

'Have you seen my inhaler?' Martha asks, looking a little frantically through the rubble on her bedside locker. She must be desperate; she is asking me to find something, despite my longstanding finding-things blindness …

> … I will regularly stand in front of the open fridge and ask: 'Have you seen the tomato ketchup?'
>
> Martha will look over her shoulder, see the tomato ketchup, see me not seeing it, and let out a long, exasperated sigh. The girls also have my gene. They couldn't find their shoes if they were in front of their feet.
>
> Martha once said to me: 'You know, I wouldn't even have to run away. I could just move next door. You'd never find me!'

' … It's okay, here it is,' she says, locating her inhaler under a book, which is good, because I never would have found it. She takes a puff.

'How are you doing?' I ask.

'What time is it?' she says, regaining her breath.

'It's lunchtime.'

She is appalled. 'How did it get to be lunchtime?' she asks.

'Well, first there were ancient sundials, and then the Egyptians got involved, and then there was Greenwich Mean Time … '

'I need another hour. Will you take Sophie for a walk to the shops?' There are afternoons when I get annoyed by this, after spending the morning with them, but I'm in good form that afternoon, so I say, 'Soph, shops?' Sophie pops her head out of the duvet; her hair is a mess, and she is naked.

'Nudeypants!' she shouts. How did she get to be naked? Then she suddenly decides that she wants to go out: 'Supermarket?' she says.

'Supermarket,' I say. 'Do you want to come, Ailbhe?' Ailbhe wants to play Minecraft until her heart bursts, so she says no, exits the scene, and goes back to her computer.

Sophie gets out of bed and makes another suggestion, which alerts Martha to the habitual visits we have been making to Sophie's favourite fast food emporium: 'Old McDonald's!' (I never stood a chance with that Father of the Year award, anyway, did I?)

When Sophie is dressed and we are ready to go, I shout up a goodbye to Martha. There is no reply. She is asleep again. 'Bye, Ailbhe!' I shout. She does not hear me because she is shouting at her game of Minecraft.

And so, we go.

Our house is a couple of kilometres from the shops in Ashbourne, as the crow flies. It's twenty minutes to Ashbourne, as the Soph walks. To watch Soph make her way down a footpath is exercise for the eyes and a workout for the soul. It is like she cannot contain all the joy in her muscles. She skips, she jumps, she runs, she picks flowers, she stands on plinths, she leaps off plinths, she reaches down to pick chewing gum off the ground and eat it.

'No, Soph! Bleurgh! Bleurgh! Spit it out!'

She spits it out into my hand. 'We don't eat off the ground,'

I say, as I wince at the glob of white and saliva in my paw with a squeamish face. I flick it off my hand, and look up to see Soph moving again. I wipe my hand off the leg of my trousers, and run up beside to take her hand, because I have spotted something up ahead. *Here we go again,* I think.

For Sophie and me, the world is a gauntlet of dogs. Every street is a canine canyon that must be carefully traversed. When Sophie spots a dog, it is as if the street has become the fire swamp in *The Princess Bride*, and she regards every hound as you or I would regard a Rodent of Unusual Size. She is terrified of dogs.

She spots this dog at the same time as I do. Immediately all her joy evaporates, and she transforms into a scared little taut creature. And this is one of the worst type of dog: a small one. She particularly hates the small ones, with their yippy, excited Brownian motions. If we meet a dog that is small and is scuttling about unleashed, as we have done on a couple of occasions, Sophie climbs me like a tree, in fright.

Luckily, this particular dog – like most dogs – comes with a responsible owner. I look at the dog owner, trying to convey an apology with my eyes. I move around Sophie, so that I will be between her and the dog when they pass. If we encounter someone with a pack of dogs, I will have to bend down, hug her tight, or pick her up, until the dogs are gone. And I try my best to reassure her – 'They're nice doggies' – but this doesn't help. I suppose it wouldn't be very reassuring for most people if I said, 'But they're nice giant rats.'

Most dog-owners, I suspect, have encountered kids like Sophie, because, for the most part, they are genuinely understanding, but on a couple of occasions we have encountered dog-owners in forest parks, with an unleashed dog that has danced around us while Sophie screams, and they have called out, from a distance, 'Don't worry, he's a lovely dog.' My right eye says 'Fuck' and my left eye says 'You.' Sometimes it's better if people can't read my eye language. I'm sure it is a lovely dog, and if it were Ailbhe with me, she would be delighted, saying things in her American-accented English, like, 'O M G, I can't stand the cute.' (When did that start, and, more important, how do we make it stop?)

When Sophie became afraid of dogs, it made simple trips out a lot more difficult. Suddenly, there were *so* many dogs. Were there that many dogs before? So when she turned six, and she was assigned a new Health Service Executive psychologist, I took time off work to go and meet her with Martha to explain Sophie's fear, as I was the one who was usually with her when she was outdoors. I said that if I did not hold her hand Sophie would run into traffic to get away from a dog. The psychologist took all of this on board and said, 'Ah, sure, a lot of kids are afraid of dogs ... '

Dee, Lisa and Laura got a dog – Holly – she's a mid-sized mongrel (labrador, collie and a bit of terrier) and a genuinely nice dog. (Much like people, some dogs are nice and some dogs are assholes.) Even though Sophie has known Holly since she was a pup, to get any peace, and not hear Sophie constantly whining all weekend, Dee and Lisa now generously put Holly into a kennel when we visit.

But not long after they got Holly, we were in Galway one weekend, when she wasn't in a kennel. We had hoped that over that weekend Sophie would gradually get used to Holly, and stop whining every time they crossed paths. But the whining and crying would kick off every time Holly was in Sophie's vicinity. This can't have been fun for Holly either.

On Saturday evening, Holly was asleep in front of the fire. Sophie walked into the room, and I waited for the whining to start again, but, strangely, it didn't come. Maybe she hadn't spotted Holly? Sophie sat up on the couch. Then she saw the dog sleeping, and, amazingly, she got down and gingerly tip-toed over and petted her. At first, this seemed like a breakthrough: one of our plans had finally worked.

But she hadn't conquered her fear, though, because Sophie is not actually afraid of dogs. What Sophie is afraid of is the unpredictable movement of any collection of animated atoms. She proved this to us by eventually becoming afraid of cats, and then birds, and then kids who scoot up quickly behind us when we are walking. Anything erratic. When Holly woke up and moved, later that evening, Sophie was still as afraid as she had ever been.

A couple of years later, Derm and his wife, Sarah, would take Sophie out to a forest park and playground. I had told them that if they saw any yippy little dogs approaching to kneel and hold Sophie until the dog was gone. Sure enough, while they were out, Derm saw a dog matching that description on the path ahead. Sophie started to whine. He did as I advised. When they were gone what Sophie deemed to be a safe distance, she turned to Derm and used a phrase that she had probably heard in a YouTube video, but he knew that she meant it.

'Oh, you saved me!' she said.

March 2013

'**G**reat news!' I told Martha. '*Singlehood* is coming back in March for a couple of nights in Vicar Street.' This is a one-thousand-seat venue, by far the biggest place I would ever have performed.

Martha said, 'That's wonderful, and you won't have to do much rehearsal, either, because you know the show.'

'Well …' I winced, 'Una's making a lot of changes to the show, there'll be rehearsals all through February, weeknights and weekends.'

Martha took that news better than I thought. She even made the cupcakes for me to bring in to rehearsals. 'There's no poison in these, is there?' I asked. In return for the cupcakes, the cast gave me a nickname. It couldn't be worse than 'Furryburger', right?

They called me 'Aids.'

Vicar Street was wonderful, the first night especially. Everything went right, and the crowd was one of the best I've ever played to. I had a serious week-long case of post-gig blues after those shows were over.

Soon after, The Guilty Folk came to an end, in much the same way as many of the other bands I had been in had done before. I was left with a load of duets that I couldn't perform, so after a short break, I started writing again, for myself.

By the time August came around, I had a new comedy set ready to go, and I did my first solo musical comedy gig under the name: 'Aidan Strangeman.'

April 2013

Martha had explained the plan to Sophie: 'Into the car, shops (meaning Tesco), café, home.' Once the plan is in place, it must be followed. It is as if Sophie sees a trip out like a large-scale version of one of her house circuits. She will not even brook a double back on a street without whining and wailing. She has a 'no retreat' attitude to shopping.

She really liked the café part of the plan. The café means she will get a cupcake, a big one, with lots of icing. She especially loves the icing. Her favourite flavour is whatever-is-on-display-that-she-can-reach-without-getting-caught, and her favourite method of consumption is the fly-by finger-scoop – Martha has bought a lot of cupcakes that she hadn't intended to buy. However, the staff are used to them now, and they are lovely with Sophie. They know to keep it simple when asking her what she wants: 'Cupcake or cupcake?'

Martha had forgotten the shopping bags. Luckily, she and Soph had only just stepped outside the house. Martha opened the front door again, turned off the house alarm and ran in to get the bags. When she came back out, Sophie was gone. Martha ran to the end of the driveway and looked. She was nowhere to be seen. Martha surmised that she must have gone back into the house when she left the door open, so she ran back in and looked around.

Sophie has never been a master of stealth. At that time, she had just started participating in hide-and-seek with Ailbhe and me. If I was 'on' I would usually walk into the room to find Sophie standing behind a mid-height curtain with her legs on view. She would immediately say, 'Hiding!' (Sadly, she's never going to be a ninja. One morning, when I was sitting at the kitchen table eating my breakfast, she tried to sneak upstairs to Mammy's bed by tip-toeing past me with her eyes closed, on the sound principle that if she couldn't see me, then I couldn't see her.)

Martha realised quickly that Sophie wasn't there, and then she began to panic, because she had wasted precious minutes. She ran out the door, and she saw one of the neighbourhood kids, who is around Sophie's age, on the green, kicking a ball. She shouted over, 'Have you seen Sophie?' Sophie does not play with the other kids in the estate, or go to school with them, but they know her to see. They know her mostly as 'Ailbhe's sister'.

'Yes, she ran around the corner a couple of minutes ago,' said the kid. At five, Sophie might not have been good at hiding, but she had become very good at running.

A few months before, Martha had been walking up from Ashbourne with Sophie when she stopped to talk to a woman she knew. As they were talking, a car slowly came around the corner, and Sophie broke free from Martha's hand and deliberately ran into the side of it. The car was moving very slowly and Sophie wasn't hurt, but Martha wasn't the better of it for days. It was a sharp reminder that the lessons we had been trying to teach Sophie about being safe around roads and car parks had not stuck.

Martha set off sprinting. She went around the first corner, and saw no sign of her. She passed the second corner, still nothing. Her panic was rising. At the third corner, she saw Sophie just crossing the road to get out of the estate. She had crossed three roads by then. It is unlikely that she stopped to look for cars. Sophie started running when she saw Martha. This was a game to her. 'Aidan, I could barely catch her,' said Martha, later.

'What did she say when you *did* catch her?' I asked.

'Shops!'

June 2013

That summer, Ailbhe was outside the house in the front garden, playing with some of the other kids in the estate. She was seven years old, and she was, apparently, making friends. I was delighted.

One day, though, she came in looking disgruntled. 'Everything okay?' I asked.

She wanted something. 'Can I have paper and a pen?'

'Of course.' She sat on the chair and started writing, furiously.

Some of the other kids had annoyed her for some reason, so what she produced was a list of rules that she wanted people to agree to before they interacted with her. The list included things like 'Be nice to me', 'Love animals and protect the planet', which were lovely. It also had, 'Play the games that I want to play' on it.

I said, 'Oh Ailbhe, you can't do that. You just have to try to get along.' She thought that her plan was better.

Later that night, when everyone was asleep, I thought about it again, and how it might save a lot of heartache if we all had contracts of friendship. I could readily imagine some of the things I would have on my list: Always have a well-stocked secret stash of Crunchy Nut Corn Flakes, in case I have a Crunchy Nut Corn Flakes emergency. There's never a conversation that cannot be improved by a well-timed Simpsons reference. Okily dokily? If you send me any Candy Crush or Farmville Facebook requests, this contract is void …

… and I wondered whether Ailbhe's idea for a list like that was born of autism, or genius.

July 2013

Much like Ailbhe did when she was a toddler, when Sophie was five years old, she chose her favourite parent. It wasn't me. It wasn't Martha. It was her 'Green iPad!' (So called by Sophie because of its green protective casing.)

We found out about a scheme where you could swap old phones for a new iPad. Our friends, and friends of friends, kindly donated theirs.

I downloaded some educational apps before I gave it to Sophie. She was delighted, and interested in the apps for a few weeks, until, like most kids, she figured out how to watch YouTube videos on it.

One day, Martha and I were standing in the kitchen, and the girls were in the sitting room, when we heard a sound we had never heard before. One of the most beautiful sounds I've ever heard.

Sophie was singing.

She had been repeatedly watching videos of the song, *'Father Finger, Father Finger, where are you, here I am, here I am, how do you do. Mammy Finger, Mammy Finger … '* and so on, on her iPad, and that day, she just started singing along.

I could tell from the way she sang that she was singing the sounds, phonetically. While she may not have grasped the meaning of every word, she could certainly hold every note. She would sing that song again and again and again. They say that Bruce Springsteen is The Boss because he plays three-hour shows. By that measure, Sophie must be the CEO.

After that, she learned a lot more songs. She started to like pop music. In the car, we listened to 'Now That's What I Call Music' compilation CDs. As anyone who has ever listened to these will know, they have a lot of hits on them, but some of the later tracks can have a tenuous relationship to the charts. That's how we realised that Sophie has decent taste. If she doesn't like a track she says, 'Skip!' She knows a hit when she hears one. Our girl is all killer and no filler.

She can sing any song that she listens to enough times. And I mean *any* song. One day Martha texted me in work, I THINK SOPHIE'S SINGING IN MANDARIN, because Sophie was singing in Mandarin.

When she sings a new song, it is heart-breaking. And when she sings that song, again, for the twenty-fifth time in a row, it is also heart-breaking.

She is strictly a soloist, though. If I try to sing along, within seconds of my first few notes she will stop and say, 'Daddy! No singing!'

One night, I took out my guitar, and as she sang, I gently strummed along, and she kept singing, and it was brilliant, for a beautiful minute, but then she stopped, and said, 'Happy!' This does not mean that she is happy. Sophie is a girl who often likes to be alone when she's doing something, so she has developed many different ways to tell us to go away.

Much like 'Bye, Daddy', 'Happy!' means, 'I need to be alone, Minion, exit forthwith.'

So the moment was over and gone. She has never let me sing or play along since, but it doesn't mean that I don't still try from time to time.

August 2013

I went to see the latest celluloid burp by the makers of *The Smurfs* with Sophie: *Smurfs 2*. Ailbhe preferred to stay at home on her computer. Clever girl. I was steeling myself for an animated nightmare. I didn't think the movie would be that popular, so I didn't book ahead, for once. When we got there the only seats available were at the front.

I was on tenterhooks, because I was worried that Sophie would get up and run around and block everyone's view.

Then the movie started, and while I wasn't expecting it to be good, I was perplexed by how bad the sound editing was. There was a persistent, regular, loud noise on the soundtrack. I saw some other parents looking around. It wasn't just me who was hearing it.

Then a hushed giggling arose. Behind me, on the other side of the aisle, a couple of rows back, there was a hefty dad asleep beside his three kids, producing the loudest snores I have ever heard. Two of his boys were trying to wake him, to no avail.

His other kid had Down Syndrome, and he was sitting in the seat beside his dad, oblivious, transfixed, and delighted by the blue blobby creatures on the screen. Doubtless, I have been that snorer. (Although my single-propeller snoring would be no match for his jet engine.)

Sophie was very well behaved that day. She never got up, seemingly happy, so long as she had a steady supply of popcorn.

I was delighted that no one woke that dad – he slept through the whole movie. He clearly needed it. Sophie giggled and squealed at the animated antics, like a lot of the little kids there, and in the lulls, the rest of the parents and I were highly entertained by the dad's shout-snoring.

It was by far the best time I've ever had at a Smurfs movie.

September 2013

It was the morning of Sophie's birthday and Martha was getting the house ready.

'So, Sophie's six today, right?' said Ailbhe.

'Yep,' said Martha, delighted that she was taking an interest.

Ailbhe was very excited. 'That's great, now she'll be able to talk properly like me!'

November 2013

Sheila came over to Ashbourne during the day, and she suggested that everyone come back to Swords with her to watch a movie. 'DVD and popcorn with Granny?' she said to Sophie, which Martha's ear translated as, 'Sleeps for Martha.' They went over.

Martha texted to ask me to come straight to Swords in the car after work and bring them all back to Ashbourne. I was delighted, as I had a gig later that night, and a nap in the afternoon would mean that Martha would be far better able to cope. NO PROBLEM, I replied, and I got to back to work, feeling better about the day.

When they got to Swords, Granny opened the door and the girls ran in together behind her. Martha was just behind them, after going to the boot of the car to get some food. When she went into the sitting room to put the DVD on, she saw that Ailbhe was on her own. 'Ailbhe, where's Sophie?' she asked.

'I don't know.'

Martha went out into the hall and called 'SOPHIE!' No answer. It was very quiet. 'Mam, have you seen Soph?' she asked, popping her head into the kitchen.

'She walked in ahead of me,' Sheila told her.

'Are the doors locked upstairs?' Martha asked.

'Yes, of course,' Sheila answered. Martha still went up the stairs and looked. It had been Sheila and Brendan's policy to lock the upstairs doors, as a rule, in case Sophie came over, so that she couldn't get at the upstairs windows.

Martha stood on the landing, at the top of the stairs, looking at the four locked doors in turn, wondering if one was accidentally open, perplexed. Then she heard Sophie, but she couldn't see her. 'Soph?' she called, puzzled. Then Soph made another little noise, and Martha had an awful realisation.

When Martha was a teenager, Brendan and Sheila had built a one-storey, pitched-roof extension on to the side of the house for a downstairs loo and a utility room. Martha saw that the landing window was open beyond the net curtain. When she pulled back the curtain, she saw Sophie standing on the apex of the roof, balancing.

Sophie had moved out too far for Martha to grab her. Martha's instinct was to shout, but she didn't want to startle Sophie either. She could easily take a tumble and land on the concrete a couple of metres below. On one side, Sheila and Brendan keep glass for recycling. A fall from a height into those bottles would make flithers of Sophie.

We often refer to Sophie as 'our mountain goat', but even mountain goats fall sometimes.

'Popcorn, Soph,' Martha said softly. Sophie looked back at Martha, framed by the window.

'Popcorn,' she repeated, excitedly. She had been about to sit down on the roof, but she got back up and teetered back towards Martha, who grabbed her the instant she was in reach and pulled her back in.

Martha called me in work and told me what had happened. 'I am never going to have any peace, Aidan, am I?' she asked.

May 2014

In the New Year, Una had asked me to try to write a new show with her. She had a concept: 'I want to write a musical about men.'

'I'd love to!' I said. As a possessor of a penis I had some knowledge of the subject matter. 'What are you going to call it?'

'*Men*,' she said. It's fair to say that, at this early stage, the project was at the saggy-arsed end of loosely conceptual.

I was delighted. A musical! Me! And, as a bonus, Una said three words that, in my limited experience, are rare in theatre circles: 'You'll get paid.' It would be a decent chunk of meat that Martha and I could throw over our shoulders as we attempted to get away from the bank's ravenous dogs.

I got paid to sit in my bedroom and write songs. Every night, after the girls went to bed, while Martha ironed downstairs watching box set episodes, I would take one of the ideas Una had emailed me, and 'quietly' write a song. I'd record it on my little table-top recorder and email it to Una. In that way, I wrote a few songs a week, for three months, while also doing comedy gigs from time to time, as my musical comedy alter ego Aidan Strangeman.

One of the most exciting parts of this project was that Una had secured a couple of weeks of studio time in the National Theatre, UK, and there were funds for me to go over for one of those weeks and work on the show with her. This would be the longest Martha and I had spent apart since we'd met. 'Are you sure you'll be okay?'

'Yes, I'll be fine,' she lied.

I stayed in digs provided by the theatre, and I got the Tube to the studios every day. Even though I had lived in Dublin for over a decade, London was so very cosmopolitan to me. I felt very much like the Little Carlow Boy Who Could.

The weather was glorious all week long. On the first night, Una and I went to see the musical *The Book of Mormon*, which we justified as 'research'. I emerged from that theatre, wrung out with laughter, and utterly inspired.

I had heard that it had taken seven years of solid work to write it, and I asked myself, 'What could I achieve with seven years of weeks like this?' *Give me time*, I thought. Possibly, a great piece of work. Definitely, no marriage.

At night, in London, I would sleep badly, because I was excited about the work, and at the same time I missed Martha and the girls. I texted: HOW IS EVERYTHING GOING THERE?

I'M OKAY, she lied, again.

In an ordinary week, I knew that Martha ached all afternoon for the sound of my key in the door. She was like a midnight driver with the two girls in the car, desperately trying to stay awake. A successful afternoon's parenting would end with a headcount: 'One, two. Not bad.'

And then I would come home, and take the wheel, and she could finally rest.

A week away had been a lot to ask for. Asking for seven years … there isn't a word to express how ridiculous that request would be.

So I enjoyed the week in London for what it was: a week of whatiffery. It was exciting to live like a professional songsmith for a week, commuting to a writing studio every day. I got a waft of how delicious it would be to write for the theatre, but I knew that it could never be my meal ticket.

On the Friday, I was leaving to go home. I left my digs very early in the morning, taking my suitcase and guitar with me, so that I could write on my own for a couple of hours. I sat in the airy studio, alone, as the dawn sun climbed into the morning.

Here's the song I wrote that morning:

I am in love with everything,
It feels like everything loves me back
It makes my heart go ding-a-ling-ling
And I'm pretty happy 'bout that
'Cos I am right where I belong,
I'm fitting right in, to everything,
Like the notes of a campfire singalong
It's everything, it's everything,
From the floor, up to the ceiling.
It's ha ha ha, *tap tap*
Happiness.

And that evening, I flew home, to reality.

June 2014

Martha went to the doctor to get her dosage of Lexapro increased. He was reluctant to do that unless she agreed to counselling. She had been taking anti-depressants for nearly seven years at that point, so she thought it might be time to try it out.

He put her name on an HSE waiting list. Martha started to feel enthusiastic about going to counselling, but HSE waiting lists are like black holes: they pull all light and hope into them, and no one really knows for sure how they work. A few months later, there was no sign of an appointment. We couldn't afford private sessions either.

Martha got chatting about it to one of my friends in the college gang. She had carried out a very large sideways step in her career by leaving the construction industry and retraining as a psychotherapist. She suggested that Martha go to Dublin City University, because there would be graduates there, eager for experience. The graduates could give her good and – importantly for us – cheap counselling, so she wouldn't have to wait.

Martha applied to the college that week and got an interview to see which counsellor might be suitable.

'What did they ask you?'

'They asked me if I had any preferences. I told them that I didn't want an older man as a counsellor, because I tend to fall for older men who are authority figures.'

'But I'm not older, or an authority figure,' I whined.

'I know; odd, that. Don't know what happened there,' she shrugged. I did a sad face. Martha said, ' … but you're my favourite aberration, if that helps?'

It did.

She was paired with a young female counsellor, and over time, counselling really did help her. We don't talk about what goes on there. That is a private space for Martha. She did tell me once that she gets a lot out of it because she can be angry, bitter and mean, and say the thoughts out loud that scare her, safe in the knowledge that nothing she says leaves the room, or leaks out onto the pages of a book.

July 2014

It turns out that Martha is a racist. I realise I should have said this earlier on in the book, but it also took me a while to figure it out.

We had a rare Sunday out as a family of four. We went to the beach in Bray on a sun-kissed afternoon. After a lovely walk, dodging the dogs, we stopped to have an ice cream down on the packed promenade. Ailbhe only likes vanilla, and often doesn't finish her portion. Sophie would eat any flavour of ice cream until she dies. She chose chocolate that day, and because she lacks a certain level of ice cream-eating decorum, she ate some with her mouth, and she tried to ingest the rest through facial osmosis.

Ailbhe, Martha and I were sitting on a low wall, while Sophie ran back and forward a few feet in front of us.

Martha looked over at Sophie, and with mock disdain said, 'Look at your dirty chocolate face,' which made me laugh. At that precise moment, an Indian family of four passed between us and Sophie, and every single head in that family turned towards Martha.

Because my male pattern baldness had become less pattern and more baldness, I had recently taken to completely shaving my head. They did not see our rambunctious little redhead, with her ice-cream covered face, what they saw was a racial-slur-spouting Irish woman and her giggling skinhead husband. They passed us, disgusted, before Martha could offer any words of explanation.

A couple of weeks later, I brought Sophie to Bray on our own. We both had vanilla.

Those days when we have all been out together as a family foursome are very rare.

When they were younger, I brought Ailbhe and Soph to all the usual places parents bring kids. But as time went on and their very different personalities came to the fore, increasingly I would take them out separately, and, eventually, usually just Soph.

For instance, where Ailbhe wanted to stop and get to know each of the animals in Dublin Zoo by name, Sophie saw the zoo the same way that Mark Twain saw a golf course: a good walk ruined. It became a balancing act between the vast amount of time Ailbhe wanted to spend at each enclosure, and Sophie's deep need to keep walking, no matter what. It was a waste of money to bring Sophie. Ailbhe eventually lost the interest she had in animals, in favour of computer games. She became the indoor child. We stopped going to the zoo.

But the three of us still went to cinema together a lot. The best movie we ever saw was *Song of the Sea*. This isn't just because it's a wonderful movie, it's because we had the whole cinema to ourselves, and it was the first movie that Sophie had a visceral reaction to.

There's a character in that movie called Saoirse, who doesn't speak. She only opens her mouth to sing. It's no wonder that Sophie strongly identified with her. When things were getting fraught for Saoirse near the end of the movie, Ailbhe was crying; I expected that. It was a scene involving expressions of intense love between a mother and her family. But when I looked over at Sophie, her face was wet too. She wasn't wailing. She was weeping. She had never cried at a movie before.

At that time, Martha was regularly drawing paper dolls for Sophie. When I came home from work, I knew immediately that Martha had been drawing, because Sophie would greet me at the door by saying, 'Laminate it!' It was my job to laminate the paper dolls and cut them into shape. The dolls were: 'Sophie Princess' or 'Sophie Astronaut' or 'Sophie Ballerina', etc. But after she came home from *Song of the Sea*, Sophie took out the paper and pencils and went to Martha and said: 'Saoirse!'

Movies really are magical.

21 August 2014
My Day

'**L**ie' is a very strong word. It is the one word that even politicians are reluctant to say of their staunchest rivals. They will say: 'He misspoke' or 'She wasn't quite truthful' or 'He gave alternative facts.' So, to say that I lied to Martha would be too harsh an accusation. It was not a lie; my sin was merely one of omission.

A couple of months previously, when I went out one night to do one of the Irish heats of the So You Think You're Funny? (SYTYF?) competition, I hadn't told her that if I got through to the semi-final round I would have to go to Edinburgh to compete.

SYTYF? is a prestigious annual competition for comedy newcomers that has been running for decades. The past Irish winners are: Dylan Moran, Tommy Tiernan, David O'Doherty and Aisling Bea. The prize that year was five thousand sterling and an all-expenses-paid trip to Montreal Just for Laughs in 2015.

So I didn't tell Martha, because I believed I wouldn't be good enough to get through to the semi-final, so why have the argument? Right?

A few weeks later, I got a call to say that I had got through to the semi-final, which would be on the Monday of the August Bank Holiday. So that evening, I went up to Martha, in bed, and said, 'I got through to the next round of that So You Think You're Funny? competition.'

I let her be delighted for me for a moment.

Then I said, 'So ... I have to book a flight to Edinburgh ... ' In mitigation I assured her, ' ... that'll definitely be the end of it.'

I went over for the whole August Bank Holiday weekend, spending money that we didn't have. I had never been in Edinburgh for the Fringe Festival, so I wanted to take what I assumed would be my only chance for a long time to come to experience it. I went to see lots of shows, and by the time my semi-final came around, I was hooked on the idea of writing a show and bringing it to Edinburgh sometime in the very distant future. To be honest, I had already been hooked on that idea. I had consumed a lot of musical comedy that year. But my favourite musical comedian, by far, was Tim Minchin. One of his prescient friends had made a documentary that chronicled his journey to stardom. In it, Karen Koren, the manager of the Gilded Balloon, had spotted him and dragged him over to Edinburgh to do a show, which led to him becoming a very big deal in the UK. The Gilded Balloon is the venue which runs the SYTYF? competition, and where the semi-finals and the final are held, and Karen is a judge.

I wasn't nervous because I knew I hadn't a hope. I had gone to see the semi-final that was on the night before mine, and the standard was ridiculously high. These were the best newcomers from hundreds of entries. *I did well to get this far*, I thought.

The semi-final was on in a room that held about 150 people, and I was on in the middle of the semi-final line-up. From the start of my seven-minute set to the end, it could not have gone better. Surely, though, another act would come along and top that, or maybe the judges wouldn't be as good to me as the audience? But as the acts came and went, I thought, *you know, I think I might have got the best reaction of the night.* When the last act finished, my heart was racing as the judges went to deliberate and the MC filled the time with a bit of his own stand-up. I had a very strong feeling that they were about to call my name as the winner of that semi-final.

The problem was telling Martha, because the final would be on right in the middle of the few days I had booked off work for our summer holiday to Gowna. 'Don't worry, I definitely won't get through this time,' I had said to Martha when I left.

When Karen came back out and announced me as the winner of that semi-final, I texted Martha to let her know. Then I turned off my phone for fifteen minutes to let her calm down. In that time, not only did I meet Karen in the artists' bar, she also said some very lovely things about my act. I was high on her compliments. When I turned my phone back on and called Martha, the first thing she said was, 'You better win this thing, now, or don't come home,' which was one of Martha's patented half-jokes.

So on 21 August, I missed our family holiday in Gowna to go over for the final. Martha still went to Gowna with Granny and Grandad and the girls, though, so I didn't feel too bad about it.

The final was in a 350-seater hall, and it would certainly be a full house. I recognised the hall from the Tim Minchin documentary, because it was the one he had done his debut show in. All day long, I had never been as nervous about a show in my life. I spent a good portion of the day staring at the back of toilet doors.

By the time the final was about to start, and I was waiting backstage with the rest of the finalists, I had become a quivering husk of a man. I wondered if I still remembered how to play the guitar.

I was on just before the end of the first half. From the side of the stage, I heard other comedians go on and nail their punchlines, getting big reactions. Bastards! Even when a set didn't go brilliantly for someone, I still envied them because they were finished. I was terrified, like a cow waiting in line to be dosed with mastitis medicine.

And then, there was no going back. It was my turn. I don't remember the set, I just remember having the thought, *This isn't going as well as the semi-final*, and once I was finished, *Well, I'm not going to win this, but at least I got to the final. That's something.*

I watched the second half of the show from the balcony and I saw some class acts. I had identified about four or five comedians who I thought could win it. They were a nice bunch and I wouldn't have felt aggrieved to lose to any of them.

At the end, all the comedians gathered in the backstage area. Third place was announced. I thought *I might have an outside hope of that.* But it wasn't me. My night was over, I thought. Second place. *Not me, of course.* Then I looked around at the comedians who were left and wondered which one was going to win it.

'And the winner of So You Think You're Funny 2014 is … Aidan Strangeman.'

I didn't move. *Did they just call my name? Me? Me?! ME?!* A couple of the others shook my hand. One of the competition organisers said, 'You need to go on stage now.'

I walked out in a daze to collect my prize. I made a short speech that began, 'I think you might have made a massive mistake … '

With the last bar of energy in my phone, I called Martha. In the background, I could hear Sheila and Brendan whooping and applauding. 'I can't believe it,' I said.

'I can,' said Martha.

There was an after-show party with free cocktails. That might account for my slightly hazy memory of proceedings after my name was announced. I know I had my photograph taken with Jason Manford, who was one of the judges that night, because there is photographic evidence of that. I spent the rest of the night talking to a blur of agents and promoters. I know that for sure because I checked my wallet the next day and I had a large bunch of business cards. They said things like, 'I deal with Eddie Izzard', 'I brought Bo Burnham over to the UK.'

I felt like saying, 'You know I'm just some eejit from Carlow, right?'

I vaguely remember being in a late-night bar after the after party talking to David O'Doherty. He probably gave me some good advice, like, 'Don't do this.'

I went straight from there to an early-morning red-eye flight home. I knew I wouldn't sleep on the flight. I hate flying. You might as well ask me to have a nap in a meat grinder.

Derm picked me up at the airport to bring me to Gowna. I was running on pure adrenaline by then. I charged my phone in Derm's car on the way down. When I turned it back on, I had hundreds of notifications and messages, which included lots of offers to do gigs – gigs that I had previously begged for and hadn't got. Paid gigs.

From then on, I didn't have to go begging for gigs, I had to sort through offers. It had been nineteen years since I'd started writing songs. When I took myself seriously, no one else did. But when I allowed myself to be silly, people started taking me seriously. There was no guarantee that I would be successful, but this win would prove to be a wonderful calling card. I really wanted to follow wherever it would lead me.

Then I remembered something: the cheque with the winning prize money! It would be enough to take a serious chunk out of our mortgage arrears. Enough to give us some breathing space. We wouldn't be losing the house this year, at least. Finally, it seemed, something was going right.

21 August 2014
Martha's Day

It was pleasant summer morning in Gowna. The door of the house was open. Sophie was eating a mouthful of breakfast, running across to have a go on the swings at the front of the house and running back to eat another mouthful. That was her circuit for the morning. Martha was sitting at the table; Ailbhe was on the couch. Sheila was in the extra cabin, asleep, and Brendan was milling around outside, enjoying the fresh country air and collecting firewood.

Then Martha realised that she hadn't seen Sophie for a couple of minutes, so she looked out at the swing. No Soph. The previous day Sophie had hidden in the wardrobe in the bedroom, so Martha checked there first. No Soph. Then she checked the kitchen. No Soph. She briskly walked outside and went around the house. No Soph.

'Dad, have you seen Sophie?' she asked.

He called over, 'No, why?'

'I haven't got eyeballs on her.' They searched in the grove of trees beside the house. Martha began to panic. She stumbled through some brambles, and ripped strips of skin off the back of her leg. Still, no Soph.

They shouted to Sheila in the cabin to get up, so she could stay at the house in case Sophie came back. 'We're going to see if she's gone down to the lake,' Brendan called. When they got into the field, there was a clear view of the path to the lake, but no Soph. They ran down expecting to see her at the shoreline. *No Soph. No Soph. Jesus! No Soph.* Martha's heart was thumping so loudly, she suspected that I might be able to hear it in Scotland.

Martha called Sophie's name at first, but then she figured that there was a better chance of her responding to 'Popcorn!' Sophie always answered to that. But, she didn't come running. No Soph.

There is a field behind the house that also has a path that leads down the lake, so Martha went back up that way, while her dad went the usual route. No Soph, either way. When they got back to the house, Sheila decided that she would go and search as well, so they told Ailbhe to stay there in case Sophie came back. 'Okay,' said Ailbhe, not stirring, seemingly unbothered by the situation.

Martha searched the surrounding fields. No Soph. Brendan went back down to the lake. No Soph. Sheila had awful memories of when Martha was a toddler in the back garden in Swords when she fell into a bin full of water, headfirst! Sheila had found her minutes later, with her chubby little baby legs sticking out of the bin, unresponsive. At the time, there was no phone in the house, so she ran out to the street with Martha in her arms, screaming for help. The neighbours called an ambulance, and Martha survived. (There are photos of her with her head shaved on one side: 'I was such a chubby baby they couldn't find a vein in my arm,' she explained to me when I first saw it.) So Sheila went straight for the nearby farms to check the slurry pits. *Please don't let her be there*, she thought.

Martha went down to the lake one more time. No Soph. It was as if in a split second on that morning it had suddenly become a Soph-less universe.

It had been an hour and a half since they had seen her. 'She would have come back by now,' Martha reasoned. *She's dead*, she thought. No Soph, for ever.

Martha has a cousin who stays across the lake, and she called him to ask what she should do next. 'Should I contact Search and Rescue?' she asked.

'I'll be over in a few minutes,' he said, and he jumped into his motorboat and started to make his way across the lake. Martha walked back up to the house, scanning desperately for a flash of red hair, but there was no Soph to be seen. She walked back up the lane with the phone in her hand. She was going to have to call me in Edinburgh. She wondered how she was going to tell me that Sophie was gone, probably dead. I would have spent the afternoon crying in the airport, frantically looking for flights home. As Martha approached the house, Ailbhe called out: 'She's here!'

Martha sprinted for the house, and when she rounded the corner of the door, standing in the middle of the room, mucked up to her chest, with no boots on … Soph! Martha picked her up, and held her, relieved, angry and terrified all at once.

We still have no idea where she went during that time, and the boots have never been found.

22 August 2014

My adrenaline buzz was finally wearing off as Derm drove up the hill to Gowna that morning. I was looking forward to an afternoon nap.

After a hug and a kiss, I gave Martha a synopsis of the night, which ended with, ' … and Karen has offered me a space to do a show in the Gilded Balloon at next year's festival … ' Behind my tired eyes, Martha could see that my brain was sparkling. She looked reticent, and I understood that. 'We'll find a way to make it work, okay?' I said.

But that wasn't it. There was something else wrong. She said, 'I have to talk to you for a second,' and she took me into the bedroom.

She told me about how her day had gone, and Sophie going missing.

'Oh, Martha, that's … ' What could I say? I just hugged her. We got so lucky. That day – our lives – could have been so different. Destroyed. In ruins.

September 2014

I had known for most of that year that there would be an Irish tour of *Singlehood* from September to November, including three nights in the Olympia. But I didn't believe it was really going to happen until I showed up at the stage door that first afternoon for a technical rehearsal and I wasn't turned away. And that is how, for my thirty-eighth birthday, I got to perform in my dream venue.

On stage, as the cast sang one of the songs with me, I wasn't nervous. It was exhilarating. I looked out at the people laughing at the lines I had written years ago, sitting on the edge of my bed, late at night after the girls had gone to sleep, and I thought, *This is the thing that I should be doing.*

After that, I booked a lot of musical comedy gigs for myself in Dublin, London and Scotland. I was so looking forward to 2015, when I would get to go to Canada, and hopefully, if I could find the money, I would bring my debut show to Edinburgh.

October 2014

By the time Sophie was seven, she had a black belt in cuteness, although I'm sure she wasn't aware of that.

One night, Martha and I were in bed together, and there was a possibility of some sort of adult action, so I had locked the door. That was the foreplay sorted. Things were starting to get hot and heavy – Martha had just finished her game of Sudoku and put down the phone – when there came a polite knocking on the door.

'Was that Sophie?' Martha asked.

'God, I hope so,' I said, 'or else we need to stop feeding the gerbils.'

Then, outside the door, we heard a little voice saying, 'Knock, knock. Who's there? Mammy's bed.' Sophie doesn't understand jokes in that way, which made it all the funnier. We fell around laughing, and all chance of adult action dissipated. I opened the door, and there was Sophie. Of course, we let her into the bed that night.

She showed us her appreciation by doing an hour-long, horizontal dance performance between us, at four o'clock in the morning.

November 2014

D o you know how you can go for a night out and somehow come home with more money than you went out with? Normally this is the result of a forgotten, drunken trip to the ATM. That was not what had happened to Martha, unless she had robbed the bank. She went out one night and came home with thousands of euro more than she had gone out with.

I was in bed and the girls were asleep by the time I heard the key in the door. I was tired, but I never sleep well when Martha's not there.

She had been out with a group of other mothers who have children on the spectrum; they called their group The Autism Mommies. (They might release a single.) 'Did you have a good time?' I asked, hopefully. Martha is often the first one to go home from these nights out. It is hard for her to enjoy herself fully when she is constantly reminding her eyes to remain open.

But the woman who jumped into the bed beside me was wide awake. 'Have you ever heard of incapacitated child tax credit?' she said.

'Did I ever tell you that you say the most romantic things sometimes?'

'Seriously, have you?'

I had filled out so many different forms, and applied (begged) for so many this-and-thats over the years, that I couldn't be sure. 'I don't think so.'

She had been told about it by one of the other mothers. 'If you have a child with a lifelong dependency, like Sophie, you can claim this credit,' she said, and she told me how much it was.

'Oh, well, that was information that would have been useful about five years ago.'

'Aidan, you can apply for it retroactively and get a rebate.' My eyes went wide. I was suddenly very much awake.

I quickly totted it up in my head. The rebate would be enough to just about cover the remaining mortgage arrears. Life couldn't be that good, so I asked Martha to tot it up in her head, since her head is better at totting. She got the same answer.

I applied for the credit the next day, and eventually we got a rebate cheque. I called the bank the day we got it, and said that I had some money to pay back the mortgage arrears, and I'd like to have a meeting.

'Martha and I got a tax rebate from a decapitated child credit,' I explained. There was a pause on the phone. 'Sorry, incapacitated child credit, I meant.'

Martha and I had taken to calling it 'Decapitated Child Credit,' and I had forgotten to switch my language settings to 'dealing with a customer service representative' mode. *Press one if you would like Aidan to be polite …*

A couple of weeks later, I had a meeting with the bank. This would be the fifth meeting we had had in total. Each time, Martha and I had met a different person. Every one of them was called Clive. Each time, they didn't have our records, or access to the computer to get our files. Each time, we had to fill out the twelve-page form before we went. Each time, we would have to tell our story again. Each time, Martha would cry from the stress and shame of the situation. Each time, the meeting would end with us kicking the can down the road.

I went to this meeting on my own, as Martha wasn't well that day. Across the table from me sat a very different beast from anyone we'd met before. He had the records. He knew the story. He was prepared to talk to me about how I could get rid of a couple of other debts we had with the bank. He was ... helpful. (He wasn't called Clive.) He told me how to negotiate. He seemed to be genuinely on my side. A nice person. (I had to come to terms with the fact that I actually liked a banker.)

'You would have been a hard case to take to court, anyway,' he said. I nodded. *Yeah, but you would have if we didn't have the money,* I thought.

When I walked out of the bank that day, I stopped and took the longest, deepest breath I'd ever taken in my life.

December 2014

The office I worked in had a panoramic view of the M50 motorway. Every day, there was a dull sound of cars and trucks rumbling by, until it came to the evening rush hour, when they would congeal into gridlock.

It was lunchtime, and the office was sparsely populated. Because I had just got paid for the tour of *Singlehood* and for some of the many gigs I had done recently, I had treated myself to a deli sandwich. It lay in an open paper wrapper in front of my keyboard, half-eaten. I was looking at my screen with watery eyes, reading an online news story about an undercover reporter who had filmed abuses at a residential home for people with intellectual disabilities.

As I read about the disgraceful care and humiliation of the elderly and middle-aged residents, many of whom could only communicate with noises and gestures, I thought about Sophie, and what might happen to her – what might be done to her – when Martha and I were gone.

There was a story about a woman whose entire day was spent sitting on one chair or another. She hadn't been taken out once during the reporter's time there. I thought of running beside Sophie while she scooted a circuit around our estate and her shouts of joy as she flew. I thought of how that could be denied to her by people who would think it too much hassle – who would see her as nothing but a day-in-day-out chore.

I was holding it together, just about, until I clicked on a secretly filmed video showing a manager at the centre sitting on a woman with autism who was in her late fifties. I thought about Sophie in her late fifties, when I might no longer be able to care for her because I was too old, or too dead, and her cries of, 'hurting,' with ever-rising intensity. I thought of her saying, 'Daddy, help,' and then 'Daddy, help, please.' I hoped that I would be dead if that ever happened to her. That happening to Sophie because I didn't have the strength to care for her … that would be too much. I couldn't help it any more: I blinked, and the well of water in one eye overflowed.

Just then, one of the guys in work came back in from his lunch. He was standing at his desk, taking off his coat, when he looked over and said, 'Hey, Aidan.' I nodded back, hoping that I had composed myself enough in the few seconds since he had come in. I hadn't.

'How are you doing?' he asked, with enough concern in his voice that I was sure the he had seen my watery eyes and suspiciously wet face.

'Just have a bit of hayfever.' He looked at me and I looked at him, and I knew what he was thinking: *But … it's … December.*

He nodded back, 'Oh right, I get a bit of that myself,' and he sat down at his desk and started to look through emails … anything but talk to me.

There is no crying in Engineering.

For a long time, Martha hadn't kept up with current affairs, because, as she said, 'I have all the misery I can handle right now,' and especially because of the potential of coming across stories like the one I had read that day.

But when I came home from work, and we were talking after dinner, I decided to destroy her peace of mind with my blunderbuss of a mouth, by telling her about my tears in work. I tried to convince her that this story was probably an aberration and not the norm, and that while Sophie might not be loved in a care home, we would find a place where she would be looked after properly, at least.

But I also remember that when I was seventeen I had partaken in the now defunct Student Summer Scheme, where you could volunteer for payments during the summer if you were in college. In my first week, I was tasked with looking after a fifteen-year-old boy with cerebral palsy, who could not communicate verbally. I received no formal training for that.

I did have to get a Garda clearance certificate, but that amounted to turning up at the Garda station with a form that basically said, 'I am a good person, honest,' which is also what all the not-good people would say. In retrospect, it seemed too rudimentary. Being the son of a well-known local homemaker and a respected senior civil servant, I had the feeling that they probably would have signed me off if I had shown up wearing a suit made of strangled kittens.

That was a long time ago, but I couldn't help but wonder, was there anything to stop that situation happening again today?

Martha didn't sleep properly at night for a month after I told her about that news story, worrying about what we could do to safeguard Sophie when we were gone. But then she came up with her own solution, and once she did, she was able to sleep again. 'Aidan, if you die first, before I become incapacitated, rather than leave her to the care of others, I will strap myself and Sophie into our car and drive off the end of a pier,' she said, calmly.

I said, 'Ah Martha, you can't don't do that: you're not a very good driver, you'll probably miss the water.'

She smiled at that, but she didn't laugh. I realised that she wasn't entirely kidding. I didn't have a good plan for what provisions to make for Sophie once I died; all I knew was that while I was still alive and competent, no harm would come to her, if I could help it.

April 2015

I couldn't think. Was this the third or fourth night I had tried to get Sophie to sleep before midnight? I was already losing count. A note came home in her school communication book. 'Sophie was cranky today.' *She's not the only one*, I thought.

'She slept on the bus home,' Martha had told me earlier, before she went to bed.

'Damn it,' I thought. I had hoped that, finally, tonight, Sophie would sleep and I would get a chance to write something – anything – for my Edinburgh show, which was booked and ready to go for August. I felt like I was running out of time to put something good together. I was often irritable with Martha when she disturbed me with awful questions like, 'Would you like tea and a biscuit?'

'You're a bit of a bollocks when you're writing, you know that?' said Martha. That was fair.

That night, it was half past midnight and Sophie was still connected to her mains supply. I wanted to just let her into 'Mammy's bed', and be done with it, but I couldn't give in. We were making our umpteenth attempt to get her to sleep in her own bed. Giving in now would render the previous evenings when I had eventually succeeded, and the last four and a half hours, a waste.

Then I heard a thud from her bedroom. She had fallen out of her bed. When I walked in to pick her up, she was rubbing her arm and going 'ooo, ooo, ooo', and 'hurt'.

I thought, *Oh no, that's all I fucking need now – a fucking trip to A&E.*

'BACK INTO BED AND STOP MESSING,' I shouted. I felt her arm. No tell-tale lumps to indicate a fracture. I picked her up and put her back in to bed, roughly. I was losing my temper. I was suddenly so very angry.

'GO! TO! SLEEP!' I shouted. She rolled over and giggled. It was the giggle that sent me over the edge. She had no idea how angry I was; how much she was pissing me off; how this shit could not continue for the rest of our fucking lives.

So, I pinched her arm. Hard. And I held it to make sure that it hurt. And it really did hurt; I could see the shock on her face. Then she screamed. I shouted 'SLEEP!' As I did, I let go and stomped out of the room. When I was outside the door, I cried. From anger. From sadness. From frustration. From shame. Especially from shame.

Do you know what the worst thing was? It worked. She went to sleep. That made me feel dreadful. I didn't sleep that night.

The next day, when I came home from work, so very tired, she was on the couch watching her iPad. I sat down beside her and said, 'Pinch. Ouch. Daddy. Sorry Soph.' Without taking her eyes off her iPad she said, 'Sorry Soph.' I pretended that was her way of saying, 'It's okay.'

But it wasn't.

May 2015

'Dad, if I never cycle a bike, then I'll never fall off a bike.'
Sometimes, Ailbhe's logic is inescapable.

She was right. Cycling is like following the Irish
football team: you will get so many good days – when Packie
guessed the right way; McAteer lashing it into the Dutch net;
the Quinn-to-Keane goal against the Germans; Robbie Brady
heading in against Italy – and that will make up for the days when
you go over the handlebars, when you feel like Steve Staunton
managing the Irish team to a five-two loss against Cyprus. Ailbhe
doesn't like football, so my excellent footballing analogy would
be lost on her; instead I promised something I could not deliver.
'Don't worry, I'll never let you fall.'

Truly, I am the Steve Staunton of teaching a child to ride a
bike. I know it's patriarchal and old-fashioned, but I wanted my
Norman-Rockwell-Gee-Willikers moment, when I would run
beside my daughter, holding on to the bike. Then I would let go
and she would wobble away, happily, for ever. 'Look, Dad, I'm
doing it!'

Every year since she was five, we had tried. And every year, it
didn't happen. I thought, 'There are probably a lot of nine-year-
olds who don't know how to cycle.' But then I had seen a dad in
our housing estate jogging beside his destabilised, pedalling little
sprout; the kid was so small he looked like a foetus on wheels.

Ailbhe and I were out on a black tarmac path that winds

through a large green space around the corner from our house, and we were going to give it 'one last go'. I could almost hear Staunton's voice in my head saying, 'I'm the dad, I'm the gaffer, and today will be the day you cycle your bike,' and I let go, and she was doing it, she was really doing it ... for a whole five seconds, before she panicked and put her feet down, and stopped. 'That was really good. We'll try again soon,' I said.

'How did you get on?' Martha asked when we got back. 'Five seconds,' I said.

Martha was a little bit more upbeat than I was. 'Well, that's a new record, isn't it?'

That is the equivalent of saying, 'That fifth goal you scored against us was offside,' but Martha doesn't like football either. My powers of analogy are as much use in my house as my ability to convince Ailbhe that she could cycle.

In school the next week, Martha mentioned it at Ailbhe's special needs assessment. She said, 'So, my husband, Aidan, is a complete failure as a father...' (She didn't, but that's what they all heard, I bet.)

That night, Martha said to me, 'Her resource teacher said that Ailbhe is to take her bike into school tomorrow. She's going to try to teach her.'

'Okay, but, I've tried everything. She's just too frightened,' I scoffed.

The next afternoon, Martha texted me in work: AILBHE CAME HOME CYCLING!

THAT WAS AUTOCORRECT? YOU MEANT 'CRYING,' RIGHT?

NOPE, SHE'S DELIGHTED WITH HERSELF!

The moral of this story is that Steve Staunton is the only player to play in every one of Ireland's 13 World Cup games, he has 102 caps as a rock-solid defender, and he has also scored direct from a corner for his country. Twice! Yes, he wasn't the greatest manager, but taking his Ireland career in totality, he is unfairly maligned. When Trapattoni took over managing the Irish team directly after him, and successfully managed to get us to the 2012 European Championships, I really hope that Steve texted him the same thing that I texted back to Martha that day.

YEAH, WELL, I LOOSENED THE LID.

June 2015

I was strapped to a rollercoaster that was making its merciless ascent up to its dizzyingly high crest, when I realised that I didn't like rollercoasters anymore, with probably the same feeling as an escapologist locked in a water tank who thinks, *Shit, I think I left my hairpin at home.*

I had always loved rollercoasters, even though I have always been afraid of heights. In fact, when Martha and I went on our short break to Paris, such was my fear that I panicked and ran off the crowded lift at the second viewing platform on the Eiffel Tower, even though we had bought tickets all the way to the top. However, when we went to Disneyland Paris a couple of days later, my love of rollercoasters conquered my fear of heights, easily.

I hadn't been on a rollercoaster since then, and I was excited at first, but then I realised that, somewhere in the last decade, my love had evaporated. I was terrified.

Sophie was in the seat beside me. She had been watching point-of-view videos of rollercoasters on YouTube for months, and was initially shrieking in delight, but as we got to the top, she looked like she needed some reassurance. I looked over (which was better than looking down) and said, 'Soph, you'll be okay, I promise.' But as the rollercoaster dipped over the crest and began its bone-rattling descents and dips and swerves, I could hear her roaring just below the sound of the rushing air, and my own screams. Yet again, I was making promises I was ill-equipped to keep.

When it was over, Sophie was windswept and shell-shocked. I didn't feel too badly about that, because it meant that for the rest of the day she wouldn't want to do any more thrill-rides.

As we walked away from the rollercoaster, I said, 'We go playground?' hoping for something more sedate for a while. 'Aeroplanes,' she said. At first, I didn't understand, but then I saw what she was looking at: it was an awful contraption nearby that was spinning sixteen souls in sickening circles, high up, and around and around and upside down – I realised that this was going to be a very long day. *I could happily live the rest of my life without doing that*, I thought, as I looked at it. 'Okay, let's do that,' I said to Sophie, with as much false enthusiasm as I could muster.

We were in Tayto Park, Ireland's Disneyworld, a fun park dedicated to the Irish love of Tayto crisps. (Truly, we have a complicated relationship with the spud.) It is fifteen minutes' drive from our house. We had gone to 'Potato Park', as Sophie calls it, on a Saturday morning, first thing, deliberately early. This meant that when we got off a ride she could say 'again!', as she often did, and the queues were not too long, so there was a good chance we could go again, quickly. I was deeply regretting that decision the second time the Aeroplane ride was taking off.

As I was being helplessly spun around by this contraption, trusting my life to its design and construction, I realised why I had suddenly become so afraid of these rides. I was thinking, *Someone like me drew this.*

After we had tried every thrill-ride twice, a few hours later, with my legs wobbling, Sophie spotted a structure that had three levels of high walkways with some obstacles, where people could gingerly make their way around, trussed up in harnesses in case they slipped. Sophie said, 'Go!' and made a run for it.

Sophie loves to climb, so, this activity would suit her perfectly. It wasn't too busy, so we waited in line.

Once Sophie and I were harnessed up, she excitedly made her way up the stairs, with me behind, dragging our safety lines along. *Good decision*, I thought. We took the lowest level, which was about ten feet (three metres) from the ground. The second that Sophie took a step onto the first obstacle (a balance beam) she made a frightened noise. *Bad decision*, I thought.

She didn't understand that she couldn't fall. How could I quickly explain the concept of a safety line to her, unless she slipped and found out that way? She was trembling all the way, as she made it across the balance beam, but at the second obstacle, she stopped in the middle. She was frozen with fear. 'You can't fall,' I said, repeatedly. I realised later that this was non-specific. It could mean, 'You can't fall because you have a harness on,' or, 'You can't fall because if you do, you will hit the ground, and might cease to exist.' It could be taken as a warning or reassurance. In that moment, I don't think Sophie was hearing me at all, though.

We had to go back. Because of the way we were harnessed, she had to make her own way back across the obstacle behind me. We were blocking other people from going. It was as embarrassing as being forced to play your way through a golf course backwards. I was hot and sweaty, and Sophie was crying. But after a few minutes of some coaxing and pleading, we eventually made it back to the first platform, and all we had to do was walk down the stairs and this awfulness would be over, and forgotten, and we could move on to the next thing.

Suddenly, Sophie decided that she wanted to go up to the second level and tried to go up the stairs. 'No Soph,' I shouted, and grabbed her.

And that's when the tantrum started. She was stuck between being terrified of this contraption and being denied the fun of it, and in her head it would not compute. She started screaming as I held her. One of the staff joined us on the platform and asked if he could help, and I immediately said, 'She's autistic, and she's about to have a massive meltdown, I'm really sorry.' I could see the other people we were blocking down below, and the queue getting longer. The member of staff was a wonderful lad. He said, 'Take your time, it's okay.'

I knelt beside Sophie as she started shouting, 'I WANT MY CLIMB!'

I said, as calmly as I could, 'No, Soph, we go down now.' And then she started to hit me, and I had to restrain her arms. There were over one hundred people standing around the ride, and it is very hard not to look. I understand that. We became the afternoon's sideshow.

I knew that the tantrum could go on and on, so after a few minutes, I decided to pick her up and take her down the stairs. The staff member walked in front of me, guiding us. Sophie was screaming, squirming and hitting me. *When did she get so heavy? When did she get so strong?* I thought.

Then she bit me.

A lot.

It was like carrying an angry hornet's nest. The first few weren't too bad, but then, at the top of my left arm, she bit hard enough that I knew she had drawn blood. I had utterly failed to handle this properly. I was queasy by the time we eventually got down. How could it take so long to get down ten steps?

At the bottom, I couldn't get the harness off Sophie quickly enough. We walked over to the bench and sat down.

'YOU DON'T BITE DADDY!' I shouted. That was too precise. I thought I had better include the entire population. 'YOU DON'T BITE.' I showed her my arm, because I wanted to see it myself. She hates the sight of blood, so she backed away from it. 'BOLD!' I shouted.

'Bold,' she repeated.

When she was fully calmed down, we walked off hand in hand. I was finished for the day, and I wanted to go home. I was making for the exit.

Then she spotted something, and said, 'Aeroplanes!'

August 2015

I took the month of August off work, with some unpaid leave included, and I went to Edinburgh to do my debut Fringe Festival Show. I had called the show *Horsey*, because I was initially going to write a show about fatherhood, 'Horsey!' being what Sophie shouts when she wants to be carried on my shoulders.

Even though Sophie was seven years old then (eight in September), she still loved all the things she had loved when she was a toddler, except she was about twice as tall. Whenever we went through doorways, I would say, 'Duck!' and she would duck and say, 'Quack!' She was also a lot heavier than a toddler as well. One day I was complaining to Martha. 'I can't bend down without her coming over and trying to ride me.'

Martha looked at me very pointedly and said, 'Oh, I know exactly how that feels.'

Still, I would always smile at the word 'Horsey', and a word that always made me smile seemed like a good name for my comedy show. It was only when I got over to Edinburgh, when I was handing out fliers, that I realised that calling the show after something that made me smile for a specific reason known only to myself wasn't the best idea.

'Is this a show about horses?' – Everyone else in the world, often.

And what was even more confusing was that most of the show wasn't actually all about fatherhood. Half an hour was about me, ten minutes were about Martha and twenty minutes were about the girls. You see, I had plenty of self-deprecating material about myself, and I had no problem writing songs about Martha:

My wife likes to do it, more than any human
I have ever met in my life
She's always, always, wanting it
There's never been a hominid
who likes doing it as much as my wife

I'm talkin' bout getting down between the sheets
My wife she likes it nice and deep
Up against a wall,
Vertically,
Seriously
She puts it down as a hobby on her CV
Frequently,
Recreationally
But if she wanted she could do it,
Professionally.
Without me,
Preferably.
She just can't get enough,
She really, really, really needs to …

… Sleep, oh sleep,
when she says she wants to sleep with me,
she really means it,
Literally
she just wants to sleep …

But I'd found it hard to write about the girls. The problem was that the word 'autism' seemed too heavy for a comedy show. In my previews, when I tried to talk about it, it hit too hard, and I couldn't figure out how to make the punch into a punchline. I needed to find a funny way to let the audience know that while it is a serious subject, Martha and I often laughed about it as well, and that it was okay for them to laugh with me. A few months before Edinburgh, I finally found a way:

I have two daughters. They are seven and nine. Now, I know what you're thinking. Odd names.

Both of my girls are on the autistic spectrum. The way I like to say it is that Ailbhe is mildly autistic and Sophie is wildly autistic. Now, Martha doesn't like it when I say it like that. She thinks that – with the whole 'mildly/wildly' thing – I am too in love with rhyming structure, and she's probably right. Not too long after the official diagnosis a good friend of mine called me up and said, 'You know, it could be worse, they could have leukaemia or something.' And I said, 'Yes, you're right. That'd be way worse. I mean, leukaemia doesn't rhyme with anything.'

And if people laughed at that, which they usually did, the rest of the show would go well.

When I got to Edinburgh, the shows went okay. Some days there would be a full house of fifty people, and some days there would be five. At some shows I would be complimented by continuous raucous laughter, but at some shows the response would be less than tepid. My skin was quite tough by the time I finished the month.

When Martha and Ailbhe came over to visit, Ailbhe didn't like that there were so many people there. She didn't want to be introduced to anyone, but she liked going to the kids' comedy shows. 'Is this what you do?' she asked me after one of them.

'Sort of, but a bit ruder,' I said.

After one of my shows, an eminent professor in the area of autism research, Simon Baron-Cohen, had come up to me. He hadn't known that I was going to do anything about autism in the show. It was just a coincidence that he was there – he must have been one of those odd people who go to see musical comedy on purpose. He asked me if I had ever thought about developing a full show about autism. He wasn't the first person to suggest it to me, so when I came home to Martha I told her that I was going to try to write that show.

I was very excited about that.

Martha was not.

November 2015

I was lying on the rocks on Bray beach, and I had just broken my hip. 'Awwwhhh,' I roared, repeatedly and aptly. As it was a soft, grey winter's day, there were very few people around, so there was no one nearby to hear me scream, except Sophie. It was Sophie who first went up on to the slippery rocks. She got away from me, and did not come back when I shouted at her. I went up on the rocks to rescue her before she fell, and with my first step, my foot went from under me and I landed on my hip. Then, Sophie skipped by my crying foetal form, off the rocks, back onto the sand and made her way down towards the waves.

She loves liquids: pouring, drinking, stirring, splashing – everything about them. One of her favourite things to do is to get a big bowl of water and mix every spice and sauce in our house to make a noxious concoction. Sometimes, she even does it with permission. If she were better able to speak, I suspect she might say of the sea, 'I like it, Dad, but I think it needs a bit more oregano.'

I never know what Sophie will do around water. On the days when I take her to the swimming pool, she could make for the deep end on her own if I let her (which I do not), but there are also days when we ease into the shallow end, and she will not let go of me for the first half an hour, petrified.

On another beach, the previous summer, I had the two girls with me, and when I turned around to play with Ailbhe, Sophie ran into the sea up to the top of her waist, and wasn't stopping. I had to run in and catch her. Since then, I had been a lot more vigilant.

Now, as I lay on the rock that day, I saw that she would be at the edge of the sea in seconds, and I wouldn't be able to catch her in time. 'SOPH! STOP!' I shouted, but I might as well have been telling the tide to turn back.

The pain from my leg was pulsing into my vision. I had a sick feeling of pain that I hadn't felt since I was a kid and had just gone over the handlebars of my bike. But I had to get up quickly and catch her. I attempted to scramble up, and I realised that my hip was not, in fact, broken, because I did manage to stand, albeit with the grace of a drunken, newborn foal. I think the pain was caused by fifty per cent soft tissue damage and fifty per cent melodramatics, but it still one hundred per cent hurt.

I gingerly made my way off the rock, as quickly as I could, to try to catch her. I wished that the sea would bark at her like a dog, as her feet splashed into the water.

We had been in Bray for an hour, and the surf had been unusually small; but just then, out of nowhere, a particularly big wave whipped up, and splashed just in front of Sophie. She turned and ran away from it, into my arms. I knelt in front of her, panting out the pain like a woman in labour (those antenatal classes have not gone to waste). 'SOPHIE, DON'T RUN AWAY FROM DADDY!' I shouted, as I held her. She didn't look at me. I moved my head to get into her eye-line and I shouted, 'DON'T RUN AWAY FROM DADDY!' again, and gave her a little shake at the same time. I wanted her to get the message.

'DontrunawayfromDaddy,' she giggled. I hugged her closer, because I could have lost her, and also because I needed the support to stay upright.

As the pain began to recede a little, I relaxed my grip, and she squirmed, broke out of my arms, and ran back up towards the stony part of the beach, which leads to the promenade. 'Ah Soph, please,' I whinged, as I got up and hobbled after her.

Sometimes, when I stop her doing something she enjoys, she has a tantrum. She is not able to deal with it very well when things don't go to whatever plan she has in her head. I had brought her to the cinema a few weeks previously, but I had misread the date the movie I told her we were going to see was coming out. There was no explaining that to her. All she knew was that there was going to be a movie and then there wasn't going to be a movie. Even though I told her we'd go for ice cream, she still screamed, 'YOU RUINED MY CINEMA!' all the way back to the car.

When I caught up with her, she offered me her hand, which meant, 'I'm ready to go now.' We went back to the train station, her skipping, singing songs from movies, and me limping.

On the station platform, I saw that we had to wait twenty-five minutes for the train. *Shit!* I hadn't planned on being that early. Luckily, I had sweets in my bag to placate Sophie, and, also, there was an empty bench, where I could finally rest.

Then I spotted three pigeons ambling over. They saw that we were eating, and they came closer, with their little bobbing, bullying heads, as if to say, *'Hey, wha'cha got there?'* Sophie began to do a high-pitched whine and climbed up the back of the bench. 'SHOO!' I shouted, but they weren't easily dissuaded, so I reluctantly stood up, and half-heartedly swished my leg at them; it hurt a lot, so I sat back down. Over the next couple of minutes, each time I got one to back off, the other two advanced. They were a clever little gang, undoubtedly descended directly from the raptors.

Sophie was shouting 'SHOO!' as well and flapping her hands. I taught her to shout 'SHOO!' at animals she didn't want near her. She was in the sitting room, one day, and she saw a cat on the windowsill and she shouted, 'SHOO! CAT!' I was momentarily proud of my teaching abilities. Then Ailbhe came over to see the cat, and Sophie shouted, 'SHOO! AILBHE!'

The pigeons persistently pecked around us, as Sophie's whines began to turn into screams. I was sure the other people on the platform were looking at this spectacle, but I didn't look at them. 'ACH! GO AWAY! SHOO!' I shouted, wondering how long it could be until the train arrived.

Suddenly, a man rushed in stage left, and he stamped and shouted loudly, and the pigeons flapped away in three different directions, defeated. He watched them go, like a hero. 'Is she okay?' he asked.

'Yes,' I said, 'Thank you,' and I saw in his eyes that he knew. I suspected that if I got talking to him he would talk about a sibling or a niece or nephew with special needs, and the difficulties of seemingly simple public situations, but he just said, 'No bother,' and walked back up the platform. This was probably for the best, as I was so grateful to the man at that moment, that if he lingered I'd probably create my own spectacle by kissing him directly on the mouth.

When the train came, we sat on the side where Sophie could look out over Dublin Bay on the way home. I was sorry we had left the beach, because the sun had come out, and the blue and green of the bay was stunning. Sophie sat quietly. She seemed content. I rubbed my hip. We would have to get the bus back to Ashbourne when we got back to the city. I looked at the timetable on my phone. We should get back just in time to make the next one. *No waiting. Excellent. Everything will be fine from here.* I had a few notifications on Facebook. I started flicking through them.

There were about ten other people on the carriage, mostly on their own, variously reading, or texting, or absentmindedly looking out the window, the only sound being the efforts of the train.

Suddenly, an almighty belch cut the silence. It was a sustained, guttural, unrepentant burp that must have surely been the explosive exhalation of every cubic foot of air in a cathedral-sized stomach. Imagine the burp a whale would do if he ate a pizza shop and a coke factory during an earthquake.

Ten heads looked up, instantly. I looked up as well, and we all saw that the sound had come from the little redheaded girl. While I had been looking at my phone, Sophie had knelt up on her chair, with her stomach resting against the seat, and let go. This burp was no accident. It was a performance. In case there was any doubt that it had been her, she said, in her cute little voice, ''cuse me.'

People looked at her and giggled, and then went back to doing the various things they had been doing with smiles on their faces. I whispered an admonishment, 'Sophie! Sit down!' and she did. She went back to looking out the window, contented, happy that her work here was done.

The burping is my fault – genetically. I can burp on command (why I haven't been more of a success at life, I don't know). Sophie had discovered recently that she could do it as well. However, she has taken this inherited art form to deeper, more resonant levels than I ever had, or could.

When we walked in the door, Martha was tidying up in the kitchen, and said, 'Hi Soph, what did you do today?' Sophie made some happy noises, and rubbed her face against Martha's belly when she hugged her. Then she ran off into the sitting room.

'How was it?' Martha asked.

'I'll show you how it was,' I said, and I started to open my jeans. I could see in her face that she was thinking, *Well, this is either a bad joke, or neither the time nor the place.* I pulled down one side of my jeans to reveal a hip that was turning from red to purple.

'Jesus,' Martha blasphemed, aptly. 'How did you do that?' I told her the story of the fall.

'Aw, will I kiss it better?' she asked, as she leaned over and planted a little kiss on my hip. A little shiver of pleasure went through me.

As I pulled my jeans back up, I said, 'You know, I think my penis is a little bruised, as well; maybe you could work some of your magic on that later?'

'Ha,' laughed Martha. 'We'll see.' Then she made a cup of tea, I told her about the epic burp on the train, while Sophie sat quietly on the couch, looking at her iPad.

While I wanted to bring Sophie out for some fun, the other point of the bringing her out was to make her tired, so she would sleep. I had been looking forward to the chance of making good on Martha's promise, but it was so late by the time Sophie was asleep that Martha had fallen asleep too.

I lay in the bed beside Martha. I'd taken a couple of codeine pills for my hip, even though I shouldn't with my hiatal hernia. I couldn't sleep. My codeine buzz was ruined by my thoughts:

What if I had broken my hip? What if I have a stroke, or a heart attack or I become incapacitated in some other way when I am out with her? Would she stay with me? But what was really occupying my thoughts was what happened when she came home, and how she couldn't tell Martha the simpler details of her day. Another seven-year-old might say, 'Daddy fell over on the beach, and was a big drama queen about it,' but Sophie couldn't even say, 'We went to the beach.' Sophie cannot tell her own story.

And then I thought, *What about the days when she is not with me, when she is being cared for by someone else? What if she had something important to tell us? What if someone hurt her? What if someone touched her? Or worse.*

And when I thought about that, I never wanted to let her out of my sight again, but then I asked myself, *What good am I? I can't even protect her from the pigeons.* True, they were a well-fed mafia of pigeons, but still, I needed help. And what if she had gone into the sea, beyond where I could catch her?

I wouldn't have been able to save her. I can burp on command, but I can't swim.

September 2015

bove me, I can hear the muffled sound of the pop music
Ailbhe puts on to help her sleep. Early in the new year,
she will be ten years old, and like most of her peers, her
musical taste has been swallowed by the charts.

When Ailbhe first cared about music, she listened to the CDs
I made for her, but that time seemed to come and go so quickly.

In one of his finer moments, Jesus said, 'Judge not lest ye
be judged,' and while I would dearly love to cast the first stone
– preferably straight into Ailbhe's CD player – I remember
that when I was a teenager I taught myself to play guitar from
a songbook called *The Great Songs of Chris De Burgh*. In case
you don't know, he's the crooner who sang 'Lady in Red'. You
may also be surprised to learn that he has other songs, and that
some of them were 'Great'. Back then, I often enjoyed performing
some of his songs, in public – you know, where other people can
see and hear the things you do – and therefore, I have no moral
authority, on any subject, ever.

That did not stop Ailbhe asking my advice about school, that
evening, after Martha went up to bed. She had just gone in to
third class. She told me that she was alone in the playground, a
lot, and she didn't like that. She found it hard to understand why
the others didn't want to do the things she wanted to do. She
wanted to talk about Minecraft and YouTubers and definitely not
make-up and clothes, but no one else was as into those things as
she was, which would be difficult, given that she was obsessed.

These are things that I was afraid I would eventually hear from her.

Not long after The Hard Weekend, we heard from a sister of one of Martha's friends, who was in a similar situation, with two kids on the autistic spectrum, one more profoundly affected than the other. 'It's the kid who will come to understand that they are different who I feel sorriest for,' she said.

While it was awful to have those fears realised, and it was sad to hear about her kicking around by herself wanting to make friends, surrounded by kids having fun with each other, I had to remind myself that there was a time when we worried about her going to a mainstream school at all. She was getting better at picking up on social cues, although she hadn't quite figured out that when it comes to making friends in school, I am not the parent to ask.

I worried about the effect being alone and feeling alone would have on her, but then I remembered that I was often alone, and felt alone, in school, and I ended up having murderous thoughts about everyone I met …

… sorry, I meant, 'fine'. I ended up fine. I'm fine. That keeps happening. Sorry.

'Dealing with other people is hard for everyone,' I told her.

Then she asked, 'Dad, what were you like in school?'

'I was anxious and I cried a lot.'

'And when did that stop?' she asked.

'I'll let you know …'

Various Dates

Today Sophie spent the entire day on her iPad while Martha and I took turns sleeping.

December 2015

S ophie didn't go to sleep. What happened that night is that somewhere between the thirty-fifth and thirty-sixth rendition of 'The Twelve Days of Christmas', in its entirety, Our Lady of Perpetual Motion eventually passed out.

Like an avaricious department store, she started with the Christmas songs as soon as the Halloween decorations came down, although her opening hours aren't nearly as sociable.

It was three weeks to Christmas, but all Sophie knew was that 'Christmas!' was coming soon, and she was excited, as any eight-year-old would be. She just likes to express that excitement by incessantly repeating the same song, in much the same way that a black-ops interrogator would torture sleep-deprived prisoners. If she's still doing this when she's eighteen – and there's no reason to think she won't be – she might yet get a steady, pensionable job in an unscrupulous dictatorship. I can but dream.

It was 'shower night,' and I committed the heinous crime of taking out a something-other-than-blue towel. 'I want my blue towel!' she said, and I got out a blue towel instead. She could just have decided that blue is the right colour for towels, although we suspect that it might have something to do with her recent obsession with *The Peanuts Movie,* and that she wants all towels to be blue, like Linus's blanket.

When I told her that it was time to get out of the shower, she didn't want to get out, so she cried, 'Five minutes!' in her annoyed Sophie voice.

I said, 'No, Soph, now!' in my stern Daddy voice.

'Five minutes' she insisted, in her whingy Sophie voice.

'NOW!' I shouted, in my raised Daddy voice.

Then Sophie looked directly at me, which she only does when she really, really wants something, and she said, 'Ten minutes?' in her quizzical Sophie voice, and I tried not to laugh, but of course I did. How could I not?

'Okay, five minutes,' I said, in my giggling Daddy voice. When I said, 'Okay, it's time to get out,' a few minutes later, she said, 'Good Grief!' just like Charlie Brown.

I knew that it was going to be a long night after she got out of the shower, because she was lepping about. Not leaping. Lepping. Lepping is like the bouncing about that drunk uncles with ties tied around their heads and trousers rolled up to their knees do on dance floors at weddings: uncontrolled joyful body movements with associated yelps, squeals and guttural roars. She was lepping when I put on her pyjamas. She was lepping when I tried to brush her hair. She was lepping when I told her to calm down. She was lepping when I helped her to brush her teeth. She was lepping when I asked her to 'Please, calm down.' I told her to get into bed, and she lepped into bed, lepped under the covers and then she lepped, horizontally.

The reason we had a trampoline was for her to lep as much as she wanted during the day, in the hope that she would be lepless by bedtime. She bounced on it that day until she was incandescent with the lep, and yet, at bedtime, she still had some leps to spare, evidentially.

She had one loud crying episode, when she thought that she had lost one of her extensive entourage of dolls, which she had taken to carrying around in a basket during the day. Her grief was on a par with a child mourning a beloved family pet. After fifteen minutes of miserable wailing, I eventually found it. It was still in the bed, under her arse. Her keening stopped immediately, and she went straight back to lepping, as if nothing had happened.

By the time she passed out, it was just past eleven o'clock. I had the rest of the evening to myself.

When I went downstairs, the first word that came to my mind was 'strewn.' I thought about un-strewing the place, but I didn't know where to start, so I didn't start. The kitchen hadn't been properly cleaned all weekend. The sitting room looked like a dishevelled clothes' club, some of them hanging out to dry, and many waiting to be ironed. I had promised Martha that I would get the Christmas decorations down from the attic, but I thought, *Christmas can wait.*

I sat at the kitchen table, pushed aside a pile of letters-that-should-have-been-dealt-with-a-while-ago, and opened the laptop to look at some videos. When I opened YouTube, every one of my suggested videos had something to do with Charlie Brown.

Martha had gone to bed at seven that night. She was very tired. So I had thought she would sleep through. At half-eleven, I heard the bedsprings moan upstairs announcing the good news: Martha has risen! *She's probably hungry*, I thought. And then, *Oh shit, she's hungry*, I thought. She advanced down the stairs and appeared at the door. Imagine a ravenous, lumbering bear, woken too early from hibernation by her hunger pangs.

With a sleepy drawl she asked, 'Has Soph gone to sleep?' 'Yes,' I replied. 'Not too long ago.' Then I said the most common sentence that couples say to each other these days: 'C'mere, you have to have a look at this video.'

She yawned. 'Yeah, okay, I'll be there in a sec.'

She opened the cupboard. She immediately looked perplexed and a little more alert than before. Something awful seemed to have happened while she was asleep. Then, more in hope than expectation, she opened the right-hand door of the same cupboard. Her worst fears were confirmed. She stood there holding both doors, looking into the cupboard, barely believing that her husband of eleven years – her friend, her lover, her confidant, inexplicably the man of her dreams – could be so callous. I knew what question was coming, and I readied my defence.

'Did you eat the last of the Crunchy Nut Corn Flakes?' she asked. Given the lack of Crunchy Nut Corn Flakes in the Crunchy Nut Corn Flakes cupboard, and the fact that all other possible culprits were currently asleep, that was an entirely fair accusation.

I tried not to give myself away, but instinctively my eyes fell upon the incriminating, milk-skinned bowl and spoon to my left-hand side. Martha's eyes followed mine to the bowl. Then our eyes met. We maintained eye contact, as I slowly slid the bowl behind the computer: 'Nope.' 'Ah, Aidan!' she exclaimed, somehow not believing me.

Our marriage is based on honesty, so I knew that I really should come clean. 'Ailbhe did it,' I said.

'I was really looking forward to that,' she whined. I felt bad for Martha. I knew exactly how she felt, because that's exactly how I had felt, just before I had eaten the last of the Crunchy Nut Corn Flakes.

Then Martha remembered something, which meant that I might yet be redeemed: 'It's okay, I think we have another box in the utility room,' and she opened the door to the utility room in much the same way that an experienced alcoholic might open a cistern.

'Yeah, so, I finished that box off on Friday,' I said, as she was about to go in.

'Seriously?' she gasped, in exasperation.

'No, not too seriously. I dribbled a bit, and then I made the sucky noise I make when I'm drinking that lovely, sweet milk at the bottom of the bowl. I wouldn't call it *classic* comedy, but it was mildly amusing at the time.' She didn't smile. 'I guess you had to be there … ' I said, trailing off.

She sighed, and looked for other sustenance. She snapped on the kettle, because a cup of tea is the very best consolation prize. 'Do you want some tea, Fuckface?' she asked. She called me 'Fuckface,' which is a term of endearment in our marriage, and she offered me tea, which meant that I was getting away lightly with this one. Given the seriousness of my crime, this was a very noble act of forgiveness on her part.

Which is why I really, really didn't want to say what I had to say next, before she got her hopes up. I inhaled deeply, before I ripped this plaster off the hairy skin of our marriage: 'Yeah, so, there's … emmmm … no milk left either.'

There would be no tea tonight.

When you are weighing the impact of this statement, you must understand that, while you might consider tea to be merely a refreshing beverage, in our house tea is a fundamental human right. We believe in tea. To tea or not to tea? That is the question.

It is a testament to our marriage, that even with no Crunchy Nut Corn Flakes for dinner, and no milk for tea, the cock had not crowed three times on me quite yet.

But then Martha spotted my third transgression, which, ordinarily, would have been a misdemeanour; however, considering my record of recent felonies, it was instantly elevated to a capital crime. I had put an un-rinsed, un-flattened, empty milk carton in the general waste bin, which is something you should never cock-a-doodle-do, and yet, it was something that I had cock-a-doodle-done. It should have gone in the recycling bin, of course, and it stuck out of the top of the wrong bin like a rasping, white tongue. This was not my first offence. When it comes to waste management, alas, I am a hopeless recidivist …

Somewhere in the Arctic Circle, there is a polar bear floating on a lonely piece of ice, which is all that remains of his once vast habitat. As he floats to his ultimate doom, tired and hungry, he

uses the last of his energy to scratch three little words into the icy
surface of his little island: Fuck you, Aidan.

I knew she was going to point it out, and even though I was in the wrong on this little thing, I could feel my back arching, because I had been stockpiling ire about the state of the house for months. I thought of how I had just spent the last three hours playing Sophieball, while Martha slept, and nothing else was done. I thought of all the times I had seen that nothing was done, and let it go. She was going to have a go at me about a milk carton in the wrong bin, and I thought of how unfair that was, how fucking unfair so many things were, and my ire began to bubble …

She said, 'You know that milk cartons go in the recycling bin, right? I have enough to be doing!'

I could have left it, thought, 'So what?' and just said, 'Sorry, you're right,' like I had many times before, but that night my mind rolled over and went as black as a shark's eye. I was about to start an argument. I was about to start *the* argument. I should have gone to bed earlier.

When Martha and I argue, there is passion, but no pyrotechnics. There is anger, but we don't engage in petty name-calling; there's more chance of a riot breaking out at a tiddlywinks tournament. We stick to the issues. It's like the opposite of an American presidential debate. We're more … Canadian. Polite, to a fault. Too polite to reach a resolution, and doomed, therefore, to have the same argument every few months.

Maybe there is no resolution to this argument? Maybe we're just two people who need to blame someone – anyone – for things that are no one's fault. Who is to blame for Martha's depression and her excessive need to sleep? I might as well kick a chemistry set. Who is to blame for the girls being on the autistic spectrum? We might as well punch ourselves in the bits. Who is to blame for the state of our house? I might as well blame Martha.

So I do.

'You're not the only one who has stuff to do. You're not the only who's tired, you know?' And then I say that while I understand that she needs to sleep, I still have go out to work every day and come home to nothing being done, constantly having to deal with the detritus of our lives – 'detritus of our lives?!' We're polite, but not that polite. I'm pretty sure I said 'shithole.'

She is up for the fight. She says she feels shitty enough about the state of the place without me making her feel shittier, and that she does clean up, but she just can't keep up. 'Do you think I can't see how bad things are? I have eyes, just like you do.' This is a fair point. She does have eyes.

And then, with my oh-so-reasonable voice, I expand on my theories on how she could use her limited energy to better effect to clean up. As I am saying this, we both know that I am being a dick, but I am too angry to stop, and she is too tired to stop me. In modern parlance, I think I am doing what they call 'mansplaining', although I prefer the more traditional term, 'Being an arse.'

Then she says that she thinks that the family have become my second priority. We've moved on to the portion of the argument that is about me going out to do gigs every week. And the odd trip away this year. A few times in London. Manchester. A week in Canada. A month in Edinburgh.

I counter by saying that there is no amount of time I could be in the house that would make her happy, and point out that even during the day, when I'm in work, she often texts me to see if I can come home early. As the words are coming out of my mouth, I hate that I am saying them, because I love it when she texts me in work.

Martha: BUNK OFF!
Me: NO, I'M BUSY.

Martha: I'M TRAPPED UNDER SOMETHING HEAVY.

Me: HA ... BUT SERIOUSLY.

Martha: SOPHIE IS EATING MATCHES.

Me: SHE'S ALWAYS DOING THAT.

Martha: AND GARGLING METHYLATED SPIRITS.

Me: AGAIN ... STANDARD.

Martha: SHE'S LISTENING TO COUNTRY AND WESTERN MUSIC.

Me: I'M ALREADY IN THE TAXI.

And then I point out that without the money I got from gigging in the last few years, we would be having this argument on the street, *sans* house – as the French say – because there is a *soupçon* of truth to that. But we both know that I am being disingenuous.

I have just got a new job, in the heart of the city again. I have finished commuting in the car and I am back on the bus every day. That means I can read books going to and from work again. The job pays more, and I love the work. We have partially emerged from our financial pit of despair, and if things keep going as they are, we'll be fully out of that hellhole soon. We don't need the money I get from gigging anymore.

And even if I hadn't been paid a cent for the last five years, would I have still gone out and performed? Yes, of course I would. The money was a very happy side-effect. It was a part of what saved us, but that hadn't been my plan at the start.

We are experts in this back-and-forward. We know all the moves. This fight is a well-choreographed event in our lives. No marriages will be harmed in the making of this movie. The argument will eventually run out of energy, as it always does. There will be apologies and tears, and the issues will remain dormant for a few months until one of us loses our temper again.

Then she says: 'I don't think I can do this any more.'

That isn't in the script. I pause, realising that I have stood up at some point. I am standing by the fridge looking at her. She has her back to me. She has her hands outspread on the counter. She isn't crying, though. I'd prefer it if she were crying, because then I could put that nonsense down to something said in passion. But the way she said it, so deliberately, it sounded like something she had carried in her heart for weeks. Maybe months? Maybe years? Something she might have said in counselling many times that she has finally said to me.

I know that the next words I say are very important. *Neither do I,* I think of saying, immediately. In that moment, I want her to go. I think that maybe without having to carry her as well, I might be better off. Maybe it would be better if it were just the girls and me. *She's barely awake most of the time anyway,* I think. It is the first time since the moment I'd met Martha that I've imagined my life without her and thought, *Maybe that would be better.*

As I open my mouth to speak, I hear the unmistakeable 'thud, thud, thud' of Sophie's footsteps as she runs into our bedroom. Martha must have left the door open. We both look up at the ceiling. 'I'll go,' I say. Martha doesn't turn around, or answer me. So I go.

When I get upstairs, Sophie is lying in our bed, under the duvet, hoping that I won't notice her. 'Come on, Soph,' I say.

'Mammy's bed,' she says. I know how she feels. I love Mammy's bed too.

'Daddy's bed?' I suggest as a compromise. She calls the bed in the spare room 'Daddy's bed' now, because, in the early morning, when she is lepping between Martha and me, showing no signs of stopping, I sometimes bring her into the spare room with me, because she tends to sleep better when it's just me and her. To Sophie, Martha means playtime. For her, Martha is intoxicating. For me too.

What if she really wants to leave me? I think, as I bring Sophie into the spare room. Sophie says, 'Snuggle,' and I say 'Snuggle' and then we get into bed and snuggle. She chirps, and buzzes, and beeps, like a little redheaded R2-D2. She babbles too, and in between the babble there are the usual movie and television exclamations. Something that sounds like Boo from *Monsters Inc*, and 'It's a disaster, Charlie,' from *Charlie and Lola*. 'Come on, Soph, sleep time,' I say. I may spend tomorrow in work jumping at shadows, again, if she doesn't go to sleep soon.

After a few minutes, I hear Martha coming up the stairs. I hope that she will come in to say sorry, but she does not. She goes into our bedroom and closes the door.

And that's when the lump that had formed in my throat becomes a soft cry. And as I cry, I would give everything I have, right then, for Sophie to turn around and say, 'What's wrong, Daddy, why are you crying?' like any normal eight-year-old would. But she doesn't, and she won't ever, probably.

She has her back to me. Soon, I hear her breathing change as she falls asleep. I cannot sleep, though. I look at her red hair in the lamplight. It is so beautiful. My favourite colour. She turns over, pushes the covers off herself in her sleep. I am surprised by the length of her, and how far her body goes down the bed now. I remember when she was a baby, blearily carrying her in my arms, trying to soothe her one night, before we knew. How small she was then.

Soon, this will go away too. She will be nine, ten, eleven, twelve, and there will come a time when there will be no more snuggles with me. I will miss it. She's going to be so much bigger, and so much harder to handle.

Her body becomes so completely settled, as she sleeps, that for the first time I notice how her pulse bounces, ceaselessly, in her neck. I think about her heart pumping in her chest. I think about our four hearts: Martha, Ailbhe, Sophie and me – my family – and how fragile all of this really is.

I remember reading the statistics on breakups amongst parents with autistic children in an article I had come across online, and thinking, *That won't happen to us, because what we have is special.* I'm sure that the couples who split up had thought that too.

We didn't talk properly for a few days. Neither of us wanted to 'touch the sore thing', as we call an issue that is difficult to deal with. We talked just enough to get through the perfunctory stuff of life. I took the Christmas decorations down from the attic. There were five boxes. Martha was going through them in the kitchen.

'Aren't there supposed to be six?'

'Okay, I'll have another look in a few minutes.' That sort of thing. I know that there are people who keep their relationships together like that for years. After a few days, though, I couldn't do it anymore.

That's not us.

I spent those few days thinking about what I wanted. I hated that I couldn't use Martha as my sounding board.

If I ever had an idea for a song or a joke, and I wasn't sure about it, I would sing or say it to Martha. If she didn't laugh that usually meant that it wasn't any good. I can remember singing her whole songs that I would have worked on for weeks and her simply saying at the end, 'You can do better.' I would get annoyed. 'I think you're wrong,' but invariably, a few days later, I would have improved it. She has a very annoying habit of being right.

When I came back from Edinburgh, my excitement about writing a new show had quickly faded. I hadn't written a word of a joke or a note of a song since I'd returned. The gigs I was playing were fine, but creatively, it all felt a bit colouring by numbers. I knew that to make it fun for myself again, I needed to move on. I've never been happy with standing still. Martha knew that too. That would mean going to the UK more often, doing more festivals, working harder. I would need to dedicate a lot more time to it. To do it properly would take years, and I didn't want to be half-arsed about it.

I understood why Martha had said: 'I don't think I can do this any more.' But when I thought about it, I realised that I couldn't really do it any more either.

I had some wonderful times performing, but did I really want to dedicate that much time to it, to the detriment of my family? When I thought about what really made me happiest in my life, I thought about that night after Ailbhe was born, as I settled down to sleep in Swords. I thought about everything, from her first smiles to the fun I had hanging out with her playing silly two-player games on the computer.

I thought about Sophie being born, the countless times she giggled with me from the first rough and tumbles to 'Daddy Sword!' I thought about the first time I heard her sing. I thought about the way Martha and I had often laughed through the shittiest of times. I remembered her, wrapped in nothing but a tie-dyed blanket, sitting by the fire in Gowna. I thought about much I loved her then. I thought about how, despite so many things not working out like we thought they would, I loved her even more now.

When I thought about continuing as a performer, I saw myself in a few years, introducing my act to handful of uninterested people at some Godforsaken foreign festival by saying: *'Hello, I am Aidan Strangeman, and I am the world's most foolish musical comedian.'*

It was time to be Aidan Comerford again.

Martha was decorating the Christmas tree. I was sitting at the table, drinking a cup of tea. I broke the silence. 'So … I'm going to give up gigging in the New Year.'

She turned around. 'That's because of me, isn't it?'

'No. It's because of me.'

'Lies,' she said. She was right, annoyingly. Well, half-right.

'How about you take a few months off and see how you feel? You might really miss it.' She was worried that if I didn't have a creative outlet we'd end up spending a fortune on toilet seats.

'Don't worry,' I said, 'If I need to, I'm sure I'll find something else to do. Maybe I'll write a book,' I laughed.

The next night, I was sitting in the spare room, with my guitar on my lap. Everyone else in the house was asleep. I was looking through pictures of gigs on the computer. In one of the folders, I came across the script of my Edinburgh show. As I looked through it, I started singing some of the songs.

After a few minutes, there was a knock on the door. I jumped, and stopped playing. 'It's me,' said Ailbhe. 'Can I come in?' she asked, opening the door and coming in before I answered.

I was glad it wasn't an axe murderer, as I had first suspected. 'Is everything okay, Bear?'

'I heard you singing,' she said.

'I'm sorry, was I being too loud?'

'No, I couldn't sleep. What are you doing?'

'I'm playing the songs from my show.' I expected her to change the subject.

'Is there anything about me in it?' She had never shown much of an interest before.

'The last song in the show is about you. Do you want to hear it?'

'Yes,' she said delightedly, sitting down on the edge of the bed, facing me.

'Okay, but then it's straight to bed, afterwards, because it's way past bedtime.'

I was suddenly very nervous that she wouldn't like it. 'It's called "Tough Audience," I said. 'And it's about how you're turning into a little teenager. It starts like this.' I played the opening chords of the song and I blew a long-winded raspberry.

… that used to make her laugh,
Now she's like '#stupidnoise #stupidDad #Ijustcant'
She's started using 'literally,' when literally is literally not the
right word

I tell her to speak properly and she says, 'Dad, you're literally
the worst'
What ever happened to my little girl?
When did she become such a tough audience?
I was her Obi-wan Kenobi; now messa be Jar Jar Binks …

As I sang, Ailbhe laughed and laughed, in all the right places. I was making my daughter, who once wouldn't look me in the eye, laugh with a silly song. Who wouldn't be happy with that?

I knew then that I wouldn't miss gigging, because I would never have a better audience than the one I had right at that moment.

Epilogue

A s you were reading this book, you might have asked yourself, 'So when did he get time to write it?'

I wrote mostly in the evenings, but initially I had to constantly get up to put Sophie back to bed, as Martha was usually asleep. I thought, *I bet Shakespeare never had to put up with this shit.* If Sophie persisted, I probably wouldn't have. What I did eventually – what I am doing right now – was to write the book with Sophie in the spare bed beside me.

I wore her pink ear defenders, and tippy-tapped away at the keyboard, while she would lep, and babble, and eventually sing herself to sleep. I didn't mind that so much, because at least she wouldn't get out of bed, so I didn't have to keep getting up, and I could concentrate on writing. I would start at eight, her bedtime. She would fall asleep between ten and eleven, most evenings, and I would finish at midnight, setting my alarm for work, falling into bed beside her, and getting up and doing it all again the next day.

One night, after a couple of months of that, I was too tired to write, so when I put Sophie to bed, I lay down beside her, with the intention of having a snooze that I would happily have let become a full night's sleep. But she looked at me and said, with annoyance, 'Daddy! Computer!'

'No, Soph, Daddy sleep,' I said.

But this would not do. It was not the way the world was supposed to be, according to Sophie, so she crawled out over me, stood beside the chair, banged on it and issued her command: 'DADDY! COMPUTER!'

I got up that night, and I wrote a chapter.

As I was writing the book, I decided to leave out a little quirk of speech that Martha and I have. In the same way that some people call each other 'Dear', or 'Darling', Martha and I call each other 'Dave'.

If I were to come home from work early, the first thing Martha would say, with surprise and delight, would be 'Daaaaave!' If she welches on going out to a party at the last minute (as usual) that I know she would probably have enjoyed once she got there, I will disappointedly say, 'Ah, Daaave.' If I cannot sleep in the early hours, and I have been louder than I thought hanging out downstairs, I might hear Martha whisper-shout from the upstairs landing, 'Dave?' and I will answer, 'No, Dave, it's an axe murderer.'

'Dave', as our term of endearment, originated with the Papa Lazarou sketch in the BBC comedy series *The League of Gentlemen*. If you haven't seen it, Papa Lazarou is a minstrel-faced circus master who calls to the door of an unsuspecting lady, eventually kidnapping her, making her his new 'wife', hilariously.

Martha, Derm and I loved *The League of Gentleman*, and after we watched that episode, whenever Derm called around, he would greet Martha or me at the door with Papa Lazarou's rasping phrases: 'Hello, Dave?' 'Is that Dave?' 'Is Dave there?' 'My wife would like to use your toilet.' Also, I may have rasped Papa Lazarou's phrase 'You're my wife now … ' at Martha during the odd intimate moment.

Derm started calling Martha 'Dave', then Martha called him 'Dave', then I called Martha 'Dave', and then she called me 'Dave'. While calling each other 'Dave' will be very handy for Martha and me in our senility, I thought it would be too confusing to have our dialogue in this book peppered with 'Daves'. (We've been to dinner parties with some very confused, actual Daves, who would certainly concur.)

One day, when Ailbhe was ten, she asked me, 'Can I watch the TV, Dave?'

'Sorry, what did you call me?' I said.

'Dave,' she said, 'that's what Mammy calls you, sometimes.'

'Mammy also calls me an eejit, sometimes, it doesn't mean it's okay for you to do it. Call me Dad!' I said in my daddiest dad voice.

'Okay, Dave,' she answered.

Writing this book, it was so hard to recall her as the taciturn, high-tempered toddler that she was. She is so different now. She is a testament to early intervention. At one time, she couldn't say 'Dada', now she asks me things like, 'Can I curse, Dave?' We've moved on from painstakingly teaching her two-word sentences, to the complexity of when it is and isn't appropriate to curse. One day she will figure out that if she wants to curse, there isn't a thing I can do about it. I just hope that she isn't fucking gratuitous about it.

We don't couch our language that much around her any more. In fact, Martha takes issue with me still saying 'piddle' instead of 'piss'. I don't think you should teach kids not to curse, because sometimes a good curse in the right place is the only way to properly emphasise how deeply you feel about something.

My biggest issue with writing this book was how Ailbhe might feel about it in the future, which is why I am going to finish this book by writing her a letter:

Bear,

When your Aunty Anita had her First Holy Communion, she wore the traditional white communion dress. Nana dressed me and your Uncle Kieran in matching outfits: we wore light blue shirts with blue ruffles down the front, dark blue velvet waistcoats and shorts, socks that matched the light blue of the shirts, and sandals. I believe this is what your generation call 'on fleek'.

Nana and Grandad took us to a professional photographer that day. The photographer liked that photograph of the three us smiling so much that every year he put it in his window to advertise his communion photo services.

At first, when I was kid, I really liked it. It made me feel a little bit famous. However, as the years went by, and I became a teenager, the photo became more and more ... off fleek, for me.

The photographer was still displaying it every year when I went to college in Carlow, and because I had the same head as I had when I was a boy, only bigger, people recognised me easily, and I got a bit of jocular taunting about it: 'The state of you in that photo!' – Everyone, often.

Eventually, the photographer shut up shop, and he sold the photo to Nana and Grandad – it's the one that they have up over the stairway.

When I was writing this book, I asked you if you were okay with me writing about you, and you said you were. I tried to explain that there might be some things in this book that, when you are older, you wished were private. You said that you understood and that it was okay, but I was worried this book would eventually become your version of my blue velvet shorts, and that you would come to regret saying yes to it. Of course, much like that communion photo, in thirty-five years, the only copy of this book still in existence might be in your Nana's house. Or not. Who knows?

In case you don't remember, you would come in to the room sometimes when I was writing the book, and you would ask me how it was going. 'What part of the story are you at now?' 'Have I been born yet?' 'Can I help?'

One day, in the last couple of months of writing, I was extremely tired, and the words weren't coming. I felt, momentarily, like I would never get to the end. You came in and asked how it was going, and I said, 'Not good, Bear.' You asked, 'What's wrong?' I sighed. 'It's not as funny as I want it to be.' You said, 'Well, you've never failed to make me laugh.' You couldn't have said a more lovely or inspirational thing right then, and I held your words in my heart all the way to the end. Thank you for that.

I will read you the bits of this book that are about you, and you might say that they are okay, but when you read the whole book, when you're (much) older, you might not like it. If that happens, I'm sorry. I would never want to hurt you, because I love you. No, I don't just love you, I fucking love you, okay?

ACKNOWLEDGEMENTS

If you are a parent of a child, or children, with special needs, I know that your time is precious, so thank you, especially, for reading this book. I tried to keep the chapters short, so that you could dip in and out if you need a laugh, or a smile, or you need to do that snorty nose noise that people do instead of laughing when they are reading a book on their own.

Thanks to everyone at Gill Books, especially Deirdre Nolan. Without you asking me, and giving me an unreasonably tight deadline, I know I wouldn't have found a way to write this book, and I had a lot of fun/dark nights of the soul doing it.

If I start listing off people who have helped Martha and me over the years, the band will start playing me off, so I'd just like to say thank you to my family and friends, and all the people who are mentioned in this book.

Thank you to everyone who ever gave me a gig or came along to my shows. I hope it was a good night/that I didn't ruin your night too much. I've met some very talented, supportive people over the years. If you're reading this thinking, 'I wonder if he's talking about me?', yes, I am.

Thank you to the people who have followed my Facebook page and who have liked and shared my stories. Every single like and share gave me a lovely little hit of dopamine. That was very nice of you (facebook.com/aidancomerfordwriting).

I'd also like to thank the lovely people I've met on the *Oh My God What a Complete Aisling* Facebook forum. You were wonderfully supportive of the stories I put up there, and made me believe that I might just have a book in me after all.

And Martha, most of all, I love you, Dave.